God's Heart Has No Borders

God's Heart Has No Borders

HOW RELIGIOUS ACTIVISTS ARE WORKING FOR IMMIGRANT RIGHTS

PIERRETTE HONDAGNEU-SOTELO

UNIVERSITY OF CALIFORNIA PRESS
Berkeley   Los Angeles   London

University of California Press, one of the most distinguished university presses in the United States, enriches lives around the world by advancing scholarship in the humanities, social sciences, and natural sciences. Its activities are supported by the UC Press Foundation and by philanthropic contributions from individuals and institutions. For more information, visit www.ucpress.edu.

University of California Press
Berkeley and Los Angeles, California

University of California Press, Ltd.
London, England

Library of Congress Cataloging-in-Publication Data

Hondagneu-Sotelo, Pierrette.
    God's heart has no borders: how religious activists are working for immigrant rights / Pierrette Hondagneu-Sotelo.
        p.   cm.
    Includes bibliographical references (p.   ) and index.
    ISBN: 978-0-520-25724-5 (cloth : alk. paper)
    ISBN: 978-0-520-25725-2 (pbk. : alk. paper)
        1. Religion and state—United States.   2. Faith-based human services—United States.   3. United States—Emigration and immigration—Religious aspects.   4. Social justice—Religious aspects. 5. Religion and justice.   I. Title.

BL2525.H665   2008
201'.7—dc22   2007046953

Manufactured in the United States of America

17   16   15   14   13   12   11   10   09   08
10   9   8   7   6   5   4   3   2   1

This book is printed on Natures Book, which contains 50% post-consumer waste and meets the minimum requirements of ANSI/NISO Z39.48–1992 (R 1997) (*Permanence of Paper*). ♾

In memory of my father, Pierre Hondagneu,
1918–2008, with love and gratitude

Contents

Preface and Acknowledgments

This book is not about me, but since it is about religious people, it's only fair to say a bit about my own religious background. I am a devout agnostic, but I grew up Catholic. My outstanding memories of going to the parish school in suburban California, back in the pre–Vatican II days, are not fond ones. The school was run by mean nuns. They paced briskly in black, full-length habits, and they ruled harshly, with long pointer sticks and public humiliation. In fear and obedience, we genuflected when we heard their clickers. Throughout the day, we girls had to kneel on command to show that our skirts were long enough to brush the ground—this was the 1960s, when even ten-year-olds were in danger of corruption by miniskirts. My family attended mass every Sunday, conducted in Latin until I was about ten. In a dark closetlike booth, I confessed made-up sins to the parish priest, adding the sin of lying to my roster. It was medieval, mysterious, and, for me, meaningless. My Chilean mother had rosaries, prayer cards, saint statues, and palm fronds around the house, and she encouraged me to pray for help with personal problems. My French father insisted we soberly and silently attend mass every Sunday. I hated Catholic school and begged my parents to release me from it and from Catholicism in general. They made me complete my confirmation at age thirteen, and then that was it for me. Mostly, I have not looked back. But once in a while, when I find myself at a wedding mass or a child's communion, or at a service honoring immigrant labor, I feel the tug. There's something about the pageantry, the mystery, and the collective effervescence that still gets to me. Sometimes I'm overwhelmed with emotion.

I came to write this book about religion not in search of personal reconciliation but out of recognition of, respect for, and curiosity about the role of religion in steadfastly pursuing a progressive agenda for immigrants in an era that has become aggressively anti-immigrant and dangerously nationalistic. I first became aware of the social role of religion, or, more precisely, Catholic social teachings, in immigrant rights during the 1980s. During the fall of 1986, I began doing research for what would become my first book, *Gendered Transitions*. President Reagan had just signed the Immigration Reform and Control Act, and in the Mexican immigrant community where I was working, undocumented immigrants were mobilizing and trying to adjust. Grassroots groups emerged to grapple with the new uncertainties of legalization, and I became active in some of these efforts. The local Catholic parish became a key site for activism, as did a smaller *comunidad de base*, or Christian base community, inspired by the tradition of liberation theology.

Although my first "aha" moment of recognizing how religion can promote immigrant rights came as I watched and participated in the mobilizations around amnesty legalization in 1986, it was not until 2000 that I began researching this topic. I began with a healthy dose of skepticism toward religion, and during the time I spent in the field, the front page news—the Catholic Church's cover-up of pedophile priests, Pope Benedict's latest regressive edict—fed my antipathy toward religiosity in general and Catholicism in particular.

Interviewing religious-based activists for this book, however, opened my agnostic eyes to the progressive potential of organized religion. In fact, I developed deep respect and admiration for these people, who, acting out of religious faith, work to make the social world a better place. Religion can act as a progressive force, lessening human social conflicts, exclusions, and inequalities. This occurs through interfaith dialogues, social services, the infusion of moral values into civic engagement, and, I think, even through prayer and the singing of songs. Religious people in America are certainly active in many of these collective projects. In this book, however, I look at other kinds of activities. In particular, I examine how Muslim, Jewish, and Christian activists rely on religion to challenge taken-for-granted definitions of migration and nation. Who can belong to the nation, and how can religion guide a more expansive, inclusive definition? This is the fundamental question that drives their activism as they challenge the notion that newcomers must accept subordination and exclusion.

This book is not about religious people coming together to pray or to offer food and charity to the poor, although to be sure, many of the same people highlighted in this book are involved in those activities. Rather, the focus here is on religious people who are advocating for the civil, economic, and border rights of immigrants. They seek inclusion, justice, and fairness for newcomers to the United States. In the current political climate in which we live, where punitive immigration policies remain popular and where descriptors like "the illegals" and "the terrorists" now dominate the popular imagination of what it means to be an immigrant, these are radical projects.

The Muslim, Christian, and Jewish activists featured in this book are using their religion to contest the uncritical application of nation-state boundaries. Relying on their identities as religious people and working with the tools of religion that I describe in chapter 1, they use religion to transcend fundamentalist definitions of the nation-state. Americans have become accustomed to thinking of religion as regressive and rigid and the state and market as more flexible institutions, but I tell a different story here. This is the story of progressive religion against a rigid, fundamentalist nation-state and against abusive practices in capitalist labor markets.

I opened this preface by stating my avowedly secular life, but during the year-long sabbatical when I wrote this book, I got heavily into yoga. This daily addiction included moments of transcendence, feelings of well-being, the experience of community, and the indulgence of an inward focus amid a busy life. When I throw that into the mix of other institutionalized yoga rituals, I think that maybe yoga has become my palatable form of midlife religion. There are, after all, moments of silence, bowing, chanting, congregating with others in appointed spaces, closing of eyes, and listening quietly to teachers read inspiring passages or even just listening to one's breath. There are also specially appointed clothing and a certain kind of yoga evangelism—although to date, my husband and kids are steadfastly refusing conversion. And just like organized religion, it requires a certain amount of self-discipline. But the inward focus of yoga, unlike the religions of the book—Islam, Christianity, and Judaism—does not promise much in terms of fueling a social agenda for justice and equality.

Yoga comes up short in promoting social change, but it is big on gratitude. Here, my list runs long and deep. First, my appreciation and gratitude goes to all of the individuals who allowed me to interview them and to attend their organizations' meetings and forums. They are, as I hope readers will come to see, an amazing group of people. I am also convinced that they are people of historical importance. To give them the recognition that is due, I have used their real names, with their permission, throughout the text.

Beginning in 2000, Don Miller, the director of the University of Southern California Center for Religion and Civic Culture, and Jon Miller, director of research at the center, generously offered me support and PEW research funding to conduct research into how religion figured into contemporary immigrant rights activism. During the five years I was researching this book, I also convened, through the Center for Religion and Civic Culture, a faculty working group on the topic of religion, immigration, and politics. This provided rich interdisciplinary conversations where I learned a lot from my colleagues, who included Professors Maria Aranda, Macarena Gomez-Barris, Clara Irazabal, Nora Hamilton, Janet Hoskins, Jane Iwamura, Roberto Lint-Sagarena,

Stephanie Nawyn, Joseph Palacios, Appichai Shipper, Greg Stanzack, Ed Ransford, and Janelle Wong. I also learned much about religion from Center for Religion and Civic Culture affiliates Grace Dyrness and Tim Fisher.

I am also deeply appreciative of the time and effort that several generous colleagues put into reading and commenting on this manuscript as it unfolded. For this, *muchisimas gracias* to Mike Messner, Don Miller, Gul Ozyegin, Joe Palacios, Mazen Hashem, and Laura Pulido. Mike Messner deserves special recognition not only for reading and commenting on my work but also for frequently discussing my research issues, large and small, in the kitchen, in the car, and over morning coffee. It seemed endless. Especially big thanks also to religious studies scholar Manuel Vasquez and to social movement expert James Jasper, each of whom read the entire manuscript and generously helped me rethink things. I am also grateful for the comments and questions that I received from audiences where I presented this material. These include the Department of Sociology colloquia at UC Santa Barbara, UC Davis, UC Berkeley, and UC Riverside; the Institute for the Study for Democracy at UC Irvine; the New Racial Paradigms Project at UC Santa Barbara; the Center for Latin American Studies at the University of Florida, Gainesville; the Colegio de la Frontera Norte in Tijuana; the Center for Advanced Study at the University of Illinois, Urbana-Champaign; the Center for Migration and Development at Princeton University; the Center for Mexican American Studies at the University of Texas, Arlington; the Interdisciplinary Graduate Student Conference at CSU Northridge; and the Catholic Theological Union in Chicago. Comments from conference presentations at the American Sociological Association meetings in Anaheim, Chicago, San Francisco, and Montreal and at Law and Society Association meetings in Vancouver also helped me.

During the time I wrote the first draft of this book, I was lucky to have a Rockefeller Foundation Resident Fellowship in the Humanities at California State University, Los Angeles. This gave me time to write and introduced me to a wonderful set of colleagues who, during seminars, offered rich insights from cultural studies, anthropology, and the humanities. Big thanks here go to Beth Baker-Cristales, Micole Siegel,

David S. Olsen, Ricardo Ortiz, John Ramirez, Mark Wild, and especially to Alejandra Marchevsky, who organized it all.

My gratitude extends to many more people, including two of the interviewees, Samer Hathout and Reverend Dick Gillet, who generously read a draft of the manuscript and gave me feedback. University of Southern California undergraduate and graduate students helped me with the research, and I am grateful to them for their research assistance, conversations, and inspiration: Genelle Gaudinez, Kara Lemma, Lata Murti, Sarah Stohlman, Stephanie Nawyn, Hector Lara, Billie Ortiz, Margaret Perez-Clark, Sharene Irsane, and Hernan Ramirez. And thank you once again to Naomi Schneider and her very capable staff at the University of California Press for support in this publication. Finally, thanks to my friends. In a big metropolitan area like Los Angeles, where we spend mind-numbing hours driving freeways, I'm lucky to have friends who are close to my heart and who live close to my home. Laurie and Oscar Narro, Francisca Gamez, Greg Molina, and Diane Laughrun have kept me going through life's dramas with laughter and restorative conversations.

My biggest thanks and hugs to Mike Messner and to our sons, Miles and Sasha. They sometimes accompanied me to street protests, the border, and into church pews, and that was nice, but most of all, I am grateful for their daily company and unconditional faith in me. Even the daily nagging came in handy. Whenever I told Sasha to shut off the TV and do his seventh-grade homework, he would tell me to get off the yoga mat and get back to writing the book. In a way, that helped too.

ONE Welcoming the Alien?

In the spring of 2006, millions of people across the United States took to the streets in what became the largest immigrant rights mobilization this country has ever seen. In downtown Chicago, Dallas, Los Angeles, Miami, and New York, and in hundreds of smaller cities throughout the nation, immigrants marched through the streets to protest a federal bill that would, among other things, make it a felony to aid undocumented immigrants. Dressed in white to symbolize peace and carrying American flags, the protestors raised their collective voices to demand legalization reform that would resolve the legal limbo of the estimated 11 million undocumented immigrants who live and work in the United States. On downtown boulevards across the nation, the marchers, who were predominantly but not exclusively Latino, chanted, "Aquí estamos, y no nos vamos" (We're here, and we're not leaving), "Hoy marchamos, mañana votamos" (Today we march, tomorrow we vote), and "Sí se puede!" (Yes, we can!). Joining them were prominent leaders from labor unions, civil rights organizations, and ethnic organizations. The American flag became the most prominent symbol of the movement, but marchers also carried crosses, votive candles, and banners of la Virgen de Guadalupe or of local congregations.[1] At one candlelight vigil that began at the historic La Placita church in downtown Los Angeles, a huge crucifix with a semicircular sign proclaiming "Cristo de los Inmigrantes" (Christ of the Immigrants) hovered higher than the sea of American flags, hinting at the critical role of faith in fueling this movement.

Religious leaders were also visible and vocal in these immigrant rights marches. Cardinal Roger M. Mahony, leader of the nation's largest Catholic archdiocese, garnered national media attention when he denounced the proposed bill as "un-American."[2] He even sent informational packets on immigration to all parishes in his district. Catholic leaders had initiated the Justice for Immigrants campaign for immigration reform in 2004, but they were not the only religious leaders involved in this campaign. In Los Angeles, Muslim, Buddhist, Jewish, and Protestant religious leaders also supported the marches and served as featured speakers.

Clergy and people of faith were not new to the world of immigrant rights advocacy. Many of them had been quietly and steadfastly working for immigrant rights well before these street demonstrations and vigils. What they are doing and how they bring their religion to bear on this activism is the story I tell in this book. Based on interviews and ethnographic research, this book provides a close-up view of religious people working for immigrant rights in three arenas: civil rights in the post-9/11 climate, low-wage workplaces, and the increasingly dangerous U.S.-Mexico border.

In the late twentieth century the United States once again became a nation characterized by immigration, and Los Angeles emerged as the premier immigrant city, rivaled only by New York for the numbers and diverse national origins of the foreign-born. That much is well known. Less well known are two other facts: Los Angeles—and California more generally—became the hub of the development of anti-immigrant backlash, and finally, coming full circle, this region has emerged as a key site of creative organizing by labor unions and religious groups working for the immigrant rights movement.[3] In all of these ways, Southern California is a harbinger of national immigrant trends. Looking at what happens in Southern California gives us a preview of what is emerging elsewhere with the immigrant rights movement.

Why should the average American care about immigrant rights? Immigrant rights activism is a critical arena in which the future of American democracy is being played out. Popular sentiment toward new immigrants remains ambivalent, even alarmist, but I believe most Americans do not want to see massive deportations or to live in a society like the Gulf states of the Middle East, where transnational migrant workers are enslaved under restrictive temporary contracts. The French model, in which economic, social, and political marginalization of immigrant communities prevails alongside the myth of a culturally homogenous nation, does not appeal either. Yet old-school American assimilation is no longer viable in an era when the steps to legalization and to economic mobility are no longer easily accessible. What is lacking in popular imagination, in media representations, and in the policy proposals of our politicians is a moral blueprint for doing things differently. The Abrahamic notions of loving the alien, welcoming the stranger, and caring for the poor provide ancient admonitions that may temper today's anti-democratic impulses.

This book, then, is based on the assumption that immigrants are not the problem. Rather, the way immigrants are welcomed into the nation is a problem. Looking at how religious activists understand the world and what they do to secure the rights of immigrants allows us to imagine new alternatives for the future. By seeking greater inclusion for immigrants, these liberal religious activists provide us with a guide for negotiating difference in an increasingly global, mobile world.

Legalization for undocumented immigrants remains an important issue. There are, however, different sites of struggle for immigrant rights, and in this book I examine the arenas of civil rights, worker rights, and border rights. This book examines Christian activism at the San Diego–Tijuana border, Muslim civil rights advocacy in Los Angeles and

Orange Counties, and the Christian and Jewish clergy mobilizations for worker rights of Latino immigrant service workers who staff Los Angeles' hotels and restaurants. Using ethnographic observations, interviews with key leaders and participants in these movements, and analyses of organizations' brochures and documents, I identify the religious "tools" that these social activists are using, or not using, and I analyze the constraints under which they mobilize and their relative successes and foiled attempts.

This religious activism unfolds in a historical moment of tension surrounding American Christianity. The United States remains a deeply Christian country, one where Christian religion has served as a force for progressive social change—and for repression too. Although post-1965 immigration has enriched religious pluralism, the United States has yet to break from the dominant Christian definitions of itself.[4] In this regard, I see two countertendencies that influence religious immigrant rights activists: the re-Christianization of the United States and a deep suspicion of using Christianity, and religion more generally, for political purposes.[5] The rise of the Moral Majority and the Christian Right, beginning in the late 1970s, contributed to both of these countertendencies. The terrorist attacks of September 11, 2001, Islamic fundamentalist violence, and the U.S. military invasions of Afghanistan and Iraq deepened this tension. This was a time when the American president referred to U.S. military efforts against terrorism as a new "crusade," and the chief law enforcement official of the nation, Attorney General John Ashcroft, publicly declared, "Islam is the religion which God asks parents to sacrifice their children, whereas Christianity is the religion where God sacrifices his son for you."

At the same time, the well-publicized money and sex scandals of Christian televangelists and megachurch leaders and the Catholic Church's institutionalized cover-up of pedophile priests in hundreds of parishes and Catholic schools exposed the moral fallibility and hypocrisy of the nation's top Christian leaders. Intellectuals and secular elites have always criticized organized religion, but in the context of religious violence and scandals galore, these critiques against religion and religious rule have become more vociferous and widespread.[6] Consequently, we see a simultaneous reaffirmation of Christianity alongside a distrust of Christian morality and, more generally, of religious influence in the realm of public policy. The Christian, Jewish, and Muslim activists for immigrant rights operate in this context of tension created by these countertendencies. This tension explains why they are able to use religious tools in some instances but not others.

These religious activists are indicative, I believe, of a new wave of religious people working for progressive causes. They are joined by religious groups working in the antiwar movement, in environmental groups, and in the efforts to end poverty, hunger, racism, and genocide. The pendulum of religious activism in the United States is swinging from right to left, away from repressive regulation of marriage, women's bodies, and Darwinism in school textbooks and toward support for progressive policies to end human suffering and inequalities.

The story I tell in this book is an optimistic one of how religion promotes social justice and inclusion, providing an important alternative to the exclusivist nationalism of the times. Listening to religious activists' stories and looking at their collective actions provide us with an analytic window into religion's contributions to U.S. immigration politics and social justice. In a more utopian vein, this allows us a glimpse into an alternative view of the future, one where strangers may be welcomed.

RELIGION AND IMMIGRANT RIGHTS

The immigration controversy in the United States has been developing for some time. This is, after all, the "age of migration." Nearly 200 million people live in nations other than the one they were born in. The United States, which includes about 34 million foreign-born, is no exception. What is exceptional, and paradoxical, is this: The United States defines itself as "a nation of immigrants," but many Americans feel ambivalent, even downright hostile, to subscribing to this legacy in practice. Consequently, recent immigrants have met with ambivalence, partial inclusion, subordination, blatant discrimination, and hostility. During the spring of 2006 immigrants and their supporters raised their voices in favor of full inclusion.

The competing legislative efforts and the immigrant rights marches in the streets surprised many observers. But this movement did not fall from the sky—it had been brewing for many years and simmering in many pots. People from the religious sector comprise one segment of this mobilization, and their efforts have been complemented and enhanced by those coming out of labor, ethnic, and community organizations. In 2000, the AFL-CIO, reversing a restrictionist policy lasting over a century, began advocating for the legal and economic rights of immigrant workers. Ethnic-identified organizations such as the Mexican American Legal Defense Fund, the League of United Latin American Citizens, and the Asian Pacific American Legal Center and legal rights groups such as the National Lawyers Guild and the American Civil Liberties Union have promoted immigrant rights for decades. Since the 1980s immigrant rights coalitions that bring together smaller community-based organizations have become institutionalized in every major immigrant city in the United States.[7] These national coalitions have also worked on immigrant rights issues for decades, and in the 1990s local organizing around immigrant issues intensified in many cities around the country. In Los Angeles alone, a plethora of community-based organizations devoted to improving the jobs of Latino immigrant workers emerged in the 1990s.[8] Alongside organized labor, ethnic groups, and legal organizations, religious groups have emerged as one of the main sectors where people are mobilizing for immigrant rights.

Mainstream observers often think of religious activists as inherently conservative, exclusively focused on abortion, marriage, sexuality, and curtailing gay rights. This view is understandable, given the high visibility of the Christian Right in recent decades. But many religious activists in the United States are dedicated to what we might call progressive peace and justice causes, such as ending the war in Iraq or solving poverty and homelessness. They do not attract the media attention devoted to the splashier activities of the Christian conservatives or to the explicitly anti-immigrant groups such as the Minutemen, but a segment of these religious-based activists has been working to expand and protect the labor, civil, and migration rights of newcomers.

Why bother looking at them? The answer is simple—new immigrants have stepped onto a slippery welcome mat, and people of faith, both U.S.-born and foreign-born, are trying to provide a more welcoming reception. Faith-based activism for immigrant rights must be understood in the context of the hostile reception that greets new immigrants, the deeply religious nature of both immigrants and the United States, and the changing role of religion in American public life.

The United States is the world's most religious postindustrial nation. No other modern, postindustrial society has a population where the majority of people regularly attend worship services. By contrast, most of the churches and cathedrals of Europe are vacant, serving more as museums for tourists' gazes rather than sacred spaces for the locals. The United States' neighbor to the north, Canada, is also a largely secular society. Congregations in the United States, however, remain lively places of worship. Churches, temples, and mosques serve as sites of civic engagement, social gatherings, and sacred musical performance. And about 90 percent of Americans say "yes" when asked if they believe in God.

Although the United States was founded on the separation of church and state, religion has always played an important role in the American public sphere. The nation itself is seen as sacred. American civil religion, as Robert Bellah argues, permeates society, enabling Americans to see their country through the lens of religious legitimation and righteousness.[9] Elsewhere, too, religion has entered public debates and political campaigns. Religion in the modern world, the sociologist Jose Casanova contends, has undergone a process of deprivatization. No longer confined to the realm of individual, private salvation, consolation, and spirituality, religion now connects public and private morality. Many examples of religion and state intersections abound. Evangelical Christians helped George W. Bush win the elections of 2000 and 2004. In many Asian and Middle Eastern countries, contesting definitions of Islam prevail and are deeply intertwined with international and intrastate politics. Elsewhere around the world, the Catholic Church, especially under Pope John Paul II, helped to oust authoritarian states, promoting democracy and space for the emergence of civil society. In this book, I am most interested in the role of religion not in elections or in revolutions but in the ways faith-based activists challenge how immigrants are treated by market and state institutions. This is what Casanova would call "the renormativization of the public economic and political spheres."[10]

The United States is once again a nation of immigration and, importantly, a nation where immigration remains controversial. Immigrant newcomers in the United States hail predominantly from Asia, Latin America, and the Middle East, and religion is salient in their lives both before and after migration. Indeed, many immigrants become more, not less, religious in their new destinations.

Although immigration scholarship once ignored religion, there is now a vast and growing literature on religion and new immigrants. The old model of viewing religion as a facilitator of immigrant assimilation has been replaced by contemporary understandings of religion as an enabler of immigrant incorporation, transnational social life, and ethnic resilience and affirmation. In this model, religion helps to create new hybrid identities.[11] Many studies of immigrant congregations highlight this fact.

Contemporary scholarship has also unveiled the multiple points at which religion may intervene to facilitate risky, dangerous migrant journeys and border crossings, can counter the anomie of immigrant life in the big city, and can serve as a transnational, two-way bridge between the immigrants' old society and the new one.[12] My contribution to this conversation highlights how religion offers a tool box that, in the hands of skillful advocates and activists, can help build a more welcoming democratic, inclusive society. This religious activism arises in the midst of formidable opponents: racialized nativism, embedded restrictionism, and new fears and anxieties about foreigners and immigrants.

FROM EMBEDDED LIBERALISM TO EMBEDDED RESTRICTIONISM

There are no hard rules in social science, but one reliable pattern is this: Repression breeds resistance, and so it is that immigrant restrictionism and racialized nativism have led to calls for fuller inclusion and enfranchisement for immigrants. Immigrant rights activists on the scene today are responding to two decades of deeply entrenched anti-immigrant laws and practices. Although the years from 1965 to 1980 were characterized by greater openness in American immigration policies and politics, the more recent era has been less friendly to immigrants.

The political scientist Gary Freeman suggests that immigration policy in liberal democracies is best explained by embedded liberalism and path dependency. "Path dependency" refers to the ways in which particular episodes or decisions either limit or enhance future possible courses.[13] This model seems to help explain the period of about 1965 through 1980. Pressure from the civil rights movement led to the signing of the Civil Rights Act of 1964, which outlawed public discrimination on the basis of race. This, combined with the cold war—with its heightened anxiety about U.S. technological and educational competitiveness, and with the discrepancy between U.S. racist legislation and the ideology of equality, which came under scrutiny by the whole world—led to the 1965 Immigration Act. The 1965 act ended racist Asian exclusions, introduced family reunification, and strengthened provisions for admitting highly educated and skilled immigrant workers. With the 1965 act, blatant racial discrimination was no longer part of U.S. immigration policy and the country's doors were opened wider, allowing rising numbers of Asian and Middle Eastern immigrants to enter as legal permanent residents. Continuing this trend toward greater openness, President Jimmy Carter signed the Refugee Act in 1980, formally removing American foreign policy as the basis for American refugee policy and admissions.

Some observers see a linear process of increasing immigration liberalism and expansionism.[14] They point to the emergence of a broad world culture of human rights, the erosion of racist national exclusions, and immigration policies moving away from, as sociologist Christian Joppke puts it, "the service of reproducing historically particular forms of nationhood."[15] In this view, once immigrants gain rights, they do not lose them. Instead, they use these to push for more, so that new rights and greater openness accumulate over time. There is much evidence to support this view, especially for the period of 1965 to 1980.

Since the 1980s, we have witnessed growing public ambivalence and even hostility toward new and future immigrants. These views have been widely broadcast in media and have found expression in numerous legislative initiatives. Immigrants and their supporters have made some major gains, but these are often accompanied by retractions and losses. Some immigrant rights and privileges that were once ratified by law have been eroded.

At the federal level, where immigration policies are created in the United States, the rights of legal permanent residents—colloquially known as "green carders" or "legal immigrants"—were actually diminished with the 1996 Illegal Immigrant Reform and Immigrant Responsibility Act (IIRIRA—the acronym is aptly pronounced as eerie-Ira). In California, after Governor Gray Davis reinstituted the right for undocumented immigrants to obtain drivers' licenses, the next governor, former body-building champion and actor Arnold Schwarzenegger, himself an Austrian immigrant, rescinded this right as soon as he took office. These were but two of the many rollbacks at the state and federal levels. At the level of public opinion, blatant xenophobia appears to reign in major media outlets. Rather than embedded liberalism, something more akin to embedded restrictionism has prevailed over immigration matters in the United States since about 1980. The 1980s, the 1990s, and the postmillennial period immediately following the terrorist attacks of September 11, 2001, have featured U.S. restrictionist immigration policies fueled by economic anxieties, racism, nationalism, and national security concerns. These efforts have become deeply embedded in legislative processes, in the media, and in the minds of average citizens.

Several strategic sites of assault on immigrants emerged in this era: the workplace, the border, and, after 9/11, the civil rights of Muslim immigrants. Moreover, these three sites of assault on immigrants are connected. The roots of contemporary anti-immigrant assaults can be traced to the Simpson-Rodino and Simpson-Mazzoli bills of the early 1980s, which first proposed fees and criminal sanctions for employers who knowingly hired undocumented immigrant workers. Employer sanctions were ultimately institutionalized through the Immigration Reform and Control Act of 1986, which also included provisions that ultimately legalized about 3 million undocumented immigrants in the United States. Although employer sanctions remain on the books, these have never been fully enforced—and neither undocumented migration nor employer willingness to hire unauthorized worker has ceased. Consequently, many undocumented workers remain employed in the United States in subservient positions, with extreme exploitation, low wages, long hours, and dangerous working conditions. Entire industries such as cleaning services, hotels and restaurants, construction, farms and poultry plants, and manufacturing sectors now feature an embedded, institutionalized reliance on undocumented immigrant labor.

Some pundits referred to employer sanctions as moving restrictionist efforts from the border to the workplace, but in the 1990s the pendulum swung back with renewed federal efforts to fortify the U.S.-Mexico border. In 1994 President Clinton and Attorney General Janet Reno, in response to public pressure to do something about illegal immigration from Mexico, inaugurated a series of enforcement measures ostensibly designed to stem illegal border crossing at the U.S.-Mexico border. Operation Gatekeeper, Operation Safeguard, and other campaigns with military-sounding names ensued. As detailed in chapter 6, these measures did not deter illegal migration but did push crossings toward sites in the deserts and mountains, increasing tragic migrant deaths.

In 1994 Californians voted overwhelming in favor of Proposition 187, an effort to deny public education and public health services to undocumented immigrants and their children. This measure responded to public perceptions of undocumented immigrants as welfare drains, and it seemed to codify the ambivalent reception of undocumented immigrants, especially Mexicans, welcomed as subordinate workers but rejected as fully human families and communities with possibilities for social reproducing themselves through schooling and health care. Women and children were to be denied public services, with gender, race, and age conspiring as mechanisms of immigrant exclusion.[16]

Proposition 187 was found to be unconstitutional, but its success in California prompted federal immigration legislation in 1996 with IIRIRA. In multiple arenas, IIRIRA demoted the status not only of illegal immigrants but also of legal permanent residents.[17] The year 1996 also brought the Personal Responsibility and Work Opportunity Reconciliation Act. This ended the system of social welfare that had been in place since the 1930s and threatened the ability of noncitizens to obtain welfare benefits. Citizenship, race, and gender constituted new, legitimate axes of exclusion.[18] That same year also saw passage of the Antiterrorism and Effective Death Penalty Act, which made it a crime to offer material support to foreign organizations identified as terrorists by the U.S. secretary of state. Importantly, the act also permitted charges to be brought against suspected immigrants based on secret evidence. As inconceivable as it sounds, the law allows the government to charge immigrants with crimes and withhold evidentiary information that might allow them to defend themselves.

The coordinated terrorist attacks on the World Trade Center and the Pentagon on September 11, 2001, inspired a new wave of Islamophobia and a suspension of immigrant civil rights. No one can deny the tragedy of the attacks, but the U.S. government's response led not only to foreign invasion and war overseas but also to domestic attacks of another sort, codified in the USA PATRIOT Act (Uniting and Strengthening America by Providing Appropriate Tools Required to Intercept and Obstruct Terrorism Act). New forms of surveillance and selective targeting of immigrants were enacted through both administrative decisions and informal practices. The USA PATRIOT Act included changes to criminal, banking, and immigration law, and it introduced more expansive definitions of what constitutes "terrorist activity" for immigrants and U.S. citizens. With this legislation, rapidly passed in the weeks following 9/11, noncitizen immigrants' rights to political association, free speech, due process, and privacy were placed in jeopardy. Thousands of Muslim and Middle Eastern immigrant men were subsequently detained and held without charges.

This is but a brief summary of recent federal immigration restrictionist legislation. The main laws have been accompanied by hundreds of federal administrative decisions and actions, and now there is something new: statewide and local efforts to punish and restrict the rights of immigrants. Regulating immigration is supposed to be a federal matter, but now states and municipalities are trying to control what immigrants can and cannot do. Over one hundred municipalities drafted legislation against undocumented immigrants in 2006, which sociologist

Philip Kretsedemas has referred to as "new immigrant profiling."[19] We have seen this in many states and municipalities with controversies over drivers' licenses, the acceptability of consular identification cards for undocumented immigrants, and law enforcement practices. Some municipalities have tried to enact city laws against renting apartments and houses to undocumented immigrants. At the turn of the millennium, the Statue of Liberty still holds the torch, but newcomers have stepped onto a slippery welcoming mat.

This anti-immigrant legislative era has been accompanied by popular, quotidian expressions of fear, suspicion, and hatred of new immigrants. These include actions and verbalizations of intolerance, contempt, violence, segregation, and exploitation. These are featured in off-the-cuff remarks and deliberate harangues at workplaces, in political speeches and social gatherings, on talk radio, on blogs and email Listservs, and in various mass media outlets. These are too numerous to cite, but even ostensibly liberal-leaning people are prone to comments implying Western, white supremacist superiority and the potentially disastrous effects of including immigrant others in U.S. society. Sometimes this takes the guise of what can be seen as legitimate concern over national security and fear of terrorism, but sometimes it is about fear of immigrant drivers, germs, or immigrant children. There is often an alarmist quality to these comments. After the immigrant rights marches of 2006, a prominent viewpoint expressed in talk radio and newspaper letters to the editors was outrage that people who had entered the United States illegally were now demanding legal rights. Criminals are walking the streets and demanding rights! "Illegals" emerged as a new noun, featured in statements such as "The illegals have won, and national sovereignty is over." "Illegals" seemed to imply the existence of a new, fixed racial category, not a momentary legal categorization.

In this historical moment, even legal immigrants have come to be seen as outsiders, as persons of ill repute. It used to be, as law professor Hiroshi Motomura observes, that Americans saw new immigrants as "Americans in waiting," as people in transition. Now, new immigrants may be permanent legal residents (law-abiding, fully employed, and authorized-to-work green carders) who "may later become citizens, but we no longer treat them as if they will."[20] Something in the current historical moment has unfolded that keeps new immigrants as permanent outsiders, rather than as people in transition, en route to becoming American.

Why has the current era become so inhospitable and mean-spirited? Certainly there are long historical legacies of immigrant and racial exclusions in the United States. As historian Mae N. Ngai has shown, practices of exclusion, restrictionist legislation, and the construction of "illegal aliens" have been constitutive elements of U.S. national identity and nationalism.[21] In the current period, we have been living through an upsurge in nationalist nativism and restrictionism. In part, this is a response to the rapid increase in global, and particularly U.S.-bound, migration, but it is important to recognize the context in which this has occurred. Below, I explain how the anti-immigrant backlash has been shaped by rapid economic, racial-cultural, and nationalist reconfigurations.

Economic transformations, particularly the massive movement of capital, have fueled xenophobia. During the last thirty years, the United States has become part of a system of economic globalization and has completed the transition from an industrial to postindustrial society. The decline of U.S.-based manufacturing, the plant closures of the 1980s, continuing deindustrialization, the proliferation of neoliberalist ideology, and free trade agreements such as NAFTA have led to employment loss and downgrading of many blue-collar jobs, compounding economic uncertainties in the lives of many Americans. As Saskia Sassen succinctly puts it, the denationalization of economies has fueled the renationalization of politics. In this context, immigrant workers appear as competitors and culprits of economic decline.

Another explanation underlines race and culture. In recent years, writers such as Samuel P. Huntington and Arthur Schlesinger have galvanized public attention, sometimes igniting controversy but also aligning sympathy with their arguments that racially different groups of immigrant newcomers are destroying the cultural fabric of white Anglo-Protestant America. There are variations of this argument. In some cases, the threat is construed as Mexican *reconquista*, in others, as non-Judeo-Christian Muslims provoking a "clash of civilizations," but the upshot is the same: The fear of racial, cultural, and linguistic difference legitimates anti-immigrant legislation. While it is no longer legitimate to frame a public campaign by appealing to a "superior Aryan race" or "separate but equal" standards of segregation, commentators such as Etienne Balibar, discussing France, and Leo Chavez, discussing the United States, argue that anti-immigrant tirades now constitute today's acceptable form of racism.[22]

Frustration and anxiety about the impotence of existent nation-state immigration policies have also fueled contemporary xenophobia. Every major postindustrial nation has erected policy barriers that have proven ineffective in restricting immigration.[23] This is true of the European Union, Australia, and Canada as well as the United States. Economic globalization and global realities such as civil wars, natural disasters, and refugee movements are powerful forces that have undermined unilateral immigration policies. In turn, this has led to symbolic efforts to bolster physical barriers at the border, as the political scientist Peter Andreas convincingly argues. Calls for fortifying the U.S.-Mexico border with more Border Patrol and Coast Guard troops accompanied the emergence of vigilante and citizen action groups bearing vaguely archaic names—Ranch Rescue, the Minutemen, and the seemingly Victorian-inspired, Arizona-based Mothers against Illegal Aliens. Can a call to bring back the Texas Rangers be far behind? Frustration and anger over the inability of existent immigration laws and enforcement efforts to have prevented the entrance of 11 to 12 million undocumented immigrants into the United States intensified these expressions of symbolic nationalism and nativism.

These economic, racial-cultural, and nationalist reconfigurations have defined an era with high rates of immigration, where many immigrants are not fully included or integrated into U.S. society. They may be physically present but not fully recognized. The back door of the United States has been opened wide enough for millions of immigrant workers to enter and find employment in the United States, but not wide enough to accommodate them with full rights at the workplace. Instead, economic exploitation, denial of equal opportunities, and the absence of full civil and social rights characterize the experience of many newcomers.

In this regard, Yen Le Espiritu's concept of differential inclusion captures the contemporary reality. Espiritu defines differential inclusion as "the process whereby a group of people is deemed integral to the nation's economy, culture, identity, and power—but integral only because of their designated subordinate standing."[24] I would add that immigrant groups are differentially incorporated into the United States. Some newcomer groups may enjoy more economic rights and privileges but find themselves more restricted in the realm of civil liberties or racial discrimination, while other groups find limited economic opportunities but enjoy great freedoms in other arenas. Similarly, Susan Coutin's concept of legal nonexistence, whereby immigrants are physically present and socially engaged in institutions but lacking in legal recognition, and Cecilia Menjívar's notion of liminal legality, which refers to the suspended or temporary nature of some immigrants' legal status, are also relevant to this reality.[25] People of faith have gathered into various organizations and groups to remedy the injustices of these differential, partial, and liminal inclusions.

DENOMINATIONAL SUPPORT FOR IMMIGRANTS

All of the major mainline religions have issued statements in favor of antirestrictionist reform. Among the most prominent are the pastoral letters by the U.S. Conference of Catholic Bishops. In 2000 they issued a statement, declaring, "We advocate for just policies that respect human rights of immigrants" and stating their opposition to policies that attempt to stem migration but do not "adequately address its root causes."[26] In 2003, together with the Mexican Bishops, they issued a historic joint statement, "Strangers No Longer: Together on a Journey of Hope." Citing the New and Old Testament and Catholic social teachings, the statement focused primarily on the world's largest and longest-running labor migration, U.S.-bound Mexican migration. While recognizing the right of a sovereign state to control its borders, the declaration is unabashedly in favor of migrant rights. If people are unable to find employment in their home societies, the bishops declared, then "they have a right to find work elsewhere in order to survive. Sovereign nations should provide ways to accommodate this right."[27] Building on this earlier momentum, in June 2004 the U.S. Conference of Catholic Bishops launched the Justice for Immigrants campaign. Even conservative Pope Benedict XVI endorsed migrant rights.[28]

Other denominations have also issued strong statements in support of immigrant rights. They became more vociferous after Congress proposed legislation to criminalize ministers and others providing humanitarian assistance to undocumented immigrants. The list of participating religious denominations is broad and impressive: The Evangelical Lutheran Church in America issued statements in favor of upholding the biblical mandate to "welcome the stranger" and legalizing undocumented immigrants currently residing and working in the United States. The Missouri Synod, a sterner variety of Lutheranism, acknowledged "the responsibility of government to regulate immigration" (citing the book of Romans for that) but also conceded that many migrants "come illegally because they have deemed that the legal route is nearly impossible." It too spoke out against proposed legislation that would make it illegal to offer charitable assistance to undocumented immigrants.[29] The presiding Episcopal bishop issued a statement in favor of a "just and humane immigration system" and called for the rejection of "punitive and impractical immigration legislation."[30] The General Assembly of the Presbyterian Church USA went further, issuing a study guide, "Resolution Calling for a Comprehensive Legalization Program for Immigrants Living and Working in the United States." And the United Methodist Church, the American Baptist Church, the Unitarian Universalist Association, and the Union for Reform Judaism have all issued statements, many going back to the 1980s and 1990s, in favor of just immigration policies.

Moreover, as sociologist Stephanie Nawyn has observed, the bulk of refugee resettlement in the United States is conducted by faith-based NGOs.[31] Many of the social services that immigrants receive are funneled through congregations and faith-based organizations, such as Catholic Charities or Lutheran Immigration and Refugee Service. Across the country, multiple small-community organizing projects in immigrant communities often center around church sites and religious-based staff. Grassroots neighborhood organizing projects, such as those run by the Pacific Institute for Community Organization (PICO), are often based in congregations and rely on religious language.[32] Many of the 2006 marches for immigrant rights included religious elements, such as candlelight vigils, emblems of religiosity, and speeches by clergy. In fact, many of the marches began or ended at church sites.

Beyond the major religions' resolutions and declarations in favor of immigrant rights, religious-based groups are working on the ground and with intentionality for immigrant rights. Legalization for undocumented immigrants remains central, but there are several arenas of immigrant rights struggles. In this book, I examine the efforts of people of faith who are fighting for immigrant civil rights, worker rights, and border-crossing rights.

I focus on individuals who have dedicated themselves to mobilizing as religious people to change laws, practices, and institutions so the social landscape will become more hospitable to the rights and full inclusion of immigrants. These are not social service providers but activists seeking social change. Some of these religiously identified people are immigrants themselves, but many are not. They are midlevel activists, neither the top brass who formulate immigration positions or policy for, say, the national Catholic Church or the Presbyterian Synod nor the average congregates in the pews. I describe them more fully later in this chapter. In the next section, I discuss the different tools of religion that these activists use.

WHAT CAN RELIGION DO?

Religion has always played a big role in American civil society and in mobilizing collective groups to pursue social change. A myriad of social and political movements in the United States draw from the well of religion, mostly from Christian religions.[33] Christianity, like other religions, has proven to be quite flexible, as abolitionists and Klansmen, antiwar protestors and "family values" conservatives have all laid moral claim to their causes by basing their movements in Christian religious teachings. In this regard, religion, and particularly Christianity in the American context, is like a tool kit that can be utilized to build different projects. If we pause to consider *what* religion has to offer political and social movements, particularly those concerned with immigrant rights, we can identify at least four critical factors.

Religion can provide social movement actors with moral justification and motivation for action. As Rhys H. Williams notes, religion can serve as a "social movement language," giving "a fairly complete 'explanation' as to why the world is the way it is and how it became that way."[34] Religion imparts not only explanation but also responsibility for setting things right. Notions of altruism and "sacrificial disposition" are deeply embedded in religious teachings and may motivate people to give time and energy to causes that entail risk and that may not benefit them as individuals, as Sharon Nepstad has noted.[35] Faith can motivate social action, and motives that are rooted in the sacred have been referred to as "transcendent motivation" by Christian Smith.[36]

Scripture allows religiously based activists to build their claims for moral authority. Ancient, deeply revered texts from the Abrahamic religions offer sacred teachings that can be applied to various contemporary issues. Notions such as Christian kinship, Jewish righteousness, and Muslim charity operate in the landscape of the immigrant rights movement. Moreover, metaphorical stories from the Bible, the Quran, and the Torah may be deployed in flexible ways. From the Bible alone, there are many stories that teach hospitality and to welcome the stranger and that encourage identification and compassion with workers and the poor. Sociologist Aldon Morris has shown how Martin Luther King skillfully recast biblical themes into calls for social action in the civil rights movement. Scriptures can be used flexibly to support new, alternative ways of seeing the world, especially ways that are not widely accepted. These "alternative frameworks of meaning" can prove critical in bringing about social change.[37]

Religion provides immigrants and their political supporters with *resources*, both social networks and concrete items (such as money and buildings). Material resources are necessary for successful mobilization.[38]

Churches and temples can provide monetary funds, offices with phones and faxes, and large multipurpose rooms with folding chairs for conducting public forums or smaller committee meetings. Clergy who become involved in organizations and advocacy groups bring their own set of resources and professional talents to these groups. They may have time to participate in meetings and coalitions and may already possess well-developed organizational and leadership skills, bringing charismatic speaking abilities to the cause. Faith-based foundations (for example, Catholic Charities, Campaign for Human Development, and Lutheran Immigration and Refugee Service) and donations from the faithful can provide money for grassroots organizing and other campaigns. Followers may donate money to the cause. We know from examining the history of the civil rights movement, the Central American solidarity movement, and the United Farm Workers movement that resources provided by churches and other faith-based organizations and the clergy were critical in those movements' successes.[39]

Existent social networks are also important in building social change–oriented organizations. Religious people are usually already involved in congregations or have other religious connections. For both the solidarity movement of the 1980s and the civil rights movement of the 1950s and 1960s, congregations and religious networks provided ready-made institutions from which movement organizations could recruit new members.[40] Operating in both existent social networks and at the level of faith or belief, religion helps sustain people's long-term commitments to social action.

In a country such as the United States, religion can offer legitimacy to causes that might otherwise be perceived as illegitimate. Religion, particularly Christian religion, carries tremendous moral weight and political legitimacy in the United States. To date, all elected presidents of the United States have been avowed believers in God and members of Christian congregations; only one was non-Protestant. An agnostic or atheist presidential candidate would not go far in the United States, and religious leaders are widely recognized as moral leaders in American society. In this regard, religious leaders who speak out in favor of ideas that are not widely accepted by the American public are not as easily dismissed by opponents as are nonreligious leaders. For example, a clergy member who expresses belief in the dignity of all human beings regardless of state citizenship is not as easily ridiculed as a nonclerical person.

Religion is uniquely suited to offer legitimacy to unpopular causes because it can operate as a relatively autonomous arena, acting as it does from a higher ground. Certainly religion is part of society, but religion is recognized as separate from secular institutions. This means that challenges to both state and market forces may be launched and nurtured through religious institutions.[41] In this regard, religious authority, faith-based morality, and the "higher law" of God and the scriptures may be used to persuade others of the need to remedy injustices in secular institutions.

Finally, religions offer ritual and shared cultural practices. Most movements for social change rely on a shared culture of beliefs and practice. Religion has much to offer in this regard. Sacred songs, religious symbols, ancient scripture, public prayer, special holy days, clerical clothing, and shared beliefs provide a rich glue holding people together. Religious-based rituals and collectively enacted rites invoke the legacy of ancestors and ancient traditions, often evoking the feelings of excitement and togetherness that Emile Durkheim called "collective effervescence."

Today, rituals are deployed in ways that bring deep relevance to contemporary social issues. As social movement theorist James M. Jasper observes, "Collective rites remind participants of their basic moral commitments, stir up strong emotions, and reinforce a sense of solidarity with the group, a 'we-ness.' *Rituals are symbolic embodiments, at salient times and places, of the beliefs of a group.*"[42] Rituals, Jasper reminds us, bring people together in a space that is apart from mundane, everyday activities, and rituals are important in stirring up appropriate collective emotional responses for social change activists. Sociologist Sharon Nepstad, who has examined the religious elements in the Central American solidarity movement, draws our attention to "the cultural resources of Christianity" and the ways in which these are used to rejuvenate activism.[43] These cultural resources include tools such as shared religious identities, rituals, and religious traditions.

The visual aspect of religion constitutes a big part of religious ritual and culture. Religious rituals, metaphors, symbols, visions, icons, and pageantry all include strong visual elements. Rituals can be important internally for a group, allowing members to share contemplative moments and to signal shared identities to one another, and they can be important in the telegenic arena, allowing groups to communicate a religious perspective on a social issue to the public through the mass media. It is in this last regard that the visual aspect of religion becomes very important in social movements, but rituals are also important for renewing activist commitments and identities. As we will see later, religious-based groups approach these tasks in different ways.

People of faith, in small groups and coalitions, are working in today's xenophobic climate to bring about just opportunities for immigrants. This book examines what Muslim American immigrants and their supporters are doing in the realm of civil rights, what Judeo-Christian clergy are doing to advance Latino immigrant worker rights, and what largely ecumenical groups of Christians are doing at the U.S.-Mexico border for migrant border-crossing rights. In the following chapters, I seek to answer the following questions:

- What are these faith-based persons and their organizations doing to promote immigrant rights?
- How do these activists and their organizations use religious language, moral authority, resources, sacred space, and symbols to pursue social change?
- How do their political and religious identities change in the process?

I answer these questions by relying on research conducted with midlevel activists working in various social change–oriented organizations. The data is rich and varied, and it is based on four sources: (1) audio-taped, fully transcribed interviews with individuals identified as faith-based advocates around immigrant rights; (2) observations from public forums, events, and planning meetings sponsored by key organizations; (3) analyses of documents, websites, flyers, and meeting agendas produced by these organizations; and (4) press coverage of these organizations' events. Altogether, sixty in-depth interviews—and an additional forty-seven very short interviews at the Posada sin Fronteras—were conducted by myself and several student research assistants. We also attended and gathered field notes at more than sixty public events.[44] Unsourced quotations that appear in the text are drawn from transcribed interviews and field notes.

PLAN OF THE BOOK

This book is divided into three substantive sections, with two chapters devoted to each case. The first chapter of each section explains what the particular group of religious-based activists do, the broader context of their emergence as social activists, and how they use religion to further their cause. Relevant historical precedents are discussed to remedy our collective social amnesia and to draw analytic comparisons. The second chapter in each section looks at the meanings and identities that faith-based activists draw from their projects.

Part 1 is called "Redeeming Citizens," and chapter 2 introduces Muslim American immigrants struggling for civil rights in the context of the post-9/11 backlash. I examine what various organizations and leaders did during this crucial period, in outreach with their own communities and the broader American public. I also interviewed some of their supporters. As a historical precedent, I also underline in this chapter the important role of black southern Christian churches and clergy in building the civil rights movement of the 1950s and 1960s and the relative absence of a religious-based resistance among Japanese Americans facing internment camps and loss of civil liberties during World War II. Chapter 3 analyzes the discursive struggle of Muslim American immigrant groups. They are seeking to carve out an identity that is at once religious and non-Christian but yet fully American.

Part 2 discusses immigrant worker justice, and chapter 4 focuses on the efforts of one organization, Clergy and Laity United for Economic Justice, to advance the rights of Latino immigrants in the service worker unions. This chapter also discusses the legacy of previous religious efforts devoted to economic advocacy in the United States, namely the social gospel movement, activists in the Catholic Worker movement, and the United Farm Workers movement, led by César Chávez's particularly spiritual form of organizing. As history reveals, there are continuities and disjunctures in the way religion has been used as a tool for worker justice. While chapter 4 focuses on what Clergy and Laity United for Economic Justice members do, chapter 5 examines the tensions that sometimes arise between clergy and union leaders and focuses on how activism informs the clergy's sense of themselves as religious leaders and as people.

Part 3 of the book, Faith *sin Fronteras*, focuses on religious activists at the U.S.-Mexico border. Chapter 6 introduces what faith-based activists are doing to address violence and migrant death, focusing on how Catholic Latino religious rituals in particular have become a key tool of social activism in responding to border policies. This chapter also details how, in the 1980s, religious people and faith played an important role in the sanctuary movement for Central American refugees. Chapter 7 explores the expansiveness of Christian antiborderism by considering the diverse meaning that participants in the Posada sin Fronteras draw from the event. Chapter 8 offers some concluding comments.

My book shows how religion is a powerful force that enables individuals and organizations to engage in civic and political action for new immigrants. This political engagement is often experienced as a "spiritual calling," even as an authentic form of worship, and this engagement revitalizes religious identities and communities. In the process, the claims for both immigrant enfranchisement and religious identities are strengthened, but this is neither a homogenous nor a seamless process. In fact, social activists must use religion strategically and in tandem with secular values and legal systems and institutions. Visiting the three sites of struggle—Muslim American immigrants working for civil rights, Judeo-Christian clergy organizing to support Latino immigrant worker rights, and ecumenical Christian efforts toward establishing border rights—reveals the multiple ways that religion is used to challenge the dominant market and state logic of immigration and immigrant rights.

PART I Redeeming Citizens

TWO Muslim American Immigrants after 9/11

THE STRUGGLE FOR CIVIL RIGHTS

There is a new movement to make people in Muslim, Arab, and South Asian immigrant communities become politically engaged and informed American citizens, but unlike the civil rights movement of the 1950s and 1960s, religion is delicately interwoven into these current efforts. I was introduced to part of this movement on a bright Saturday morning in December 2002 when two thousand people convened at the gargantuan Long Beach Convention Center for the annual convention of the Muslim Public Affairs Council (MPAC). The large convention halls, the registration desks, the speakers dressed in expensive suits and business attire, and the prominent MPAC banners—in red, white, and blue and featuring stars and stripes—prompted my student and me to think we had stumbled into a Democratic or Republican Party convention. All that was missing were balloons, booze, and major television media.

On closer inspection, most of the participants were not fair complexioned, as one would find at the mainstream political party conventions. Joining the predominantly South Asian and Arab Muslim immigrant participants were prominent civil rights attorneys and leaders from African American and Japanese American groups. Organizations such as the American Civil Liberties Union, the Mexican American Legal Defense Fund, and the National Lawyers Guild joined the Muslim American leaders in denouncing federal government legislation and administrative decisions and practices. This was a moment defined by civil liberties violations of foreign-born Muslim Americans. These violations were enabled by the quickly passed legislation, the ominously titled Uniting and Strengthening America by Providing Appropriate Tools Required to Intercept and Obstruct Terrorism Act (USA PATRIOT Act).[1] This legislation was accompanied by the following: hate crimes and harassment against Muslims, South Asians, and Arab Americans; massive government registration and roundups and prolonged government detentions of Middle Eastern immigrant men; the denial of civil rights and due process; the freezing of Muslim charities' assets; racial profiling at airports; and institutionalized use of secret evidence.

One year after the attacks of 9/11, U.S. government efforts at fortifying national security had expanded from terrorist prevention to terrorizing practices that violated basic civil rights.[2] At the MPAC convention, panelists warned of the need for community vigilance against racial discrimination and loss of civil liberties. In one session, an Iranian American attorney, Banafsheh Akhlaghi, denouncing the detention of her clients and as many as several thousand male immigrants from the Middle East, warned ominously that Muslims were not the only targets.[3] "It's not a Muslim thing. It's not an Iranian thing. It's not an Arab thing. It's a human thing," she proclaimed to a rapt audience. This presented a new, virulent form of nationalism, where national origins, she observed, figured more importantly than legal or civil rights. "They don't care what your citizenship is—they look at where you were born. . . . It's a wake-up call."

A MUSLIM THING?

Was the post-9/11 barrage of hate crimes, discrimination, and federal administration directives "a Muslim thing"? Muslim American immigrants were the primary, preferred targets of post-9/11 backlash, and they emerged as key leaders in the effort to end these practices and to promote civil liberties. But as the above quote makes clear, and as many panelists at the convention reminded us, the conflation of race, religion, and nativity seemed to outweigh protections promised by U.S. citizenship and the Constitution. Muslim immigrant men from the Middle East became the preferred, intended targets of post-9/11 backlash, but they were not the only ones. Because of the way in which racialization of Muslims unfolded in this process, Hindu, Egyptian, Arab, and Sikh immigrant men were frequently misidentified as Muslims by attackers as well. Just minutes from my home in Los Angeles' San Gabriel Valley, an Egyptian-born Christian Coptic grocer was murdered on September 22, 2001.[4] Muslim immigrant women who wear hijab in California and other states found themselves harassed, and out of fear for their own safety, many of them responded by staying in self-imposed home confinement in the aftermath of 9/11. And government agencies reported an upsurge in hate crimes and discrimination.

In the wake of 9/11, many non-Muslim South Asians and Christian Arab American immigrants became both victims and activists, as did some Latinos and Asian Americans of various religions. White, U.S.-born Christians and Jews were generally not targets, but many of them, particularly those in the clergy, also worked tirelessly in interfaith dialogues and formed new alliances with these groups. In this chapter I focus particularly on the Muslim response, but also on the collective South Asian and Arab American immigrant response to 9/11. I provide a snapshot of what these community organizations and leaders did in Los Angeles and Orange Counties to restore civil liberties and how, in this process, they renegotiated religious and racial identity with media and government realities. The leaders and organizations discussed in this chapter constitute part of a new movement for immigrant civil rights and for Muslim American identities in the United States.

Muslim citizens and immigrants are a growing and increasingly visible part of the population in all Western, industrial, and postindustrial societies.[5] Syrian immigrants from what is today Jordan and Lebanon, most of them Christian, came to the United States, mostly to the Midwest, during the late nineteenth century as labor migrants and peddlers.[6] Racist exclusionary laws in the 1920s curtailed midcentury immigration from Asia and the Middle East. But the 1965 immigration act, with its preference system for highly educated, skilled migrants and its lifting of the racist exclusionary immigration laws, reopened the doors. Consequently, in the 1970s highly educated, urban-origin Muslim immigrants began coming to the United States from nations as diverse as Pakistan, India, Iran, Indonesia, and Jordan. They were seeking economic and academic opportunities in the United States and fleeing political violence.[7] Many came as students and started student organizations, such as the Muslim Student Association and the Islamic Society of North America, to keep their religion alive in their families and communities.[8] Shared religious identity allowed them to forge connections even though they came from diverse nations. Since the census does not collect data on religious affiliation, the precise number of Muslims in the United States is disputed, but a population of 6 million Muslims is the figure most often cited. About one-third are African American, with the remainder split among Arabs and South Asians.[9]

A plethora of Muslim organizations, most of them built in the 1980s and 1990s, emerged in the forefront of the response to post-9/11 backlash against Muslim, Arab, and South Asian American immigrant communities. I studied a handful of these organizations in Los Angeles and Orange Counties, which is where approximately six hundred thousand Muslim Americans reside. Most of these organizations are directed by first-generation immigrant men who were educated in U.S. universities, many of them in the sciences or business.[10] These men are the antithesis, in substance and physical appearance, of the dominant media representations of bearded, bomb-throwing, foreign, Muslim masculinity. They are clean-shaven and telegenic, they wear exquisite business suits, and they appear equally adept at speaking at press conferences, on panels with the FBI or officials from the Department of Homeland Security, or with Christian interfaith groups. They are not formally trained Islamic religious scholars or imams but savvy, eloquent spokesmen for Islam in America, and they were already making optimistic headway into mainstream American politics before 9/11.[11]

These Muslim American leaders seek to work within the system. They threw their support to the Bush-Cheney ticket in the 2000 presidential election, driven in part by Bush's campaign promise of less support for Israel and by Bush's pledge to repeal the 1995 Antiterrorism and Effective Death Penalty Act—which allows the government to use secret evidence against non-U.S. citizens.[12] While these groups gained momentum in the 1990s, it is the post-9/11 assaults on their communities that propelled them headfirst into the struggle for civil rights. These Muslim organizations, built on the model of modern, professional organizations—with executive directors, public relations specialists, administrative support, newsletters, websites, boards of directors, and small but skilled staffs—were well positioned to take political action, and they were joined by other groups, as I detail further below.[13]

As I see it, this collective effort constitutes a traditional struggle for civil rights and civil liberties. The goal of these activists is both discursive, to carve out an identity as American Muslims (or as American Arabs or South Asian Americans, as the case may be), and instrumental, to end racial and religious discrimination, detentions, profiling, and harassment based on religion, race, and nativity. In this regard, the struggle waged by Muslim, Arab, and South Asian immigrants in the United States runs parallel to the civil rights movement waged by African Americans in the 1950s and 1960s. It is also parallel to the experience of Japanese Americans during World War II internment. Here, it is instructive to pause for a moment and contrast the religious contours of these movements.

IN THE STEPS OF BLACK AMERICANS AND JAPANESE AMERICANS?

There appears to be much in common between the experience of Japanese Americans during World War II and Muslim Americans in the current era. In both instances, the United States government responded to violent attacks from outside the nation by seeking to define and retaliate against an enemy within the nation. Both instances rely on racial discrimination against citizens and immigrants of Japanese or Muslim, Arab, or South Asian origins. And not surprisingly, in the post-9/11 period, there has been an outpouring of support from Japanese American organizations to Muslim, Arab, and South Asian American communities affected by the post-9/11 backlash and new affiliations between these groups.[14]

What happened to Japanese Americans is well known. Soon after Japan attacked Pearl Harbor on December 7, 1941, President Franklin Delano Roosevelt signed Executive Order 9066. Everyone of Japanese ancestry on the West Coast was subjected to curfew and, eventually, forced removal from their homes, schools, and workplaces. Entire families were freighted into internment in camps in remotely located rural places in Utah, Idaho, and Montana and deserts in California. Approximately 110,000 people of Japanese descent, 70,000 of them American citizens, spent the duration of World War II living in cheaply constructed wooden barracks in places like Manzanar or Topaz, with armed sentry guards posted along the barbed wire enclosure fences.

Where was religion in this process? Although there is some evidence that Buddhist priests were among the first Japanese Americans to be targeted, religion was not an effective organizing principle among the Japanese Americans who tried to protest and resist internment.[15] This is not to say that religion was not important to Japanese Americans. It was. The majority were Buddhist, and a substantial percentage were Christian.[16] Religion and religious traditions from both Buddhism and Christianity were important resources for coping with the brutality of the evacuation and interment experience. As historian David Yoo summarizes, "In the concentration camps, temples and churches offered comfort and a source of meaning through a variety of religious activities. Religion, far from being an opiate, served as a venue in which Japanese Americans explored the meaning of their plight."[17] According to Yoo and others, religious leaders and churches helped Japanese Americans adjust to harsh life in the camps and provided social services and a place to seek racial-ethnic solidarity and understanding of what was happening.

For the Japanese Americans, religion did *not* provide a venue for contesting the evacuation and internment. Religion allowed people to keep their ethnic identity and express solidarity in the face of extreme circumstances—but neither Buddhism nor Christianity were used to organize protests against the basic injustice.

By contrast, the civil rights movement of the late 1950s and early 1960s was built on the religious foundations of black Christian southern churches. Respected, charismatic clergymen, already skillful orators, became the movement's most famous and effective leaders. Biblical scriptures provided the rationale for condemning racial discrimination and oppression, and the example of Jesus served as a model of both social action and personal sacrifice for the common good. Moreover, churches provided autonomous, ready-made meeting sites for tactical and strategic planning. According to Aldon Morris, the scholar who has most comprehensively analyzed the role of religion in the civil rights movement, "The black church supplied the civil rights movement with a collective enthusiasm generated through a rich culture consisting of songs, testimonies, oratory, and prayers that spoke directly to the needs of an oppressed group. Many black churches preached that oppression is sinful and that God sanctions protest aimed at eradicating social evils."[18]

Community allegiance to charismatic clergy leaders was a key factor in this movement, and the local, regional, and national leadership of Dr. Martin Luther King personified this dictum. Christian scripture served as a rationale for the struggle, while the organization of black churches and the tradition of charismatic religious leaders provided the key resources for organizing the movement.[19]

The contemporary Muslim struggle for civil rights shares much with the goals of the civil rights movement of the 1950s and 1960s. These Muslim American leaders want to put an end to unfair treatment and discrimination against their communities, and they want the right to claim a Muslim American identity, just as blacks sought to become fully enfranchised American citizens. Religion, however, gets used differently by these groups. In the contemporary instance, religion is the central basis for discrimination and is a primary means of mobilization, but religion does not serve as a rationale for making claims for the restoration of civil liberties. While civil rights leaders in the 1950s and 1960s regularly quoted the Bible to give religious relevance to social injustices, the contemporary Muslim, Arab, and South Asian civil rights leaders do not appeal to Islamic sacred scriptures to claim their rights. Instead, they evoke the American Constitution as a textual source of justice. The Quran is not the warrant for making claims about inclusion in the American polity, nor is it a means of motivating people to social action. Rather, as we will see, the Quran is used variously, as a text that helps unify Muslim organizations and Muslim collective identity, and when it is engaged in public discourse, to show that American values and political traditions are compatible with Islam's major tenets.

The relationship of religious places of worship to the civil rights struggles also differs. Unlike Christian congregations, mosques are not always congregational centers. Observant Muslims need not congregate weekly as part of a mosque. While some of the early post-9/11 public forums were held in mosques, the key organizing entities in this movement were not mosques but professional religious-political organizations, and they tended to hold their events in decidedly secular sites, in large halls that could accommodate big crowds, usually in hotels and convention centers. Similarly, charismatic imams were not the principal leaders. Rather, leaders were professional, highly educated executive directors of nonprofit organizations that specialize in civil rights.

Religious freedom is a foundational American narrative. The central struggle for these groups, however, is not the right to practice Islam but to lay claim to rights and civil liberties as Americans and as immigrants who are racialized, "alienized," and oppressed because of their religious identification. While these groups claim to share experiences of minority subordination with other U.S. racial-ethnic minorities, especially with Japanese Americans who were also held suspect during World War II, their struggle is to disestablish Christianity as a precursor to American national identity. To be clear: They are not against Christianity. They are against the idea that one must be Christian to be American. In this regard, their goals go right to the heart of the origins of the United States.

For the first- and second-generation immigrants active in this project, religion and ethnicity act as an organizing net. But in an era when being foreign, Islamic, and Middle Eastern is conflated with "terrorist," they cannot deploy religion in overt, highly visual public ways. Organizations such as the Council on American-Islamic Relations (CAIR) and MPAC seek to represent themselves as both Muslims and Americans, while the South Asian Network (SAN), the American-Arab Anti-discrimination Committee (ADC), and the Palestinian American Women's Association (PAWA) are also working to represent themselves as Americans. In this struggle for recognition and self-definition, they use established, institutional modes of political engagement. These include town hall meetings, conventions, press releases, and formal meetings and collaborations and informal meetings with federal, state, and local government and law enforcement authorities. They organize as members of racialized immigrant groups, and in the post-9/11 era, they establish coalitions and working relations with other groups, such as Japanese Americans and Christian clergy as well as government representatives from the FBI, the Department of Homeland Security, and the local sheriff's office. They seek to influence public opinion and the state, but they refrain from bringing highly visible expressions of Islam to the political arena.

"WE SHOULD BE ABLE TO DEFINE OURSELVES"

Constructing and promoting an identity is at the heart of the struggle for all the ethnic-religious organization leaders I interviewed. For the leaders of CAIR, MPAC, PAWA, ADC, and SAN, civil rights is, at core, a discursive struggle. This is their primary challenge. At stake in the post-9/11 era is who will control the image of Muslim Americans, Arab Americans, and South Asian Americans. What will be included in the content of this identity? And will this identity be used to promote inclusion or justify exclusion? These groups want inclusion, and they are actively seeking a place in the American polity and society that reflects their position both as Americans and as immigrants who will no longer be racialized and persecuted because of religion and phenotype. They want to contest the images of them that circulate through the media. As Hussan Ayloush, the executive director of CAIR, put it when I interviewed him, "The raison d'etre of CAIR is defending the image of the Muslim community." No other group in American society, he said, is as vulnerable to constant barrages of racial epithets and openly disdainful commentary as Muslim Americans."At the bottom of the food chain are Muslims," he plaintively explained. "For years we allowed others to speak on our behalf, to define who we are, and I can assure you, we didn't like the way they defined us." Similarly, Ahmed Younis, the national director of MPAC in Washington, D.C., declared, when speaking in 2005 to a gathering of journalists in Los Angeles, "Identity is the fulcrum of the discussion about Muslim participation in U.S. society."[20]

These groups seek inclusion as Americans, but not an inclusion that compromises being Muslim. Their remedy focuses on educating the larger society, to show that they are American *and* Muslim. As Salam Al-Marayati, the Los Angeles director of MPAC, told me, "We're stressing the American Muslim identity. We're trying to be more vocal and set America straight." For those who are South Asian or Arab but not Muslim, the struggle is to retain (or construct) those ethnic-national identities as American. These leaders were involved in many projects to educate Americans about Islam prior to 9/11, but that crisis intensified their efforts.

Among the organizations at the forefront of this effort in Southern California were CAIR and MPAC. Founded in 1994 to promote positive images of Islam and Muslims, CAIR defines itself as "America's largest Islamic civil liberties group." Today it maintains headquarters in Washington, D.C., and twelve regional offices in the United States and Canada. The CAIR-LA office in Orange County has become one of the most active chapters in the nation. Although it does not maintain a strictly dues-paying membership, CAIR has a large mass following. Hussan Ayloush, the executive director of CAIR's Orange County office, estimated in 2002 that about three thousand people donated locally through their annual banquet and about three hundred people donated monthly. To my eyes, it certainly appears to have an affluent constituency that donates generously. At a 2002 CAIR fundraiser that I attended in Anaheim, I saw the group raise a half-million dollars in one evening.[21] In this, too, these organizations differ from black civil rights organizations of the 1950s and 1960s.

MPAC, founded in 1988, defines itself as "a public service agency working for the civil rights of American Muslims, for the integration of Islam into American pluralism."[22] MPAC had established some visibility and legitimacy with the federal government, but the pro-Israeli lobby prevented MPAC executive director Salam Al-Marayati from being appointed to the National Commission on Terrorism. MPAC maintains a small staff with offices in both Washington, D.C., and Los Angeles, but the MPAC conventions that my students and I attended at the Long Beach Convention Center in 2002, 2004, 2005, and 2006 drew big audiences. Each time, we saw over one thousand people in attendance, and perhaps closer to three thousand in 2002. Until then, the main immigrant events and fundraisers I had attended were sponsored by Mexicans or Central Americans, and the difference in class resources was striking, to say the least. At the MPAC and CAIR fundraising banquets, the parking lots boasted plenty of late-model Hondas and Toyotas as well as luxury cars, and my students and I witnessed public outpourings of generosity from affluent Muslim American immigrants. Abundant resources, however, do not shield these groups from harassment or discrimination. Below, I detail how some of these groups responded to this post-9/11 reality.

KNOW YOUR NEIGHBOR, KNOW YOUR RIGHTS — AND SHOW YOURSELF TO THE FBI

Immediately after 9/11, organizations like CAIR and MPAC were thrown into high gear, initially responding reactively, defending and protecting members of their communities, and then proactively, educating and informing members of the Muslim immigrant communities and other Americans as well. The aperture of collective self-definition opened up as it never had before, and the leaders saw this as a new opportunity and obligation. The Islamic-identified organizations were most deeply affected by these imperatives. They set about the task of educating Americans about Muslims and of informing their own ethnic communities about civil rights. We can think of these, respectively, as "Know Your Neighbors" and "Know Your Rights" campaigns.

The executive director of the Muslim Public Affairs Council told me that in the Los Angeles area, MPAC had sponsored or participated in over four hundred public forums and outreach events between September 11, 2001, and February 2002, the time of the interview. MPAC sought not only to inform and protect community members, but also to educate the government and the larger public.

How did organizations with small, already stretched paid staffs accomplish this? They dipped into their general membership to develop a new pool of leaders. As Samer Hathout, a lawyer, MPAC board member, and daughter of a key leader reflected, "We feel so behind, so overwhelmed. There's so much to do now. . . . Everyone wants to know about Islam, so there is this overwhelming demand for speakers and appearances." MPAC developed new spokespeople during this period, and she noted, "People that didn't necessarily want to do public speaking are finding that it's not as scary as they thought it was. So it's really brought out some more leaders for us."

The ways in which these groups responded to these urgencies signaled organizational maturity. Salam Al-Marayati, the executive director, remained proud that the organization had stepped up to the new challenges. Speaking of this period, in our interview he said, "It intensified the work and there were much more opportunities because it showed that MPAC was an organization that was ready, able to really represent Muslims in the public eye and defend Islam in the public eye." Among MPAC successes he counted the following: "We've had major addresses at the State Department, major meetings with the administration, the Senate, the House. So everyone has looked upon Muslim organizations in general in the field, and on MPAC in particular, to give them advice on dealing with the politics of the Muslim world and the Muslim community." Lest this assessment sound thoroughly optimistic and satisfied, I must note that in the following breath, Al-Marayati expressed his frustration with problems "of reception." New venues had opened, but "people aren't listening to the [moderate] voice."

At the Council on American-Islamic Relations office in Orange County, the response was initially reactive and service oriented—taking reports of hate crimes, employment discrimination, and school and workplace harassment—but it also did proactive work aimed at information and outreach. Speaking of the immediate post-9/11 months, the executive director of CAIR, Hussam Ayloush, said, "We've been doing the same thing for the last almost eight years nationwide, and the last six years in Southern California. But what's happened is the degree or the amount of what we were doing has changed—the intensity. In the past maybe we used to give one presentation at a church maybe every two months, at a school every two months; we would deal maybe with twenty cases of discrimination. Within a few months after September 11th, we had to deal with over—if I'm not mistaken—close to two hundred cases in our area of hate incidents." Like other organizations, CAIR was not equipped for this barrage of activity. "As a small office," explained Ayloush, "we weren't prepared to deal with a flood of phone calls." They brought in more volunteers and hired new staff, but this required devoting more resources to training.

More time and resources were subsequently devoted to civil liberties issues. CAIR, for example, has continued to issue "action alerts" through the Internet, alerting Listserv recipients to instances of prejudice, discrimination, and violence against Muslims. For affluent, literate, educated, professional-class immigrants, the Internet is a useful resource. One observer has called this "action alert activism."[23]

Organizations such as CAIR and MPAC did not sponsor public forums entirely on their own. They worked together with other, smaller South Asian and Arab organizations in the Los Angeles–Orange County area, such as SAN, PAWA, and ADC, and, importantly, they formed coalitions and collaborated on projects with traditional civil rights organizations. These included legal organizations such as the American Civil Liberties Union and the National Lawyers Guild, the Department of Justice's Community Relations Service, as well as interfaith Jewish and Christian groups and clergy leaders. New alliances were formed with racial-ethnic civil rights organizations, such as the Mexican American Legal Defense Fund and the Nikkei for Civil Rights. Prominent African American civil rights leaders in Los Angeles, such as Connie Rice (Condoleezza's progressive cousin) and the Reverend James L. Lawson, a veteran leader of the civil rights movement in the South, became featured speakers at the annual convention. The Muslim, South Asian, and Arab organizations also established formal collaborations and received support from the Orange County and Los Angeles County Human Relations Commission, the state agency formally in charge of monitoring and preventing hate crimes and racial discrimination. They also participated with law enforcement agencies, such as the sheriff's offices of Los Angeles and Orange Counties.

Among the most controversial collaborations formed, however, were those with agents of the federal government. After the FBI began a series of raids and detentions and an administrative call from Ashcroft's Department of Justice was issued for Middle Eastern men to present themselves for "voluntary" questioning, the community organizations faced the decision of how to deal with the federal government. Should they collaborate in an effort to prove their innocence and to protect themselves and their communities? Or would compliance and connection with government agencies lead to further repression and surveillance, to mass detentions, and to more civil liberties violations? Fear and anxiety, emotions that can easily paralyze people, suggested that either route might exacerbate the repression, and the organizations were clearly, as one interviewee said, between "a rock and a hard place." Victor Narro, a progressive Los Angeles–based immigrant rights and labor lawyer, was involved in these coalitions, and when I interviewed him, he reported, "There was a lot of conflict within groups about collaborating with government agencies who were creating the danger." Narro, then with the Coalition for Humane Immigrant Rights (CHIRLA) of Los Angeles, recalled a meeting at the ACLU offices where the executive director I interviewed related how the FBI had approached him with the request to give names of community leaders, so that the FBI could then presumably offer those people protection against possible hate crimes. Narro recalled telling him, "Man, they're setting you up for surveillance."

I do not know the extent to which the FBI used intimidation to get names, files, and other information from these organizations. Clearly, it was a dangerous and difficult time for the organization leaders and staff, and government intimidation, anonymous hate emails and phone calls, and even bomb threats appear to have kept the groups from vociferously protesting legislation such as the USA PATRIOT Act. When I asked why they had not been stronger in publicly decrying this legislation, Salam Al-Marayati suggested that protesting the detention of thousands of Muslim immigrant men in the United States and the closing of Muslim charities would have been too much for MPAC to take on at that point. "As a young organization," he said, "you can just offer your voice, and that's what we do." He recognized, he said, that "it's very little, but still, it's an important step." Working together for civil liberties with other groups, "whether it's ACLU or it's interethnic or interfaith groups, Hispanic groups, Asian American groups," holding teach-ins and public forums, and doing media outreach were preferable, he said. When I asked Sarah Eltantawi, who was then in charge of MPAC media relations, about MPAC efforts to directly counter the USA PATRIOT Act, she said that efforts were "not as much as I would have liked." When I asked what prevented a stronger stance, she stated, "Intimidation. After September 11th, a lot of voices and a lot of these organizations were really just trying to cooperate as much as possible." Why? "Just scared," she replied. "The community was scared. The period right after September 11th just didn't seem like the time to kind of say to the FBI, 'Get out of our affairs.'" Interestingly, none of the male respondents put it quite this bluntly.

Instead of a policy of noncooperation with government authorities, the groups decided to participate in town hall meetings, which brought together Muslim, South Asian, and Arab American community leaders and members with FBI, INS, and Department of Justice functionaries. I attended the second in the Southern California series of town hall meetings in January 2002, four months after 9/11. It was officially sponsored by the U.S. Department of Justice Community Relations Service, through the efforts of Ron Wakabayashi, a Japanese American with a long history of civil rights activism.[24] The meeting was held on a Saturday afternoon in a ballroom of a Holiday Inn in La Mirada, a city just off Interstate 5, near the industrial area where northern Los Angeles and southern Orange County meet. There were over one hundred people, most of them Arab American or Muslim, and a handful of Sikhs. In the lobby, where various groups set up tables to distribute leaflets, I saw newspapers in

Arabic, but I was most struck by how prosperous the people looked. In fact, I remember wishing that I had dressed up a bit more. The men—and it was mostly men—wore suits and ties, and the women wore professional attire. Many women wore headscarves that matched their outfits. Once in the ballroom, the audience mostly listened attentively—but sometimes heckled—as speakers from the FBI, INS, and the Department of Justice addressed questions of concern. Joining the three white middle-aged men representing the government were four community representatives, including one woman, and the moderator, Tareef Nashashibi, who introduced himself as president of the Arab American Committee of the Republican Party of Orange County. He began on an upbeat note, celebrating and thanking the FBI for incarcerating Irv Rubin of the Jewish Defense League, who bombed offices in 1985, killing Alex Odeh, and he emphasized the rights of citizens and the importance of working together with government. "We are aware," he stated at the outset, "of the FBI looking closely at us, and we want to look back at them." He identified the use of secret evidence as a major threat, and he said, "These issues are important to us, the recent immigrant group. We are all citizens of this country, and we need to be treated alike." At the meeting, the government representatives addressed questions from the audience about the use of secret evidence, racial profiling, detentions, and visas. The INS representative claimed that the term "racial profiling" had been abused by the media in "unsettling ways," and he tried to allay fears by saying that less than one hundred people in the INS western region had been detained due to post-9/11 investigations. The audience response varied, from polite questions and nodding heads to outright heckling.

The diversity of views expressed by the community organization speakers and the audience was also evident among the leaders I interviewed. Some of them saw the town hall meetings as important for building relations with local government bureaucrats and for educating government officials about their communities. They saw these meetings as "building bridges," as ways to keep their own communities abreast of developments, but also as educational efforts, so that government officials "will know that Arabs and Muslims are not what they see on TV." As one leader said to me in an interview: "We wanted to make sure that people do not have this fear of the FBI, so we arranged several town hall meetings with the FBI, the INS. . . . They had very pleasant people working with them. . . . It helped us both, both communities. I think it helped them realize that as they attended those meetings they saw that the Muslim community was not just a bunch of bearded men shouting, 'Death to America!'"

Not everyone agreed with this strategy of government collaboration. This dilemma is common to many social movement organizations. In this instance, some of the organizers were criticized for organizing and participating in these events. Tareef Nashashibi later told me he had been criticized for being the master of ceremonies at such events. His critics alleged, he said, that he was "dealing with the secret police, with the *migra*." (Interestingly, *migra*, the Spanish word for immigration police, has seeped from Mexicans to Muslims.) Nashashibi's response was that the gains outweighed the risks. Now, he said, "They know who we are. They know what we feel, what we think. . . . Now we have contacts. The INS wants to have sensitivity training on Arabs and that's never happened before. This is an achievement." Other leaders also cited the benefits of contacts with local federal government officials. This "could help to get visas or certain things taken care of," said one. Hussan Ayloush added that prior to the town hall meetings, CAIR had "always hit a wall" with the INS, a federal agency widely known for its thick bureaucracy and disorganization. But the INS had actually brought a little entourage of agents who consulted with the audience after the La Mirada town hall meeting. After the meeting, Ayloush reported, "We were able to get a hold of names of people who are high-ranking officers or INS officials, and these people were instrumental in helping us resolve a number of unfair cases." Other community leaders found little to celebrate in these new collaborations. One critic had this to say: "We had three town hall meetings with the FBI, the INS, and the Justice Department, and I felt like it was group therapy. We talked . . . they listened and they did not do anything. There's still a lot of people being detained, still a lot of people going to jail. The idea about democracy that we are innocent until proven guilty no longer stands. There is no due process for the Arabs or the Muslims."

These internal conflicts speak to the diversity of Muslim American, Arab American, and South Asian American immigrant communities. Just as there is no monolithic voice in the Muslim world, there is no monolithic voice among these various communities in the United States. One interviewee candidly noted that the diversity of the Muslim community makes the advocacy work a challenge. Some members favor traditional party affiliations and congressional causes, while others advocate grassroots connections with labor and civil rights organizations; others bitterly disagree about the relative merits and dangers of participating with the FBI, INS, and Department of Justice. Fighting domestic surveillance of Muslim American immigrant communities and yet working with the federal government is the tightrope these groups walk. The groups want to work with the government, but they want to stop government surveillance based on racial-religious profiling and unspecified standards. While there are disagreements on approaches, they all agreed that a big part of the problem is the United States' ignorance of their communities.

Of the organizations I examined, none were as explicitly focused on the project of addressing imagery in media and among opinion makers as CAIR and MPAC. Within MPAC, no one was out on the frontlines more than Sarah Eltantawi. Freshly out of graduate school, female, and still in her twenties, she had only been on the job for a few months before 9/11. Suddenly, she found herself on Fox News and CNN. By February 2002 she had debated Daniel Pipes on the *Gretta Van Sestren Show* and had been on the *O'Reilly Factor* three times. "The first time was with John Gibson," she said. "That was absolutely horrific. . . . I was supposed to go on and talk about American Muslims' response to 9/11, and as soon as I got on there, he immediately started screaming at me about 'Why do you people have a problem with the United States after all we've done for the Palestinians? After all we've done for the peace process, you ungrateful, blah, blah, blah.' I mean, he really just screamed at me, wouldn't let me get a word in edgewise." From her experience, she concluded, "O'Reilly's people just want Muslims up there, like sitting ducks." That television appearance was followed by more where she was often pitted against so-called terrorism experts like journalist Steve

Emerson and Daniel Pipes, editor of the *Middle East Quarterly*. Both of these men frequently write and speak about the dangers of radical Islam and promote the view that Arab and Muslim American communities harbor terrorist sleeper cells. As Eltantawi recalled of the news shows, "The question of who Muslims are and who Arabs are is never approached objectively, but more like, 'The Quran says this and this about infidels. What do you have to say?' We're always on the defensive, always having to answer questions that are posed with a certain kind of bias in mind."

While the media spokespeople routinely questioned the patriotism and innocence of Muslim and Arab Americans, interviewees from various groups said that the media refused to report their organizations' condemnations of the terrorist attacks. CAIR, ADC, and MPAC regularly issued press releases condemning terrorist attacks, suicide bombings, and the like. These, however, typically went ignored and received no press coverage. Ra'id Faraj of CAIR noted the selective bias. The media asks, he said, "Where are the Muslim organizations who are condemning 9/11? And we're saying all along, you know, read our statement, read our press releases and fax and this and that." He added, "From day one the Council on American Islamic Relations has unequivocally condemned, and we will continue to condemn, any act of terrorism and violence against innocent civilians."

Bombings are news, and statements of pacifism are not. Advocates understand this. "We shouldn't feel that radio and television and print should just print our press releases through their outlets," offered Salam Al-Marayati. "Having said that, though," he continued, "we had a conference on the rising voice of moderate Muslims, and we didn't get a single media outlet to cover it." The conference was held in December 2001, perhaps the high point of public interest in Islam and Muslim Americans. "It was eye-opening for me because even though we had all these positive relations with these journalists, we couldn't get a single one to come out," he recalled. When asked to explain this outcome, he noted that moderate Muslims are not perceived as a sexy or sensationalistic media topic. "If I get three people to have a conference to say that Bin Laden is a good guy, you'll get the media and they'll cover you ad nauseam. But if you say, 'Here are the moderates . . .' they just don't find an interest." Hussam Ayloush concurred. "You know, media is a business, and like any other business, in order to survive you have to be able to sell your products," he said. "A demonstration by a couple of hundred extremists in Pakistan or Bangladesh burning the U.S. flag and saying, 'Death to America!' is very sensational. Take a picture of it with a nice comment, and you get a lot of viewers."

Moderate, peaceful Muslim Americans do not fit the narrative of what is profitable to print, and this determines, in part, how these communities come to be viewed by society at large. During the first few months after 9/11, a counternarrative appeared in the media news, as we saw the debut of a series of "human interest" stories on Muslim American families. These constituted the mass media's approach to the "Muslim moment." On the one hand, these stories presented humanizing quotidian portraits of Muslim American families. The features focused on Muslims as average American families, were typically shot in the domestic sphere of kitchens and dining rooms, and showed glimpses of all-American mortgages, children with homework, and family members gathered around a dining table for an evening meal. On the other hand, these portraits may have played into the new American paranoia of sleeper cells. Regardless of how these "American family" narratives were ultimately read by viewers, they did present a significant departure from the media-as-usual representations of Muslim and Arab Americans. Ra'id Faraj, the public relations director of CAIR, was among the most charitable in his assessment of the media. "The mainstream media," he said, "has been okay. After all, they've definitely worked with us on all kinds of stories. We've assisted them on stories, we gave them numbers and statistics, and we helped them to find individuals in the communities [to feature]." Nader Abuljebain of the ADC was less sanguine with his succinct assessment: "So I'm glad at least they know we exist, and we don't all have tails, and we are not all terrorists or millionaires or belly dancers."

The "Muslim American family" media narratives were relatively short-lived. By the spring of 2002, with Palestinian suicide bombings and Israeli military attacks raging in the Middle East, the tenor had changed. Samer Hathout told us that her assessment of the media had changed over time as well. When asked in April 2002 to state her opinion of media coverage of Muslim Americans, she said, "I think my answer would have been different three months ago when there was a lot more interest, because now it's degenerated back to that Middle East political brouhaha. A couple of months ago, I think it was very positive, good stuff on Islam and Muslims." Speaking in reference to a news show that featured a Muslim family who had lost a loved one in the World Trade Center, she said, "I think the media has really made an effort to humanize us." Still, she was quick to note the significant vacuums: "I'd like to see more coverage of civil liberties issues."

In the discursive battle for civil rights, the media is a site of struggle for Arab American, Muslim American, and, to a lesser extent, South Asian American immigrant communities. Media constructs of their communities are consequences, the interviewees said, of control of the news media by corporate conglomerates, the government, and "special interest groups," which generally refers to Zionist lobby groups. Mass media in the United States, for these commentators, does not fit U.S. ideals of free speech. Several of them noted how state controlled the media is in the United States in comparison with other democratic nations in Europe. Citing examples of army generals providing analyses and shaping opinions in the media, Michel Shehadeh of the ADC concluded, "There is a militarization of the media." Other interviewees agreed that, increasingly, the media serves as a tool of the government, the military, and "special interests."

In spite of the range of critiques of the media, nearly everyone we interviewed cited the media as a tool for reshaping and contesting the distorted imagery. Some groups cited new relations built with reporters, but they explained that the news stories still often remained stymied by editors or the larger structural obstacles. Still, they held hope that the media system might ultimately reform, or perhaps that different modes of communication might counter the negative media images of their communities.

These groups sought to inform other Americans about their communities, but the mass media was not the only venue. The organizations explored different routes toward this end in the period following 9/11. Hollywood was one venue. As Michel Shehadeh, who had been invited to speak about images of Arab Americans at a television production company, noted, "Now I am not speaking in [only] the traditional places, like campuses, churches, now it's [also] businesses, corporations."

In 2002 CAIR debuted a series of billboards along Southern California freeways showing photos of smiling, multiracial Muslims—the photo was reminiscent of a Benetton ad—with the text "Even a Smile Is Charity," to suggest that Muslims might be kind and compassionate rather than dangerous. CAIR also invested in getting books and videos with accurate portrayals of Islam into public and school libraries. MPAC members were encouraged to write letters to the editor, and they did, and some of these were published in the *Los Angeles Times*. In the post-9/11 period, MPAC actively encouraged members to become media spokespeople. "We are learning to do the sound-bite thing," explained Samer Hathout.

A long-term route to remedy media distortion involved getting more Muslim Americans and Arab Americans into media jobs. This is part of the larger Muslim American project of cultivating leaders in the second generation. As one leader said, Muslims should be "encouraging more Muslims in those fields, fields of media, journalism, communication, educating members of the media, sensitizing them." First-generation Muslim immigrants and their children tend to concentrate in science and engineering jobs, so as one interviewee said, "encouraging them to be journalists or [in] any area of the liberal arts . . . to consider politics as a career" is part of the solution.

In at least one instance, Hollywood stars were mobilized to fight prevailing negative Hollywood images. In the immediate aftermath of 9/11, the Los Angeles County Commission on Human Relations sought to deter hate crimes with the help of Hollywood celebrities. Robin Toma said that after the movie star Patricia Arquette, herself the daughter of a Muslim American father, came forward to volunteer "to do something about what she saw was the anti-Muslim, anti-Arab backlash in this country," celebrities were recruited to do radio public service announcements against hate. Arquette visited public schools to talk with youth and apparently used her personal networks to recruit celebrities for the radio spots. Hollywood was also rewarded by MPAC for fair and non-stereotypical portrayals of Muslims. To encourage fair representations in film, MPAC had already introduced a media awards program. Past winners now include Denzel Washington, Morgan Freeman, Spike Lee, George Clooney, Kevin Costner, and Yusuf Islam (formerly known as Cat Stevens).

Many interviewees, like Sarah Eltantawi, expressed frustration and doubts about the media's ability to change. From her perspective, this is a classic chicken-and-egg problem. As she reflected aloud, "Can we change the media? Can we change the way media covers us, or do we need to change public opinion first? How does this work exactly? I still haven't figured this out." While she had established rapport and respect with some journalists, she still found her interactions with the media to be very problematic. "It's a real uphill battle, the media," she sighed wearily.

Leaders of these organizations worked hard to allay fears and anxieties and to inform their communities of their civil rights. It was a tough sell. Fear prompted people to stay away from mosques and Islamic centers and to withdraw their financial contributions to Islamic charities. Randall Hamud, a third-generation Arab American civil rights attorney and ADC board member who was defending detainees, reported at an ACLU-sponsored public forum his frustration with raising bail money—no one now wanted to take the risk of association with detainees, even though they were not proven to be guilty of anything. Hamud also reported accompanying clients from San Diego who were asked to come forward for questioning. The FBI asked them, "Why were you trying to change your license plate?" Neighbors had reported seeing Hamud's client changing his license plate at night, but the client had merely been tightening a license plate that was coming loose.[25] In this context of surveillance and accusations, community members were less likely to volunteer information and were reluctant to report hate crimes out of fear and stigma. Ra'id Faraj of CAIR said that the attitude of many victims was "It's already happened. I don't want to talk about it." Even ethnic organizations providing health services such as mammography screenings to the South Asian community said they were unable to do so because of the new fear. "We felt the change especially three months after the September 11 attacks," said the program director at SAN. "They were just not giving their names or phone numbers, nothing," and this negatively affected delivery of basic services such as breast cancer screening, those offered at domestic violence shelters, and so on. As Hamid Khan, executive director of SAN, put it, "Right now we feel besieged, because of detentions, because of dealing with the FBI, we are having extreme difficulty in documenting needs because people are unwilling to share stories, but they tell us, 'We just had a raid.'" Michel Shehadeh of ADC concurred: "The community is not coming out to join organizations and to fight back. This is a scared community, and the challenge is to empower the community." Most agreed that the fear was greatest among the foreign-born.

In the aftermath of 9/11, the organizations discussed here devoted a good deal of their outreach and educational efforts to their own communities, particularly first-generation immigrants. Large public forums at Islamic centers, churches, town hall meetings, and hotels attracted thousands of people. Informational materials were distributed at these meetings and in ethnic newspapers. Yet the community leaders reported that immigrants in the Muslim American, Arab American, and South Asian American communities presented particular challenges: ignorance of their rights and entitlements in the United States; the legacy of having grown up under despotic rulers and being unaccustomed to freedom; and intensified fear and anxiety due to government repression following 9/11.

If information is power, knowledge of basic civil rights and entitlements, the leaders reasoned, may help deter abuses. Toward this end, the organizations distributed thousands of "know your rights" brochures and cards. The pocket-sized, fold-up cards such as the ones distributed by CAIR, for example, included titles such as "Know Your Rights as an Airline Passenger," "If the FBI Contacts You," "Your Rights as an Employee," "Your Rights as a Student," and "Reacting to Anti-Muslim Hate Crimes." These were brilliantly prepared, informative, pithy documents and included simple, sequential steps to take in a variety of problematic circumstances. Similar brochures and cards were distributed by the other organizations, and they were translated into multiple languages, including Arabic, Farsi, and Hindi. Some of the organizations set up websites. MPAC, for example, featured one with information ranging from First Amendment rights, Miranda rights, and the rights of due process for noncitizens to the difference between hate crimes and hate incidents, including online forms for downloading hate crime reports. The document on hate crimes instructed the aggrieved to do the following:

- Report the crime to your local police station immediately. Ask that the incident be treated as a hate crime. Follow up with investigators. Inform CAIR even if you believe it is a "small incident."

- Document the incident. Write down exactly what was said and/or done by the offender. Save evidence. Take photographs.

"Know Your Rights as an Airline Passenger" advised people of their rights and told them what to do in instances of racial profiling:

- As an airline passenger, you are entitled to courteous, respectful and non-stigmatizing treatment by airline and security personnel.

- You have the right to complain about treatment that you believe is discriminatory. If you believe you have been treated in a discrimina-tory manner, immediately:

  – Ask to speak to a supervisor.

  – Ask if you have been singled out because of your name, looks, dress, race, ethnicity, faith or national origin.

  – Ask for the names and ID numbers of all persons involved in the incident.

  – Ask witnesses to give you their names and contact information.

  – Write down a statement of facts immediately after the incident. . . .

  – Contact CAIR to file a report.

As the reader will observe, this information does not make reference to God, the Quran, or religion. Not only do the materials urge nonviolent responses, they are all based on protections offered by the U.S. Constitution and U.S. laws. The materials instructed the aggrieved to take proactive steps, to remain calm and seek witnesses, to gather evidence and documentation that might be used in court, and to contact legal advocates and start a paper trail of documentation. These efforts, however, sometimes fell on frightened ears.

Reporting discrimination is one thing, but getting immigrant communities involved in collective mobilization and proactive political advocacy is even more daunting. As Nader Aduljebean of the ADC said, this is the biggest "inside challenge." Many Arab American immigrants, he said, "remain fearful and apolitical" because they grew up in nondemocratic nations "ruled by dictators or kings . . . so whenever it comes to the issue of politics, [they say,] 'Oh, no, no, no! Don't talk about politics! They [the authorities] will come and do this and this.'" The wave of government repression that struck Muslim and Arab immigrant communities after 9/11 exacerbated this fear and reluctance. "Now what's happening in this country after September 11th, and after the passing of these laws [the USA Patriot Act] is that those people say, 'See, didn't we tell you this would happen?'" While he and other community leaders tell them, "You as Americans are still protected by rights," the only ones brave enough to speak, he said, are some of the highly educated first-generation immigrants and the second-generation, U.S. born. Others agreed with this assessment. As Samer Hathout said, "The biggest challenges are from the Muslims, especially the immigrant Muslims. There is really a lot of resistance to get involved politically, to donate money, to write letters to the editor, especially from the immigrant community. They just didn't do that where they came from. There wasn't that freedom of the press." The raids on homes and charitable organizations, the threat of detention and surveillance, and the mass detentions and racial profiling all worked to further stifle the immigrant community's receptiveness to the "know your rights" information. In spite of these obstacles, the crisis galvanized an upsurge of public engagement among Muslim American immigrants and the advancement of a particular collective identity. It is this topic that I explore in the next chapter.

THREE The Moderate Mainstream

Muslim American immigrant organizations responded to the post-9/11 backlash leveled at their communities through public engagement, civic participation, and outreach to their own communities and beyond. In all these efforts, they put forth an image of community members as moderate, mainstream, middle-of-the-road, middle-class Muslims.[1] In this chapter, I examine this image. Based on what leaders of these organizations told me and what I observed of their organizations' activities, I came to see four dimensions to this collective Muslim American—and sometimes, more expansively, Middle Eastern, Arab, and South Asian—identity project: (1) showing involvement with national domestic issues; (2) promoting moderate political views; (3) avoiding overt forms of religious piety in the public sphere; and (4) regularly offering public declarations of American patriotism and denouncements of Islamic fundamentalist violence and terrorism.

HIGHLIGHTING THE NATIONAL

Being associated with religious fanaticism and suicide bombers prompts these groups to actively disarticulate images of themselves from "foreign Others." Muslim American and Arab American immigrants must convince the public that they are different from the Middle Eastern terrorists regularly featured in the media. One aspect of this strategy involves a focus on national, domestic politics. As Sarah Eltantawi said, "We're really trying to move away from the impression that American Muslims only care about foreign issues." American Muslims, the thinking goes, should be concerned with American domestic issues. In the period after 9/11, the stepped-up focus on violations of civil liberties provided a ready-made and urgent outlet for this need.

Involvement in community service and domestic charities also fulfilled this need, and such involvement allowed these groups to identify with acceptable American public engagement styles in a society where church civic engagement is admired by White House staffers and liberal scholars alike. Mosques sponsor community public forums on a number of topics relevant beyond Muslim communities and charity campaigns for less fortunate others.[2] In 2001, for instance, mosques formed the Coalition to Preserve Human Dignity, a humanitarian effort to serve homeless and needy American citizens in fourteen cities across the country. By providing blankets, food, and clothing, Muslims are showing their participation in an all-American faith-based volunteer and charity activity.[3]

Underscoring that many Muslims are American-born is also part of this strategy. As one of our interviewees emphasized, "You know, we have a lot of U.S. Muslims who have never lived anywhere else but here." Hussan Ayloush, speaking of CAIR founder Omar Ahmad's concept of the "Muslim Moment" immediately following 9/11, used the opportunity to underscore how many Muslims are American-born. "I think for many years, for the longest time, many perceived Islam to be a foreign religion, a religion of the immigrants," he said. "People are finally realizing that, wait a minute, we have six to eight million American Muslims, of whom many are born and raised in this country.

In fact, two to three million of them are African Americans who had been in the country, since, you know, they were brought from Africa."

In this regard, these leaders also underscore the nondiasporic character of the American Muslim population, including those who were foreign-born immigrants, and the need to cultivate a space where the new second generation can be both Muslim and American.[4] This project involves not only grooming the second generation as Muslims and as participants in American democratic and civic institutions, but also showing that Islam is a domestic religion, not foreign and from outside, but rather part of American pluralism. Putting American-born Muslims in visible positions is part of this strategy. One American scholar of Islam advised these organizations to put women and U.S.-born, accent-free English speakers in key positions of power.[5] This advice would seem to have come to fruition in the 2006 election of a white, Canadian-born woman, an Islamic convert, to lead the North American continent's largest Islamic organization.

The dilemma facing these groups is reminiscent of struggles facing Asian Americans. Americans of Japanese, Filipino, and Chinese origin are frequently taken to be foreigners, even if they and their parents were born and raised in United States. This perception, and in particular the construction of a racialized "Other" as perpetual foreigner and alien, was responsible for the incarceration of Americans of Japanese descent during World War II.

Today's Muslim, Arab, and South Asian American immigrants live in a world saturated by media coverage of the violence in their countries of origin. Due in part to these media frames, they are conflated with violent foreigners. As one interviewee said, "International events have always been that unfortunate factor that dictates the discourse, and we have to overcome that challenge." In fact, he went even further and suggested that "to us, these are not foreign policy issues; these are domestic issues because they have a direct impact on the image of Islam in America." The activities of a strong pro-Israeli lobby, at both the national and local levels, also contribute to the blending of the domestic with foreign policy issues.[6]

War and violence in the Middle East get far more attention in the mass media than do violations of Muslim American and Arab American civil liberties. In this way, media coverage then casts Islam as a "foreign" religion. When the Palestinians or Muslims in the Middle East are identified as a terrorist threat, so are Muslim and Arab Americans, and this is why the symbolic and discursive struggle for self-definition is crucial to a campaign for civil rights and equal political participation.

Another way the groups emphasize their American and domestic character is by reiterating that their funding comes from domestic sources. At the CAIR and MPAC fundraisers, donations are elicited from the attendees with exclamations such as "It is on us! Get out your checkbooks, because all of our operating funds are coming from us." This line was repeated by the executive directors of the organizations. The thinking here is that the money is domestic and so are the Muslim constituencies. In the context of a national campaign of terror against Muslim charitable organizations and allegations that they are tied to foreign terrorist organizations, the executive directors of the Muslim American organizations took pains to underscore that their funding was domestic. As Salam Al-Marayati of MPAC said: "Our funding is all based in America. We do not accept any funds from overseas and we do not accept any money from governments. . . . We're not acting as agents of any foreign government, and I think . . . one of the major accomplishments of MPAC is that it really has established that American Muslim identity. All of our donors are basically private sources, and they are individuals who reside in the United States [and] have residency as Americans."

The organizations direct this sort of statement at outsiders in an attempt to legitimate the projects of their organizations. Legitimacy increases with the perception that these efforts are solely national and domestic. Here, legitimacy derives not from religion, but from the association with being American and domestic.

These organizations want to create inroads for Muslim American participation in government and civic engagement. They want to be involved in local, state, and national politics. In the November 2006 elections, Keith Ellison, a Democrat from Minnesota, became the first Muslim to be elected to the U.S. Congress. This was a tremendous achievement, but he drew the ire of Islamophobes when he announced his intent to be sworn in with his hand on the Quran rather than the Bible. In fact, a Republican congressman from Virginia used the occasion to send a letter to his constituents, warning that without further immigration restrictions, "Many more Muslims will be elected."[7] Never mind that Ellison is a U.S.-born nonimmigrant who converted to Islam.

It is clear that MPAC and CAIR want to see more Muslims engaged in U.S. politics and that they are actively trying to prepare members of their communities for political leadership and service. This usually means focusing on the youth and the second generation. At the 2006 MPAC convention, I attended a breakout session that presented concise nuts-and-bolts directives on how Muslim Americans can obtain employment with the federal government. At this session a career diplomat described how to prepare for the Foreign Service exam, noting that there was now a preference for Arabic speakers, while a young Arab American Republican appointee advised the group on how to best prepare for a White House appointment. A deputy officer from the Department of Homeland Security (DHS) went over the benefits of DHS employment, enticing the audience with descriptions of flexible work schedules, 401(k) programs, paid holidays, transportation subsidies, and so on. The young Muslim Americans sitting in my row, professionally attired women and clean-shaven men in their late twenties, took copious notes on the presentations and collected cards and brochures advertising employment opportunities with the DHS. In the same session, a Muslim American grassroots political activist from Houston offered tips on cultivating Muslim American voters. These presentations were part of a push to get Muslim Americans working in the government and on local and national political campaigns so that their voices may be heard. It was a crash course on basic civics, and the audience seemed poised to follow through on the directives.

These groups are also asserting their domestic national identity by claiming minority status and joining with other racial-ethnic and immigrant groups. Muslim, Arab American, and South Asian immigrant organizations are consolidating coalitions with other U.S. racial minority groups and with organizations that are pursuing immigrant rights. Publicly announced accolades and alliances are common. For his efforts in promoting immigrant civil rights, the executive director of SAN received a major award from the Coalition for Humane Immigrant Rights in Los Angeles in 2003. During the spring of 2006, when massive immigrant rights mobilizations emerged across the country, MPAC, CAIR, and other major Muslim American organizations formally announced their support of the massive May 1, 2006, immigrant rights rally. "We are America" was one of the main rallying cries. This mobilization advocated legalization rather than criminalization of undocumented immigrants. These are all indicators of greater involvement in domestic issues and affiliation with multiculturalism and immigrant rights more generally.

MODERATE AND MIDDLE OF THE ROAD

The second aspect of this strategy is to denounce extremism in favor of moderation. This is defined by American inclusion, working within the system, and the deployment of adjectives such as "moderate" and "middle of the road." Salam Al-Marayati, the director of MPAC offices in Los Angeles, explained the dynamic: "The moderate voice aims to preserve the [Muslim] identity but within the context of being American citizens, responsible American citizens, and that's the middle road that we are trying to achieve. And I think that's the major civil rights issue for the Muslims." He ominously warned that failure to attend to this project of showing others that Muslim Americans are moderate would ensure draconian oppression. Working within the system, and cooperating with the FBI, local law enforcement, and the DHS, as we have already seen in this chapter, is one way of accomplishing this.

Engaging in open dialogue with a range of political actors is also part of this strategy. The CAIR and MPAC conventions, for example, feature multiracial, non-Muslim panelists who span the political spectrum. At the MPAC conventions, the progressive, Left-leaning Pacifica radio journalist Amy Goodman, the daughter of a rabbi, is a favorite speaker. But MPAC conventions also feature mainstream Democrats as well as those from the Right, such as high-ranking Republicans and members of the

Libertarian Party.[8] Open dialogue, where divergent viewpoints are expressed, is encouraged and celebrated. Appeals are made to reason and to U.S. constitutional law. While Islamophobia is condemned, free speech is celebrated.

Being moderate involves undergoing training on multiculturalism and promoting pluralism. Muslim, South Asian, and Arab American immigrants must partake in the post–civil rights movement era of diversity and "sensitivity training." As we have seen, groups like ADC, MPAC, and CAIR engage in these types of outreach activities. They regularly speak at interfaith gatherings and conduct workshops for the media. To counter misconceptions about Islam, CAIR distributed eighteen thousand books or DVDs on the legacy of Mohammed. This is part of a project of sharing and bridging within the paradigm of pluralism and multiculturalism.

In the immediate aftermath of 9/11, Islam was delicately woven into these efforts. Religion, and in particular relying on Islamic scripture for moral authority and legitimacy in taking the "middle" or "moderate" road, became part of the discourse only after sufficient time had elapsed since 9/11. At the 2006 MPAC convention, where the organizing theme was "Reform, Renewal and Relevance: Understanding Islam for the Future," keynote speakers emphasized the scriptural basis for moderation. Dr. Asifa Quraishi, a professor at the University of Wisconsin Law School, argued that moderation is the truly authentic expression of the Abrahamic faiths. In her talk, she cited Quranic scripture to argue that "moderation is a theological, moral, and ethical concept, one enshrined by the Prophet," and she cast this as "the opposite of extremism." She praised moderation not only among Muslims, but also among Jews and Christians. Her talk was followed by Professor Sherman Jackson, an African American professor of Islamic studies at the University of Michigan, who also emphasized the need to access "the real Islam." "We don't need twenty-first century moral pragmatism," he said to the attentive audience, most of whom nodded affirmatively, "but Islam going to its essence." Moderation based in Islamic foundations was the main message at this keynote opening to the December 2006 MPAC convention, but of note here is the observation that it was only several years after 9/11 that the *scriptural, religious* underpinnings for moderation were voiced more strongly. Will this continue? Perhaps, but it is striking that the pendulum seemed to swing back in the opposite direction the following year, when MPAC adopted a 2007 convention theme that echoed American Muslim affinity with U.S. foundational narratives and doctrines: "Islam: A Call for Life, Liberty, and the Pursuit of Happiness." Whether relying on Islam or the U.S. Declaration of Independence, the emphasis is the same: moderation.

Denouncing terrorism and decoupling it from Islam are also part of the moderate Muslim identity project. In this regard, the organizations emphasize their cooperation with U.S. law enforcement and their united efforts against violence and terrorism. Moderation is posed as the opposite of extremism. The theme of MPAC's fourth annual convention in 2004, for example, was unambiguous: "Countering Religious and Political Extremism." MPAC speakers spoke out against political extremism and terrorist violence and in favor of the compatibility of Islam and democracy. "The authentic teachings of Islam are incompatible with extremism" became a common refrain of that year's convention. Al-Marayati closed a session of the conference by underscoring that MPAC seeks to amplify Islam's opposition to terrorism, and as he summarized MPAC publications on this issue, he urged the audience to redefine "moderate" this way: "Moderates are those who have authentic representation and authority in the Muslim community." And in the next breath, he invoked the U.S. Constitution as "the number one protection of rights."

DOWNPLAYING RELIGION

The third facet of the moderate strategy is that leaders downplay religion in public venues. This conclusion—which I hasten to add is my own and is not necessarily shared by the leaders—may appear to be contradictory. While organizations such as CAIR and MPAC mobilized under a religious umbrella as Muslim Americans and on behalf of largely Muslim American immigrant communities, they gingerly embrace religious icons, texts, and symbols in their public advocacy work.

A glance at the MPAC and CAIR web pages illustrates how Muslim identity interfaces with American identity in ways that assign Muslim religion a backseat to national U.S. symbols. The MPAC logo, three red, wavy stripes with five blue stars floating above, integrates elements of both the American flag and Islamic symbols. But, glaringly, there is no crescent. At a glance, we see an icon flashing in colors of American patriotism, red, white, and blue, and outfitted in stars and stripes. The logo, to my eyes at least—and I recognize that all symbols are open to multiple interpretations—seems to subordinate Islam to American patriotism and pluralism. The MPAC web page includes shots of the U.S. Capitol building and of Mecca, and these look similar to my eyes (although I do not know if this was the intent of the web page designers). Meanwhile, the top banner on the CAIR website shows the light image of the U.S. flag with the inscription, "In the Name of God, Most Gracious, Most Merciful."

The town hall meetings or the conventions may open with a Quranic recitation, but the Quran is never cited as the rationale for civil liberties and civil rights. Instead, appeals are made to secular constitutional law. Religion stays in the background. The Quran is never repudiated, but when the Quran is cited as a rationale for public behavior, it is to show its basic compatibility with the U.S. Constitution, democracy, and the Declaration of Independence. Since 9/11, Muslim American leaders have written Op-Ed pieces seeking to show the fundamental similarities between these sacred texts. In a book that reflects the discourse of MPAC and the Southern California Islamic Center, *The American Muslim Identity: Speaking for Ourselves,* Aslam Abdullah and Gasser Hathout explain the compatibility between Islamic law and American law. In this book, quotes and basic tenets from the Quran are shown to be parallel with those from the Constitution. According to these authors, "It is clear that the pillars of justice, equality before the law, due process, and absence of cruel and unusual punishment, as they are present at the heart of our Constitution, were cornerstones of Islamic jurisprudence for a millennium before the writing of our Constitution."[9]

In fact, the leaders of these organizations put forth a secular image of their religion. This is not to suggest they are not religious or pious. Rather, my point is that religion gets defined as something that is internal, confined to private spaces in mosques or, as during the conventions, in prayer rooms that remain separate from where the political discussion takes place. At the conventions, pluralism reigns; it is never assumed that all convention participants will go off to pray, nor that all women will cover their heads. Some women do, and some women don't. At the conventions, a large room is set aside for prayer. I have seen some women washing their feet in the restrooms, preparing for observant collective prayer sessions, but it is clear that not everyone goes to the prayer rooms. There are always hundreds of people milling around, chatting, eating, and looking over the literature and merchandise for sale.

When these leaders discuss Islam in the context of the United States, it is also singled out not for its difference, but for its similarity to the dominant religions. Here, Islam is identified with Judaism and Christianity as part of the trio of Abrahamic faiths that are in accordance with the dominant foundational ideals of the United States. Here, religion is paradoxically highlighted to show its similarity to the majority culture.

Religious rituals and symbols are used sparingly. At the conventions, Islamic symbols are not highlighted. I was unable to attend the 2004 MPAC convention because it was held on the same day that I was at the border, at the Posada sin Fronteras, but I sent my research assistant, PhD student Lata Murti. I asked her to keep an eye out for symbols and signs of Islamic religion, and she keenly observed that these were spatially separated from the Muslim civil rights and political engagements. In her field notes, she wrote:

> As I browsed the stalls, I realized that it was here that I was seeing Islamic symbols, not in any of the conference sessions. The bookstall sold copies of the Quran, some leather bound. The stall where I saw the greatest use of Islamic symbols was one featuring beautiful etched-glass sculptures. The etchings, as far as I could tell, were all Arabic script, most likely passages from the Quran. . . . Next to the glass stall was a stall selling prayer rugs and mats. The rugs had images of Mecca on them. Near this stall was a stall selling children's books and software programs on Islam.

Here, it is important to acknowledge divergent approaches to sacred iconography in different religions. Islam, unlike Christianity, does not favor representational images of the divine. This is especially true in the area of Islam's genesis, the Arabian Peninsula, and less so in areas to which it expanded later, such as Iran and South Asia. Still, it is important to underscore that at venues such as the MPAC conventions, even Quranic calligraphy is confined to spaces separate from discussions of civil rights and politics. In this case, the sacred blends more easily with commerce than with the political sphere. Symbols of Islam were available for private consumption, not for public collective action.

This is quite a contrast to the ways in which religion was used by African Americans in the civil rights movement of the 1950s and 1960s. Those activists, as we saw, relied on clergy and used a sacred text—the Christian Bible—to push for inclusion and against oppression. They could do so because they were Christians operating in a Christian country. Appeals to Christianity allowed those civil rights activists to reshape the U.S. Constitution and add the Nineteenth Amendment. In the current moment, we see Muslim American immigrants appealing to a Christian-influenced document, the U.S. Constitution, to safeguard their rights as Americans and as Muslims.

Religious sites are also not central in this movement, as the civil rights work is mostly occurring outside of the mosques. In Orange County, the very first post-9/11 town hall meeting was held in a mosque in Mission Viejo, and it was organized by the Orange County Islamic Foundation. But these meetings quickly moved to secular venues. Tareef Nashashibi, who helped organize these, said the second and subsequent ones were held in secular venues, because of diversity of the communities: "I decided that it was time to take it out of the mosques, because there are Arabs, not just Muslims. There are Christians, there are Jews, so the other religious groups would not go to the mosques to have a meeting to see what the FBI would say. And the FBI and the government will realize that not all Muslims are Arabs, and not all Arabs are Muslims."

Some of my interviewees also emphasized the personal rather than the political nature of their religion. Sharene Irsane, a hijab-wearing University of Southern California student, accompanied me to interview the president of the Palestinian American Women's Association, Sameera Sood. When Sharene asked if she focused on Islam in her work,

Sameera retorted: "I don't work for Islam. Actually, I work with government." She clarified her position on religion and politics by stating, "I am not a scholar of Islam [but] I know how to pray; I know the Quran." Sameera Sood went furthest of all the interviewees in suggesting that Islam is a culture rather than a religion, and she believed that this expansive identification had grown because of the post-9/11 oppression. "Like I said, religion is personal," she explained. "It shouldn't divide us, but right now, for instance, even my Christian friends . . . work for the Muslim cause; they work to defend Islam because to us, Islam is also a culture. For the Christian Palestinians, Islam is *the* culture. For the patriotic Palestinian Christians, they feel more Islamic than Christian. . . . They are closer to Islam than their own Christianity." In this instance, Islam acts as a cultural-ethnic net for mobilization of civil rights.

South Asians' reasons for downplaying religion are more deeply rooted in their own communities' diversity and internal conflicts. South Asian immigrants have diverse religions, linguistic communities, and national origin groups. Here, religion can be divisive among South Asian Christians, Hindus, and Muslims. In some cases, elite Hindu Indians attempt to impose their own religion and culture as the ultimate arbiter of authenticity.[10] Homeland politics and conflicts between Muslims and Hindus have also created deep cleavages in South Asian immigrant communities.[11] For these reasons, SAN, devoted to civil rights and social advocacy, has remained deliberately nonreligious so as to avoid divisive homeland politics and to foster collective unity. As Hamid Khan, SAN's executive director, explained, "When SAN was first introduced, here was an organization that was claiming to be nonreligious, nonpolitical—nonpolitical in the sense of not bringing . . . homeland politics into the issue."

DECLARING PATRIOTISM, DENOUNCING TERRORISM

A fourth facet of this collective strategy involves constant statements declaring American patriotism and denouncing Islamic and Palestinian terrorism. Moments after the first plane crashed into the World Trade

Center on September 11, 2001, major Muslim American organizations issued a press release condemning the attacks. The joint statement proclaimed in no uncertain language that "American Muslims utterly condemn what are vicious and cowardly acts of terrorism against innocent civilians."[12] One week after the attacks, the Council on American Islamic Relations took out a full-page advertisement in the *Washington Post* expressing condolences for the victims and survivors, gratitude for the rescue workers, and condemnation of the violence, calling for apprehension and punishment of the perpetrators.

This practice of denouncing terrorist attacks was already a mainstay of these organizations' activities before 9/11, but it intensified in the aftermath. Not only do American Muslims have to denounce terrorist attacks in the United States, they must denounce terrorist attacks anywhere in the world and regardless of whether Muslims are involved in committing the violence. When the suicide bombings in Ramallah intensified during spring 2002, CAIR issued frequent press releases and mass emails denouncing the violence. When the Oklahoma bombings at the Federal Building occurred in 1995, before the world knew that white Christian U.S.-born men had committed the violence, the Muslim organizations also rushed forward to issue declarations condemning the violence. And in 2006, when violence in Syria erupted after cartoons ridiculing Islam appeared in Danish newspapers, organizations such as CAIR urged restraint and reason. In a separate case, CAIR's national director, Nihad Awad, went to Iraq to plead for the release of a Western journalist.[13] On the fifth anniversary of the 9/11 attacks, when Al-Queda released a videotape, CAIR director Nihad Awad issued a statement denouncing Al-Queda's worldview, saying, "We will not allow terrorist groups like Al-Queda to be the voice of Muslims."[14] The leaders have grown weary of expending so much energy on denouncing violence committed by other groups and then having it fall on deaf ears. As one MPAC member said, "Everyone's like, 'Why doesn't MPAC condemn other [terrorist] Muslims?' And we're like, 'Hello! Just show up at a press conference or read the press release!'"

In the wake of 9/11, national security rhetoric became part of the narrative of American patriotism, and both MPAC and CAIR developed campaigns blending civil rights with antiterrorism work. Here, American patriotism meshes with Islamic faith. CAIR developed a "Muslim community safety kit," a guide meant to ensure community safety, on March 17, 2003, the eve of what appeared to be the American attacks on Iraq. The guide not only instructed people on how to protect themselves from hate crimes but also stated, "Muslims must do their part to ensure the safety and security of our nation. If anyone notes suspicious persons or activities in their community, they should report it immediately to the local Field Office of the FBI." CAIR also collected more than 690,000 signatures denouncing hatred in the name of Islam. MPAC developed an even larger campaign, the Civil Liberties and Security project, complete with a crest that meshed Islamic and American symbols (red and white stripes from the American flag, white stars on a blue foreground, and the Islamic crescent moon and star, together with a peaceful dove). This national terrorism prevention campaign, which debuted in 2004, included recommended mosque guidelines for imams and mosque etiquette for law enforcement officials, and it was endorsed by more than six hundred mosques nationwide. The materials state: "It is our duty as American Muslims to protect our country and to contribute to its betterment. Since September 11, 2001, intelligence reports indicate that international terrorist networks continue to plan attacks against the United States. . . . It is obvious that Muslims should be at the forefront of the effort to prevent this from happening."[15]

In 2006 this campaign crystallized into a collaborative initiative, the Muslim-American Homeland Security Project, established by Los Angeles County sheriff Lee Baca and Muslim American leaders. This larger initiative brought together efforts to prevent terrorism and to enlist the Muslim American community to serve as "the eyes and ears" of law enforcement. As Sheriff Baca reported to journalists, "I don't think we can ever believe for one minute that the battle against terrorism can be won by secular society alone."[16] Sheriff Baca announced at the press conference that this alliance would further "the mutual goal of protecting and defending America and its entire people," while Congresswoman Jane Harman simply stated, "We cannot solve the problem of terrorism without the support of the Muslim American community."[17] In this instance, Muslim American leaders from MPAC, CAIR, and other organizations stated they would encourage imams to speak out against terrorism and to prevent extremism among youth. As Salam Al-Marayati said to reporters, "We are playing the most critical role in America's national security because of our partnership with law enforcement."[18] The U.S. federal government has yet to create avenues for cooperation or partnership with Muslim Americans.[19]

The Palestinian activists that I interviewed also underlined their American patriotism. Michel Shehadeh, then executive director of the regional Southern California offices of the ADC, invoked the iconic American figure Benjamin Franklin, the protections offered by the Constitution and the Bill of Rights, and free speech when he spoke with me about why he is committed to his civil rights work. "I've never invested in any country as I've invested in this country," he said. "It's not that I own land or properties," he clarified, "but it's the first time that I invest in a country that is built on ideals. . . . and I like it very much. I hate countries that are built on race or built on ethnicity or birth, and this is the first country that is not based or built on that. . . . My kids were born here and I just feel comfortable; I feel at home, and despite everything else, this fight is really a real fight for who I am, not just a place to stay."[20]

I heard similarly strong statements of American patriotism from Sameera Sood, a board member of the ADC and the president of the Palestinian American Women's Association. "I am an American by choice and I love this country," she said. "I'm going on thirty-five years [here in the United States]; I raised a beautiful family of law-abiding citizens, all graduates from colleges and all professionals. This is the land of opportunity; if you work hard, you get your dream." In the wake of 9/11, however, she expressed doubts about her American dream. In fact, she compared her shattered dream to those of Native Americans in the United States. At the shop she operated in upscale Laguna Beach, she now felt cautious about discussing her identity with other shopkeepers and customers. "Now when they ask me," she said, "I hesitate. I feel my religion is personal. I think religion should be personal, but I am a Muslim."

Transnationalism, which has emerged as an important paradigm in the immigration literature, is not easily applicable here. Transnationalism has been variously defined as the social circuits and networks that transcend national boundaries, allowing immigrants, for example, to continue participating, through politics, culture, or financial or social remittances, in their countries of origin.[21] The groups under discussion in this chapter, however, do not hold strong transnational or homeland identities. Moreover, they must fight the public perception of their affiliation with and similarity to "bad" foreign Muslims. The leaders I interviewed said there were other reasons for the underdeveloped transnational identities and practices in their organizations. First, many Muslim American immigrants hail from countries ruled by deeply antidemocratic governments and rulers, and there is thus little space for building the sort of transnational civic associations that Mexicans, for example, energetically built as the institutionalized political party, the PRI, started faltering in the late 1980s. In fact, Muslim leaders said that the legacy of having lived under dictatorship and repression dampened Muslim American immigrants' civil and political participation in the United States.

At the same time, Muslim identity emerged as a strong pan-ethnic, cross-national identity, one in line with the global *umma*. With the exceptions of the Palestinian leaders, who are members of a national and ethnic group fighting for the right of nation-state recognition, no leader that I interviewed identified by national origin, as a Saudi American, Iraqi American, or Jordanian American, for example. None of them spoke of ties to their country of origin. They saw themselves as Muslim Americans. I also encountered cases where non-Muslim Christian Arab American immigrants felt tremendous solidarity with Muslims in the post-9/11 world. At the 2006 MPAC convention, a young Arab American political appointee was warmly introduced by Ahmed Younis, MPAC's executive director, as "not a Muslim, but definitely part of the Muslim community." The Muslim American identity not only is a new reactive ethnicity, one forged in the context of the post-9/11 backlash, but is one that is readily expanded to include people who are not Muslim.

While not overtly transnational in their institutional practices, these activists and organizations do underscore the connections between U.S. foreign policy in the Middle East—such as U.S. support for Israel against Palestine and for the military invasions of Afghanistan and Iraq—and

U.S. domestic policy toward Muslim American communities of South Asian and Middle Eastern origin. U.S. foreign policy, the leaders said, is one of the biggest obstacles to achieving civil rights as Americans, because it prompts other Americans to see them as Middle Eastern enemies.

In the post-9/11 era, Muslim American and Arab American community leaders found that their rights to free speech were curtailed and that they were unable to criticize U.S. foreign policy—especially with regard to the Middle East—without being called unpatriotic. "If we were ever critical of Israel at any time in our life," observed Hussam Ayloush, "then that makes us, according to them, not worthy of being active in our country's affairs. . . . Our patriotism is being questioned because of our criticism of a foreign country." Michel Shehadeh, commenting on the U.S. role in recruiting, arming, and training Afghans to fight against the Soviet Union, said, "Nobody mentions that, and if you mention that, then you become a nonpatriot." Spring 2002, when the violence between Palestinian suicide bombers and the Israeli military offensive reached its highest point since the 1967 war, presented a trying time for these activists. As Samer Hathout reflected, "What's going on in the Middle East is a huge setback—not just for the Middle East but for the Muslims in this country, because every day there's a suicide bombing, and they think we're all a bunch of suicidal maniacs." The United States and Israel were not the only ones to blame, she said, but Saudi Arabia as well. "Sending our troops over there to keep the dictators in power infuriates me. Saudi Arabia has most of the blame for the image of Muslims."

While these groups seek to end government-sponsored or -condoned discrimination and harassment, their struggle is fundamentally a discursive struggle for self-identity as Muslim Americans and for the right to be American citizens. As the political scientist M. A. Muqtedar Khan has observed, this proactive orientation characterizes this new generation of Muslim American activists: "They are not satisfied with the mere preservation of Islamic identity. They want it accepted and recognized as a constituent element of the American identity itself."[22]

In the post-9/11 era, the project of claiming an American identity means claiming and protecting civil rights. It is a civil rights campaign, but religion is used in quite different ways than it was used by the 1960s civil rights movement, which organized through the black churches. Religion is not used to organize through the mosques, nor is it used in the highly public, visual way in which Jewish and Christian religions are used in many social justice campaigns for new immigrants or other marginalized groups. Rather, there is a serious appeal to American constitutional law and to the legacy of civil rights struggles and values in the United States. Appealing to "Muslim" law would further cast Muslim activists as foreigners, dangerously close to the terrain of "terrorists." Thus, they must work in the opposite direction and cast themselves as Americans who are Muslim. These groups put forth a deliberately nondisruptive, institutional, and nonpious public identity.

Yet Muslim Americans do not forfeit their Muslim identities. Instead, Islam is presented in ways that mesh with being American. The Quran is certainly not forgotten, but it is interpreted in ways to show how its tenets are fundamentally in alignment with American principles of inclusion, tolerance, democracy, and pluralism.

What is the relationship between religion and immigrant civil rights? To embrace a non-Judeo-Christian religious identity and to be American at the same time, these groups find they must adopt secular American modes of political participation. Unlike the cases covered in the other chapters of this book, and unlike African American clergy in the civil rights movement, the contemporary Muslim civil rights advocates do not read from scripture to legitimize their political goals. The sociologist Rhys Williams (2003:329) has noted, "The price of getting into the playing field of American politics is a willingness to play by the dominant—and admittedly secular—rules." But in fact, the dominant rules accept religion in the public square so long as it's Christian—Jews get a little space, but not much. To the extent Muslim American immigrant leaders are having success in their civil rights and identity project, it is a success predicated on following a different set of rules—keeping their religion in the prayer rooms, mostly separate and apart from political engagement.

PART II Worker Justice

FOUR

Take Your Good Friday to the Streets!

In a church hall in South Los Angeles, during a breakfast meeting held by clergy and laity concerned about the plight of the working poor in Los Angeles, Reverend Dick Gillet, a pale, retired Episcopal minister wearing a clerical collar and a gray tweed jacket, stepped to the podium. Speaking into the microphone, he urged those in attendance—who were mostly dressed in street clothes, with a few clerical collars present—to contact their city council representatives and to tell their congregations about the need to support low-wage workers in their struggle for dignity, justice, and a living wage. "Sign the new Declaration of Conscience," he said, referring to a document with policy recommendations designed to achieve these goals. But talking, praying, and signing papers was not enough. "You can't just repent and feel holy in church. You have to take your Good Friday to the streets!" he exclaimed. "Take your Exodus to the streets!" And with that, he told us that he expected one hundred clergy and three hundred people of faith to attend the fourth annual Holy Week–Passover Procession, which this year would be held in Santa Monica, to demand justice for hotel workers.

When I arrived at the interfaith procession, which gathered in front of Santa Monica City Hall on an April evening in 2001, I found a crowd decked out in a rainbow-hued collection of clerical robes and union T-shirts. About one hundred fifty clergy wore religious robes signifying a particular denomination, clerical rank, and racial heritage. The Catholic priests wore loose-fitting black robes, while a Catholic bishop stood out in a form-fitting black cassock with scarlet buttons, matching red trim and sash, and a big gold cross dangling close to his waist. The Episcopalian, Presbyterian, Methodist, and Lutheran clergy dressed in variations of collars and floor-length robes. Many of them also donned long, slender scarves of kente cloth, Mexican serapes, or Guatemalan woven fabric around their necks. Rabbis came in yarmulkes and prayer shawls. Union members and staffers and community supporters were there too, some carrying staffs, crosses, and banners. Banners proclaimed the support of various local unions and congregations for the hotel workers, who marched alongside, some dressed in white cooks' jackets and others carrying the tools of their trade, such as feather dusters, mops, and brooms. To be sure, banners and images of La Virgen de Guadalupe were there, while the police politely stood along the curb of the palm tree–lined boulevards, wearing helmets and riot gear, just in case anything crazy should happen in this newly sacred space.

After an invocation and blessing, recited in Spanish and English, those gathered processed through the posh streets of Santa Monica, singing songs and stopping at hotels that represented the stations of the cross. At each stop, different clergy offered spiritual reflections and a prayer, followed by musicians and singers performing songs. Ancient religious symbols played a big part in the procession. At the first station, we all dropped matzo crackers in a basket, offering thanks, as our program reminded us, "for the sustenance of labor and the journey from oppression to liberation." When we stopped at the Loews Santa Monica Beach Hotel, where a particularly nasty labor struggle was under way, we left bitter herbs as a reminder to the hotel "to not make the lives of their workers bitter anymore."[1] People in suits came out to stare, but the procession participants remained undeterred. We stopped next at the Pacific Shores Hotel, which had ratified a union contract, and here, offerings of milk and honey—and parsley, a Passover seder symbol of abundance— sent a message of congratulations for good labor relations to the hotel management. The procession concluded with offerings of *nopales*, an ancient Aztec and contemporary Mexican food of cactus, to the Santa Monica City Council, given to remind them that their vote on the then-pending living wage ordinance could produce either flowers or thorns in the lives of workers. That the last offering was more ethnic than scriptural hints at who the afflicted workers are in this story. They are overwhelmingly Mexican and Central American immigrant workers.

After decades of declining rates of unionization, a revitalized labor movement emerged in the United States at the turn of the millennial century. Unions had dedicated more than a century to organizing white male citizen workers, and, in fact, had been historically key to pushing for nativist, restrictionist policies, but they have now deliberately diversified their strategies and also the kinds of workers they include. Spearheaded by progressive leaders working at the grassroots level and in the AFL-CIO, the movement gained momentum with the rise of service-sector unions, the concerted cultivation of community allies, and a new commitment to organizing women, minorities, and immigrant workers.[2] We have seen this new face of the labor movement chronicled in newspaper headlines, weekly newsmagazines, and even a docudrama-style movie, *Bread and Roses*. Less well publicized are the new mobilizations of clergy marching in the street to support these unionization efforts. Religion is a critical part of this newly revitalized style of unionism, which relies on building allies and cultivating community support. Often in clerical robes and regalia, rabbis, priests, and ministers from various denominations are marching in the streets, holding prayer vigils, engaging in civil disobedience, and visiting workers at their homes and workplaces. Through their actions, they collectively offer their moral authority and spiritual support to the struggles faced by low-wage workers, many of whom are immigrants.

How did this happen? The development of these religious support groups for workers follows on the heels of the new openness in the labor movement, but it also reflects the clergy's pent-up desire for meaningful social engagement. Religious people who had grown weary of the limitations of religious charity—and who longed to once again, or perhaps for the first time, experience participating in something like the civil rights movement—coalesced to form labor support organizations such as Clergy and Laity United for Economic Justice (CLUE) in the 1990s. Many of these clergy groups around the country are coordinated through the Chicago offices of Interfaith Worker Justice, an organization founded by Kim Bobo in 1995. As Bobo told me, "There were a lot of folks in the religious community who had done twenty or twenty-five years of soup kitchens and shelters and were beginning to realize that this was just a complete dead end." These were religious people looking for a way to put their faith into action for social change. "We had to find," Bobo explained, "some new ways to challenge what was going on in society."

CLUE is located in Los Angeles, and it is among the strongest of the sixty religious-based labor support organizations in the country. These groups support workers by relying on religious moral authority, scripture, and a mixture of modern political persuasion techniques (such as street protests, phone calls, and delegations to authority figures) and ancient religious symbols (such as stone tablets, bitter herbs, and milk and honey). In Los Angeles and Santa Monica, CLUE has acted quite militantly in demanding economic justice for workers and the working poor. Sometimes their opponents, the managers and employees of corporations, allege that the CLUE clergy are not authentic religious leaders or that they are merely puppets of the union. For example, when CLUE members organized civil disobedience and clergy delegations at a major luxury hotel in support of service workers and their union, the hotel management circulated a flyer warning workers not to be duped by "phony priests." Leaders in CLUE were outraged and exacted an apology from the management. CLUE members also bristle at the insinuation that they were simply manufactured by the union or that they follow union orders. "We're not on their payroll," they say. Rather, they see themselves as an autonomous organization, constituted by people of deep religious faith who have embraced the cause of worker justice as their own, precisely because it is a direct expression of their religious beliefs and doctrines. For many of them, supporting the struggles of low-wage immigrant workers has become an integral part of their religious identity and practice. A CLUE board member and minister of a small congregation told me, "Faith is what you do." Many of the clergy said that the experience of participating in CLUE has brought them spiritual renewal and positive transformation.

In principle and practice, CLUE is not devoted exclusively to the economic struggles of immigrant workers. Members seek to remedy economic injustice and the plight of low-wage working conditions across the board, in different industries, on behalf of white, African American, and Asian American workers and for immigrant workers and U.S.-born citizens, too. In 2004, for example, CLUE organized a highly publicized pilgrimage to the Northern California home of the Safeway CEO to support the striking supermarket workers, who are largely multiracial and U.S.-born. CLUE has also advocated for security guards, who are largely African American U.S.-born citizens, and CLUE has supported convalescent home workers, who are quite racially diverse.[3] CLUE has participated in Wal-Mart Watch, a nationwide campaign designed to benefit all communities.[4] Contemporary labor markets, however, are deeply stratified by race and citizenship. At the bottom are immigrant workers, especially Latino immigrant workers, who have borne the brunt of the new, intensified forms of labor exploitation that emerged from economic restructuring during the late twentieth century.

In cities like Los Angeles, where Latino immigrant workers constitute the majority of those in the low-wage, super-exploited jobs, labor organizers of the 1980s and 1990s concentrated on a particular set of industries that seemed organizable. Consequently, much of the sparkle and success in the new labor movement comes from immigrant workers in the hotel and restaurant industry, in home health care, and in the janitorial sector.[5] Organizations such as CLUE support the cause of economic justice broadly, but some of their biggest and most successful efforts have concentrated on union campaigns where Mexican and Central American immigrant workers predominate. Like the new union movement, CLUE is concerned about racial inequalities, and recent campaigns are devoted to organizing around jobs in which African American workers are concentrated. Negotiating racial tensions and bringing justice to all low-wage workers, black or brown, U.S. citizen or immigrant, is part of the CLUE mission. The clergy support the rights of all workers, but because CLUE worked with key unions in organizing Latino immigrant workers, such as the Hotel Employees and Restaurant Employees (HERE) and the Service Employees International Union (SEIU), a good deal of CLUE's energy has been channeled toward advocating for Latino immigrant workers' rights.[6]

So what are these religious leaders and supporters doing, and how are they bringing their faith to the struggle for immigrant workers' rights? This chapter and the next one attempt to answer this question by examining the activities of CLUE in Los Angeles. The portrait of activist clergy and the analysis of the religious tools they use suggest the effectiveness of a religious sector steadfastly dedicated to improving the wages, working conditions, and dignity of immigrant workers toiling at the bottom stratum of the economic hierarchy.

HISTORICAL PREDECESSORS

Clergy and people of faith who are today actively working for immigrant worker rights believe that religious-based political expression is compatible with democratic action. Faith compels them to act, and their actions are directed toward making the world a better place by remedying labor exploitation and the many problems faced by low-wage workers. In this respect, they stand on the shoulders of faith-based actors of the nineteenth and twentieth centuries. Many Protestant clergy of the late nineteenth century, along with Catholics and Jews in the twentieth century, did more than pray, proselytize, and pursue personal salvation. They used religious morality to speak out against immigrant labor exploitation, poverty wages, and sweatshop conditions. In the 1960s and 1970s clergy and religious congregations from various denominations did so also, as they supported the United Farm Workers (UFW) campaign for better migrant working conditions and the right to unionize. The social reformers and activists of the social gospel movement, as well as Dorothy Day and those in the Catholic Worker movement and César Chávez and the United Farm Workers movement, relied on religion to construct their activism. Religion was deeply implicated in these three historical movements, but as we will see, it was deployed differently in each instance.

The Social Gospel Movement

The United States is built on immigrant labor exploitation, and at key historical junctures, clergy and laity have tried to challenge these injustices. The Progressive Era of the late nineteenth and early twentieth centuries, when people of faith joined with reformers, radicals, and unionists, constituted one of these moments. As new forms of American industrialization and urbanization created deep wealth for the Rockefeller, Ford, and other dynasties, new forms of inequality and poverty intensified. The social gospel movement, a Protestant religious movement led by clergy that took place from the 1860s to the 1920s, responded to this social landscape. The social gospelers went beyond their Protestant predecessors, who had pursued the project of saving souls through social ministry or providing services. The social gospelers believed they could achieve "the Kingdom of God on earth," and toward this end, they worked to clean up slums, eradicate unfair working conditions, and ameliorate the problems of poverty and alcoholism. They wanted nothing less than to reconstruct urban social conditions, and to achieve this, they integrated their religious beliefs into the modern apparatus of politics and society.[7]

What did the social gospelers actually do? In the realm of labor reform, they worked to establish laws against child labor, to regulate the work hours of mothers, and to prohibit the twelve-hour workday for men. These projects were not exclusively focused on immigrant workers, but immigrants were certainly well represented among the working class in cities such as New York, Boston, and Chicago. The 1880s–1920s brought 25 million immigrants to the United States, the majority of them

Italian, Polish, Slavic, and Russian. These Southern and Eastern European immigrants settled into eastern and midwestern cities, where many of them encountered racial discrimination, substandard housing, and labor exploitation in factories, meatpacking plants, the construction industry, and sweatshops. Upton Sinclair's 1906 novel, *The Jungle*, became famous for its portrayal of shockingly grotesque and unsanitary conditions in meat production, but the novel also described in great detail the grim poverty, unscrupulous real estate predators, and grotesque public health dangers suffered by a Lithuanian immigrant worker and his family. Social gospelers were responding to precisely these kinds of urban social problems as they worked to reform housing and implement mandatory schooling and public health measures. Jane Addams and others who opened settlement houses in Chicago were not exactly representing a religious group, but they too were inspired by the social Christianity of the social gospelers and were responding to the same harsh realities. Other social gospelers fueled the Woman's Christian Temperance Union, which was fighting for prohibition, and worked for women's suffrage, so not all of their efforts were focused on remedying labor exploitation and the problems of poverty. They approached urban social reform more broadly than that. These activists relied on religious motivation—often based on lifetime dedication—and the legitimacy provided by religion to pursue social justice for workers.

Dorothy Day and the Catholic Worker Movement

The Catholic Worker movement, founded by Dorothy Day in 1933, represents another faith-based response to the injustices of industrialization, but in many respects it was, and remains today, far more radical in vision and activity. Day was more influenced by radical movements of the time, by the Wobblies, socialism, and industrial unionism, than she was inspired by Christian reform and salvation. A bohemian journalist, she converted to Catholicism in 1927, and after witnessing the government's callous treatment of poor workers marching on Washington, D.C., during the Great Depression, she developed the Catholic Worker Houses of Hospitality—homeless shelters—as well as farm communes and a newspaper. These were guided by a deep sense of spirituality. She launched these programs together with Peter Maurin, who has been described as a French "illegal immigrant" and "worker-scholar," a man who was motivated by the teachings of Jesus and utopian desires for a perfect society.[8] Day took a vow of poverty and, unlike the social gospelers, lived among the poor and developed ties with the labor movement.[9] The legacy continues. Today, unpaid volunteers, many of whom have taken on voluntary poverty, operate over one hundred Catholic Worker houses in poor urban neighborhoods throughout the country. Catholic Worker activists regularly protest against racism, war, unfair labor conditions, and policies of the Catholic Church that they perceive as unjust and regressive.[10]

Participants in the social gospel and Catholic Worker movements shared a dedication to remedying urban poverty and injustices, but they diverged in method and form. Unlike the social gospelers who came to help the working poor, the Catholic Workers lived, and continue to live, among and with the poor. Their name alone speaks to their allegiance with workers, but they have devoted themselves to many social causes.[11] While the social gospelers were led by clergy, the Catholic Workers have been less hierarchical, composed primarily of laity, often with a kind of loose organizational style that some observers have called anarchistic— a paradox, considering the organizational conventions of these religious denominations.[12] Religious idealism, utopian dissent, and an ideal of social perfectionism have characterized Catholic Worker efforts.

Supporting labor became a key concern among the Catholic Worker activists in the 1930s. At that point, they were successfully supporting industrial unions, especially in Pittsburgh, Chicago, Detroit, and Seattle. With this momentum, in 1937, a separate organization, the Association of Catholic Trade Unionists (ACTU), formed in the New York House of Hospitality. This group supported sit-down strikes and provided Catholic sanction to the newly formed CIO labor-organizing efforts. Religion and papal dictates fueled their efforts. According to one commentator, the ACTU "used the papal encyclicals to persuade the Catholic working class that they had not only a right but a 'duty' to join unions and to strike for 'just cause.'"[13] From 1939 to 1949, the ACTU supported over three hundred labor strikes, and some of their tactics—such as carrying protest signs that suggest biblical or papal notions of justice—are echoed by CLUE today.[14] Various offshoot organizations that supported labor came out of the Catholic Workers too, but with growing antiunionism in the 1950s, these groups eventually lost clout.[15]

Rerum Novarum, an encyclical issued by Pope Leo XIII in 1891, provided an important document for both Catholic Worker efforts and contemporary clergy and laity struggling to support workers and unions. This encyclical, a document distributed to all Catholic bishops, proclaimed the rights of workers to form unions. It was an explicitly antisocialist statement, reaffirming the property rights of capitalists at a time of possible socialist revolutionary change, but it was the first time that the Catholic hierarchy came out in support of worker rights under industrialization. Later encyclicals, such as Pope Pius XI's 1931 Quadragesimo Anno, reinforced these views, but Rerum Novarum was the first to recognize the rights of workers. It is still cited by labor-religious activists today.

César Chávez and the United Farm Workers

César Chávez, the founder and organizer of the UFW, is easily the most celebrated Latino public figure in U.S. history. He started the UFW with Dolores Huerta in 1962. Most Americans know about his efforts to organize workers deemed unorganizable as well as the historic nationwide grape boycotts and the strikes by Mexican migrant farmworkers as they mobilized to negotiate union contracts with California agribusiness in the 1960s. Less well known is the religious dimension of these efforts. Chávez brought a deeply spiritual aspect to the UFW. This resonated with Mexican migrant farmworkers and with many religious UFW supporters around the nation.[16] More than the social gospelers or Dorothy Day and the Catholic Workers, César Chávez and the UFW innovated a way of seamlessly blending religious ritual, spirituality, and labor advocacy. This lives on in CLUE today.

As others have convincingly argued, religion and spirituality were not simply added on as an afterthought to the UFW. Religion was an integral part of the struggle for justice in the fields.[17] César Chávez grew up in a migrant farmworker family, living and working in almost unimaginable poverty, and he was deeply influenced by the Catholic popular religiosity that he learned from his mother and grandmother. As a young man, after he moved to San Jose and began working with the Community Service Organization, a Catholic priest, Father Donald McDonnell, introduced him to religious social justice teachings. He read widely and was influenced by St. Francis of Assisi, who emphasized sacrifice and living among the poor, by Mahatma Gandhi's teachings of nonviolent struggle for social justice, and by the labor encyclicals of the popes. Chávez creatively incorporated these teachings and elements into his struggle to build the movement for social justice for migrant farmworkers. Prayer vigils, fasts, pilgrimages, mobile religious altars, and masses held in the fields wove spirituality into the daily texture of the UFW. César Chávez's moral vision of justice resonated beyond the ranks of the farmworkers, and clergy of various denominations came to lend their support. César's home and UFW office were decorated with crosses and religious icons, and the UFW newspaper regularly quoted the labor encyclicals of Pope Leo and praised the support of bishops and priests who helped the UFW. Still, 1966 was something of a turning point for religion in the UFW.

During Holy Week 1966, Chávez and a group of grape strikers began what would become a historic march from Delano, California, to the state capital. He had laid out the plan for this event in a short document, titled "Pilgrimage, Penance and Revolution."[18] This pilgrimage was led by a Catholic priest and incorporated prayer, clergy of various denominations, a crucifix, banners of La Virgen de Guadalupe, and even the Star of David. Mexican farmworkers, clergy, and progressive supporters gravitated to the event, and the march ended with nearly twenty-five thousand people; not all the UFW organizers enthusiastically embraced the Catholic idea of doing penance and the visible religiosity of the march.[19] But the notion of penance, suffering, and sacrifice—central to Catholicism—were palpable aspects of this march and were central to César Chávez's labor organizing. He identified the suffering of the exploited farmworkers, and he built a movement based on the notion of sacred self-sacrifice in the service of others.

This historic political pilgrimage–protest march was followed by a two-month prayer vigil which began in May 1966. As Chávez would later recall, some women in the union asked about doing a prayer vigil because of the court injunction against pickets at DiGiorgio agribusiness. They devised a mobile altar, and at night hundreds of farmworkers and supporters came to pray and support *la causa*. "Every day we had a mass, held a meeting, sang spirituals, and got them to sign authorization cards," Chávez said. "Those meetings were responsible in large part of keeping the spirit up of our people inside the camp and helping our organizing for the coming battle."[20] In 1968 César Chávez began the first of his many fasts to show commitment to nonviolent struggle for labor justice. This was at once a private and spiritual statement, requiring suffering and self-sacrifice, but it was also a public and telegenic way of publicizing the issues. Farmworkers from around the state came to show their support; during the fast, Chávez revealed that he had received a revelation from God, and he developed a paper called "The Mexican American and the Church."[21] The fast ended with Robert Kennedy coming to Delano to break the fast with César Chávez, and with new UFW efforts toward voter registration.

After major gains in 1975, the UFW declined as a labor union. When César Chávez died in 1993, the Catholic leaders eagerly claimed him as one of their own. Although the UFW continues today largely as a social justice service organization, the most important legacy is twofold. It trained and inspired future leaders, many of whom are leading, among other things, today's labor movements among immigrant workers in the service unions. And it pioneered, under Chávez's leadership, a completely new and modern way of injecting religion into labor organizing campaigns. In recent years, critics have come forth with exposés of Chávez's flaws and dictatorial tendencies, questioning the hagiographic narrative of César Chávez's life. They may or may not be right, but there is no denying the continuing legacy of the UFW mobilizations.

The use of fasts, crosses, clergy support, prayer vigils, and special masses continues to define the contours of the labor movement among Latino immigrant workers in the service unions of today. When we look at how CLUE functions and the integration of clergy into national immigrant labor campaigns, such as the Immigrant Workers Freedom Ride, we see that these religious-based activists have creatively taken as templates models that were first innovated by the UFW. They also borrow from civil actions and projects from the sanctuary movement of the 1980s and the civil rights movement of the 1950s and 1960s. In this regard, there is continuity. What *is* new is the development of an autonomous, labor-supporting religious organization such as CLUE. CLUE continues the tradition of social advocacy for the urban poor pioneered by the social gospelers and Catholic Workers, but like activists in the UFW, the civil rights movement, and the sanctuary movement, it takes a more radical stance when it comes to its style of protest and its demands. As we will see, CLUE does not shy away from deploying public expressions of religion for political purposes.

LABOR'S GENESIS OF FAITH IN THE CITY OF ANGELS

There have always been low-wage workers in Los Angeles, so why did CLUE emerge in the mid-1990s? The benefit of hindsight allows us to see how the social, political, and economic context of Los Angeles was ripe for such a movement to emerge at this moment. While Los Angeles had once boasted good unionized jobs in manufacturing, by the 1990s the L.A. economy was split between the haves and the have-nots. Many of the poor were Mexican and Central American immigrants laboring in downgraded manufacturing, construction, and service-sector jobs and in sweatshops in the garment and textile industry. By the 1990s Los Angeles enjoyed the dubious distinction of having the largest income inequality of any U.S. city. As well-heeled business owners, managers, and professionals enjoyed luxury restaurants, country clubs, and hotels, Latino immigrant workers cooked the food, made the beds, and mowed the lawns. Meanwhile, although some African American workers enjoyed good jobs, many in the public sector, others remained visibly and painfully underemployed. Moreover, the African American population of Los Angeles was steadily shrinking as many black families moved to safer and more affordable neighborhoods in the San Bernardino and River-side region. After the civil unrest and violence of 1992, which emerged in response to the acquittal of white police officers in the videotaped—and highly televised—Rodney King beating, Los Angeles witnessed a heightened sensitivity to the damage wrought by racial conflict and employment-based poverty. This provided what social movement theorists would identify as a textbook political opportunity structure, a historical moment ripe for an organization such as CLUE to emerge.

Like a phoenix from the ashes, a new social movement of labor and community emerged. Not just political opportunity structures but also key people and new social movement practices and coalitions were an important part of this unfolding history.[22] Women, especially women with connections to Latino immigrant communities, would prove to be central players in leading the organizations that constitute this story. A union then called HERE Local 11 emerged as a strong force under the leadership of the indomitable, charismatic, and seemingly tireless Maria Elena Durazo. In my estimation, Durazo has done more than any other person to put immigrant worker rights on the social map of the contemporary United States. Reverend James Lawson has often referred to her as *the* civil rights leader of the current moment, and it is hard to disagree. As the child of Mexican immigrants and one of ten siblings, all of whom worked in California agricultural fields, she stems from roots strikingly similar to César Chávez's. Durazo, who trained as a lawyer, began her labor-organizing career in the garment sweatshops and then moved on to organizing hotel and restaurant workers. In 2006 she became the executive secretary-treasurer (the leader) of the Los Angeles County Federation of Labor, representing 850,000 union members and 350 local unions. As she would later testify before Congress, when she began as an organizer with Local 11 she witnessed unfair treatment of the immigrant workers not only by the employers but also by the union. "I got hired as an organizer at Local 11 in 1983 and for 4 years I witnessed a Union deteriorate right before my very eyes. The leadership of that Local had a policy of exclusion. 70% of the members are immigrants from Mexico and Central America. The meetings were held in English only; the publications were sent out in English only and members rarely attended meetings. The office closed down at 4 PM—the time most members were getting off their shifts."[23] Durazo led a rank-and-file effort to change union leadership and policies. The cooks, dishwashers, and housekeepers she organized were, like those in the garment industry, predominantly Spanish-speaking, Latino immigrant workers. Under her leadership, Local 11 emerged as a union at the forefront of the struggle for Latino immigrant worker rights, a union not shy about using aggressive tactics, such as strikes, boycotts, fasts, and street theater. When Local 11 was fighting for a contract at the University of Southern California (USC), union members, together with CLUE clergy, held a sit-in that shut down traffic during graduation ceremonies. Due to Durazo's efforts, the union has become a formidable political force.[24] While serving as president of HERE Local 11, she helped to start the Los Angeles Alliance for a New Economy (LAANE) and became chair of its board of directors.[25]

LAANE was founded in 1993 as part of the national living wage movement.[26] It was headed by Madeline Janis, formerly the director of the Central American Resource Center, more popularly known as CARECEN, an organization that came out of the sanctuary movement and responded to the urgent needs of Central Americans relocating to Los Angeles in the 1980s. Dedicated to fighting employment-based poverty, LAANE spearheaded the city of Los Angeles' Living Wage Ordinance, which passed in 1997.[27] Winning the Living Wage Ordinance took the efforts of many people and groups. In 1996, when the director of LAANE, Madeline Janis, tapped key clergy for support in the living wage campaign, CLUE was born. As Janis would later tell an interviewer, "One of the innovations introduced by LAANE has been the strategic creation of coalitions and satellite organizations that could wage battles on different fronts." She went on to say, "I would describe LAANE has having an incubator or catalyst approach to the movement" (Nicholls 2003:890). Organizations such as CLUE, Santa Monicans Allied for Responsible Tourism, and Strategic Actions for a Just Economy are some of the results of this approach.

CLUE is a multidenominational, multiracial group of clergy and lay leaders in Los Angeles. When I started studying it in 2000, it claimed two hundred fifty members, but by 2006 its ranks had grown to over six hundred fifty. While the prompt for CLUE's genesis came from the campaigns already being waged by labor and labor advocates, the group crystallized on its own. Today it supports a multitude of economic justice campaigns. It would be a mistake to say that CLUE is the creation of the labor movement. The director of LAANE, Madeline Janis-Aparicio, came to the religious leaders with a very specific request, with particular parameters, but the clergy were adamant—they did not want a single-issue campaign. In the wake of the riots and civil unrest of the early 1990s and in the midst of the then-prevalent economic and social despair of urban Los Angeles, they wanted to build a social movement for economic justice. The Episcopal reverend Dick Gillet, who brought rich life experience in blending labor justice and religion and who would emerge as a key leader in the organization, recalled the beginnings of CLUE this way when I interviewed him: "A group of less than half a dozen people came together and were asked to form a religious presence and form a strategy for [a] living wage coalition, and so that got going. The mission, the theological statement, developed because Jim Lawson, who was probably the leading light in that earliest group, said, 'Well, we ought not to just say we're going to work on the living wage. We have to take advantage of this and say we're going to address ourselves to economic justice.' So out of that came that theological statement." Reverend James Lawson had already established himself as a major religious leader in the civil rights movement in the 1950s and 1960s. He is widely credited with teaching Martin Luther King the nuances of nonviolent civil disobedience, and he brought many of his religiously inspired organizing talents to CLUE. He still serves as chair of the CLUE Board of Directors, and he is proud of stating that he has been arrested more times during his recent work with CLUE than he was during the heyday of the civil rights movement.

The newly formed CLUE began showing its support for economic justice in multiple ways. Members testified at city council sessions and spoke out on behalf of the Living Wage Ordinance, which passed in 1997 and required the city to pay higher than state or federal minimum wage salaries for workers employed in companies contracting with the city.

They met privately with city council members and spoke to the media about economic injustices faced by minimum-wage workers in Los Angeles. As they engaged in these activities, they emphasized the ethical and moral dimension of their support for low-wage labor.

CLUE's next step was to lend direct support for several union campaigns then underway by HERE Local 11, under the leadership of Maria Elena Durazo. In 1998 the union had just won agreements with several downtown hotels to raise housekeepers' wages from $8.15 to $11.05 an hour. The union was determined to bring these achievements to the luxury hotels located in the exclusive Westside enclaves of Beverly Hills and Bel Air, but when union members met with resistance, they asked for CLUE's support. They got it.

Scriptures and Protest

As one of their first direct actions in support of the hotel workers, CLUE inaugurated Java for Justice. Seemingly inspired by the lunch counter sit-ins of the civil rights movement, small groups of clergy dressed in clerical collars and ministerial garb ordered coffee at the hotel restaurants. They used these opportunities to preach about the injustices of hotel managers who refused to sign union contracts or allow for workers' demands. Reverend Dick Gillet recalls one of his first experiences with the Java for Justice campaign this way: He and about a half-dozen other clergy, several of them in clerical collars, visited the restaurant of one of the luxury hotels and ordered coffee. "We finished our drinks and coffee and stuff and then I got up," he related, "and said, 'May I have your attention?'" Speaking in as loud a voice as he could muster, he recalled saying, "I know this is a bit unusual, and certainly not my real congregation, but I would like you to know that we are here in support of the people who are waiting on you, who make your beds, who are tending to you while you are in this hotel. They need your help, and you can help them if you go downstairs to the front desk after you are through here and tell them that you personally want the hotel to sign a fair contract."

CLUE would continue to develop and refine this tactic. In 2002, after Elba Hernandez, an employee who had worked for Santa Monica's

Doubletree Hotel for eleven years, was fired, allegedly for union organizing, CLUE participated in a "lunch-in" action at the hotel restaurant. Twenty-two CLUE members filtered into the hotel restaurant, and after ordering drinks and lunch, they stood up in unison, holding placards that read, "Support Your Workers' Rights." Reverend Jarvis Johnson led them in prayer and declared, "These walls of Jericho," the ones that separate rich and poor, "need to come tumbling down." The clergy activists were quickly ushered out of the building, but outside they gathered to pray while Reverend Sandy Richards read a letter of support from the Muslim Public Affairs Council's senior advisor, Maher Hathout. Letters in support of reinstating the fired worker were also sent to the hotel from bishops of the Methodist, Episcopal, and evangelical Lutheran churches.[28] Following this event, Father Michael Gutierrez, also a CLUE member and a priest at a Santa Monica church, had a private meeting with the general manager of the hotel, a fellow Catholic. At the meeting, he expressed his dissatisfaction with the hotel management decisions, and he suggested the manager face the moral contradiction of being a Catholic and treating employees so unfairly. A few months after these actions, Elba Hernandez was reinstated with back pay.

Later in 2002 CLUE took inspiration from the sanctuary movement of the 1980s. On March 17 of that year, about fifty CLUE supporters gathered for an interfaith service at St. Anne's Catholic Church in the city of Santa Monica to show support for all low-wage workers in the tourism industry. Santa Monica is known as a high-income town of progressive political bent, but it is also an exclusive seaside residential city that draws significant numbers of local and international visitors. At the religious service, Latino immigrant workers gave testimonials of how management at high-end Santa Monica hotels intimidated them for organizing, threatening to fire them if they joined the union. Reverend Salvatierra, CLUE's executive director, explained that the idea of sanctuary was not to offer refuge and safe havens to the workers, as the sanctuary movement had done for Central American refugees in the 1980s, but rather to show spiritual, material, and personal support for the workers. The pastor of St. Anne's Church, Father Michael Gutierrez, held a series of educational forums at his church to garner support for the issues among parishioners. Still, clergy, not congregational laity, remained at the forefront of CLUE's efforts. Direct visits to the workers at their workplaces and their homes became part of CLUE's institutionalized activities.

CLUE members have used a variety of tactics to express their support for union mobilization. To show their support for workers to the public and to corporate management, they have marched in picket lines, spoken out publicly in support of the union mobilizations, and participated in several instances of civil disobedience and a well-publicized fast at USC. Many clergy were also arrested at USC in their attempts to win union contracts for the food service workers. Some clergy also visited the offices of hotel and USC managers.

The battle with the Westside hotels reached a high point in April 1998 when CLUE, together with the Westside Interfaith Council and the Jewish Labor Committee, organized what would become the first annual Holy Week–Passover Procession. At that first event, sixty priests, rabbis, and ministers outfitted in robes, shawls, collars, and yarmulkes walked alongside another one hundred lay supporters and workers on that iconic boulevard of consumer dreams, glitzy Rodeo Drive in Beverly Hills. By the time the procession occurred, two of the three Beverly Hills hotels had already signed the contract with Local 11, so these hotels were publicly rewarded with symbolic offerings of milk and honey, referring to the land where Moses set the Jews free. The managers at the Summit Rodeo Hotel received bitter herbs after a brief street-side seder, symbolizing the plight of the ancient Jews. Soon after, the Summit Rodeo signed the union contract.

In all of CLUE's actions, biblical references and faith-based morality are used as justifications. One of CLUE's earliest declarations in support of the living wage cited Deuteronomy 24:14–15: "Don't withhold the wages of poor and needy laborers—including those of 'aliens.'" In the struggle at USC, CLUE relied on the biblical story of David and Goliath to call attention to how "the University of Southern California, like Goliath of old, has unleashed its enormous economic and corporate power on its own little David, the 340 Food Service and Housing working men and women members of H.E.R.E. Local 11."[29] And Moses and stories of exodus (e.g., "You must welcome the alien, the stranger as yourself") as well as references to Incarnation have been frequently invoked in various CLUE campaigns.[30]

CLUE participates in many splashy, public collective actions, but what does it do behind the scenes? What do the clergy do as members of this organization when they are not protesting? Below, I provide a glimpse into some of their nonpublic actions. These are the small steps they collectively engage in to advance economic justice in Los Angeles and, more specifically, to help Latino immigrant workers at the workplace. Below we look first at the CLUE breakfast meetings and then at the practice of worker home visits.

Breakfast Meetings and Testimonials

CLUE sponsors large breakfast meetings for its members and potential recruits. Four times a year, clergy and laity gather in a church hall on a weekday morning to informally "greet and meet," to share a buffet breakfast, and then to listen to an array of speakers, most of them union representatives, who provide updates on the various union campaigns.[31] The meetings serve multiple purposes, allowing CLUE to recruit new members while providing socializing opportunities for progressive clergy who might otherwise feel isolated. The meetings also provide a forum for information and updates on various union campaigns. The featured speakers generally include Latino immigrants in low-wage service jobs who give testimonials about their struggle to win union battles. The testimonials are critical to bridging the chasm between CLUE members and low-wage service workers.

The meetings are held in the multipurpose room of Holman Methodist Church in Central Los Angeles, not far from the USC campus. Holman is a church with a predominantly black congregation and is led by Pastor Emeritus Reverend James M. Lawson, founding member and board director of CLUE. At the first breakfast meeting I attended in July 2000, the meeting opened with a prayer and introductory comments before going into the testimonials, which the meeting agenda listed as "workers sharing their personal stories of suffering, courage, and union organizing in the tourism industry." All but one of the testimony givers—an African American worker who wept freely as she recounted her fear of being arrested on a union picket line—were Latino immigrant workers. Most of them spoke in Spanish, and their words were translated by Reverend Altagracia Perez, a charismatic Episcopalian minister who is black and Puerto Rican. She emerged as a highly visible leader in CLUE during this time, one of several prominent female clergy leaders.

Who was there? The one hundred or so clergy sitting around the round tables, ten to a table, were predominantly African American and Anglo men. There were certainly women present, but they were outnumbered by men, many of them with gray hair and quite a few of them clerically attired, wearing religious collars or clothing items that unambiguously identified them as clergy. Some of the African American clergy wore elegantly coordinated suits and ties, while the white, Latino, and Asian American union organizers were clad in jeans or baggy khaki pants with union emblem T-shirts. With the exception of Reverend Perez, few Latino clergy seemed to be present. Union organizers, workers, and LAANE staff were also present.

The testimonials that morning centered on personal stories of hardship and injustice suffered by Latino immigrant workers. A group of them took turns narrating their struggles to support their families, and they described employer abuses and threats, finely orchestrated anti-union campaigns, and various techniques used to harass unionization efforts. The immigrant workers implored the clergy to support their union efforts.

The first speaker that morning was Jose, a diminutive man who was introduced as a father of six who works full time as a dishwasher at a luxury hotel in Santa Monica. He said he wanted a union so that he would no longer have to ask for food handouts to feed his family. Hotel managers had responded to him, he said, with threats, harassment, and intimidation. After consulting with a priest, he reported that he had decided to stay with the union and had won a pay increase from $6.47 to $8.91 an hour. Now, he said, he could actually feed his family with his wages. "Pope John Paul II said the church should support workers and the union," he said in closing, and he urged the clergy to do the same.

The next speaker was Lupe, a worker at the New Otani, a hotel in downtown's Little Tokyo. She announced that she had worked there as a hotel maid for twenty-one years and had been trying to organize for a union contract for the last seven. She also spoke in Spanish:

> *Soy de El Salvador.* . . . I'm from El Salvador. I came here at age fourteen, and I started working when I was eighteen years old. In El Salvador, I was very comfortable, but when I came here, I had to work, and that was something difficult for me. I saw the mistreatment they show the workers here at the hotel. . . . We started showing the manager that we could organize, that we wanted a voice in the workplace and to be treated like people. So, we've gone seven years, struggling. . . . I'd like to invite all of you to join us for August 3rd. Fifteen of us workers are going to allow ourselves to be arrested, and we'd like to invite all of you ministers. As a Latina, the role of the clergy is very important to us. It means a lot to us when the clergy will come to our home or march to support us.

Another Latina immigrant woman, Francisca, also a hotel employee, described how hotel managers had forced immigrant workers who support the union to meet clandestinely. Hotel security guards had threatened some of the workers, and now they feared losing their jobs. The woman said, "I'm here to ask all of the priests to support us in this campaign. I know that once our coworkers see the church is behind us, they will join our union. Right now, they are too frightened. . . . *Sacerdotes* [priests, ministers], we need you to support us on August 3 and accompany us on our march." Around the room, clergy responded by initially shaking their heads in disapproval and anguish at the employer's action and, finally, by nodding their heads, as if resolved to meet her appeals for support.

These testimonials were followed by announcements and pleas to attend an upcoming protest at Loews Hotel in Santa Monica. Someone shouted out, "What else can our congregation do to support the workers?" A CLUE member replied that they could fill out "commitment cards," committing themselves to pay a personal visit to a worker's home or workplace or to protest or picket. Then, to encourage both the workers and themselves, the one hundred or so clergy rose, clapped, and raised their voices to chant, "Sí se puede! Sí se puede! Sí se puede!"

What is the purpose of these worker testimonials? Like the testimonials given by Central American refugees for the solidarity movement, they provide informational and educational material for the clergy, but the testimonials are perhaps most critical in mustering the proper emotional response necessary for collective action. Like the sanctuary movement's testimonial events, the CLUE breakfast meetings allow clergy to hear and see what low-wage Latino immigrant workers endure in the luxury hotels of Los Angeles. The testimonials establish a shared understanding of what is unjust and a shared emotional response. When the workers were testifying, the clergy had empathetic expressions on their face, and some shook their heads in visible signs of disapproval. They signaled this to one another and back to the workers. A few shed tears, and on several occasions, both workers giving testimonials and clergy in the audience wept. Compassion is the central, shared emotional response to the worker testimonials. And compassion deepens clergy's commitment and resolve to pursue social justice activism as an expression of faith.

Clergy are deeply transformed by these testimonials and by the interactions they have with the workers during the home and work site visits. The clergy said they feel inspired by the hardships as well as the courage shown by the low-wage workers. Listening to the testimonials and participating in these labor struggles were experienced as a new religious awakening for some. "My work at USC was really transformative for me," explained Reverend Altagracia Perez. "It was the fact that folks who had so much less than I did, or than I do, were taking risks and making sacrifices. Hearing them talk about what it meant for them to have it [a fast for a union contract at USC] be religious. . . . They felt that God was working in this movement for their getting a contract and security in their jobs. I was in tears! It was wonderful for me. It was moving. It transformed my ministry." Her reflections on these interactions were all the more remarkable because she was leading a congregation that included poor Latino immigrant workers. Yet she claimed that it was through working with CLUE, in the direct actions, testimonials, home visits, and fasting for labor rights, that she had come to know more intimately the daily life struggles of these people.

The power of the testimonials goes two ways. The testimonials help to educate and hook the clergy, and at the same time they deepen the commitment of the workers who narrate their own stories. CLUE favors the testimonials, as these strengthen the workers' religious faith and faith in the union. The executive director of CLUE, Alexia Salvatierra, said that she actually needed to persuade the union leaders to devote more time to these worker testimonials.

> When I take workers to speak in the educational piece of what we do, I always have to fight with the organizers about the time involved when a worker/leader is coming to speak. I always say, "Don't worry, because it's going to make a big difference for him or her. They are going to have articulated his or her faith, their commitment in front of a whole bunch of people, and that is going to strengthen them immeasurably." The organizers are not quite on board with me yet on that, but I think it is really a pastoral perspective that I am assuming. Evangelism is all about telling your story.

Salvatierra, recalling a special service organized by a priest with the help of a union organizer and CLUE, said that opportunities for workers to verbally express their faith and fears were vital to building commitment. "There was a lot of space in the service for workers to share," she said. "It was just this spiritual experience that happened for everybody who was in that room. And organizers were crying, and you know, it was a really powerful experience of affirmation and strengthening and mutual care."

The Home Visit

> I don't think it's fair to expect them to say, "Oh yeah, the church is with us," if the church isn't there. So I think we need our bodies there, and that's one thing I've always realized I could provide. I could provide my body, my presence. And even more concrete [are] home visits, because some of the workers are afraid to come to union meetings, and we have to convince them that it'll be safe.
> Reverend Bob Miller

Workers are fearful. At the luxury hotels in Los Angeles, they fear retaliation on the job and even losing their jobs if they join the union. If they are immigrants, working with or without legal status, they fear harassment from immigration authorities and deportation. To quell these fears, CLUE members personally visit, usually together with a union organizer, the workers' homes and work sites.

More than the breakfast meetings and formal testimonials, these visits provide clergy with intimate, face-to-face, and sometimes one-on-one contact with the workers. These visits are eye-openers, as the clergy learn firsthand the fear and vulnerability that many immigrant workers feel. They see the crowded, substandard living conditions of the workers and learn, as one CLUE member said, that the American dream is not alive for everyone. These lessons are especially stunning for clergy who do not minister to poor immigrant congregations. But even clergy who minister to immigrant congregations, such as Father Mike Walsh, a priest at a large Catholic parish near downtown Los Angeles with thousands of Latino parishioners, learned a few lessons. Although Father Walsh ministered to Latino immigrants in his church, it was the USC workplace and home visits that made him aware of "just how intimidated workers feel." The visits made him realize the risks the workers take and the vulnerability they feel. "I'm not facing, you know, deportation, and harassment, and being fired," he reflected. "It's a longer road than I thought for the workers themselves, especially the undocumented, to get any sense of empowerment, and also we need to be careful that we're not encouraging people to take risks that we are immune from. It's been something that is still slow to dawn on me: number one, how much exploitation is out there, and how much need there is to help immigrant workers to act on their own dignity."

When the clergy see the workers in their home surroundings and among their family members, they begin to understand more about the daily dilemmas the workers face. The clergy offer their moral support to help make the workers strong, but in the process, they themselves become educated and transformed. They do not enter the home ready to proselytize, bring salvation, or force the workers to join the union, but in the process of bolstering the workers, the clergy find themselves bolstered, too. As Jarvis Johnson, an African American minister and CLUE staff member, put it, "Many times when we go to minister to the workers, to talk to them about their fears and doubts, we hear their struggles and we hear some of the obstacles that they have in their lives. Sometimes we sit there and wonder, How are they able to make it?" Indeed, even clergy who lead congregations of the working poor find that it is visiting the homes of workers that shows them how the workers are juggling complex job and family arrangements. Altagracia Perez, who led a small Episcopal congregation of middle-class African Americans and Latino immigrant workers in Central Los Angeles, was shocked to see the crowded and substandard living conditions of hotel workers. Reverend Miller, a retired minister, recalled being particularly moved by a "very wonderful mother who took us into her cluttered kitchen." When he learned that this woman, a single mother, also juggled food service jobs at both UCLA and USC, requiring that she travel about twenty miles back and forth by bus, he gained new respect for the workers' struggles. Other clergy said the same. "They have so much courage," Johnson continued. "They are asking me for courage, and they exemplify courage. The home visits can be very enlightening, [especially] taking other ministers there; they don't exactly know what the plight is." The home visits are humbling for the clergy.

Clergy realize that they cannot accomplish miracles on these visits. Sometimes, workers are so fearful or so resentful of the union that they do not open the door. When I interviewed her, Reverend Salvatierra insisted, "If the door doesn't open, that's fine. They can see that there is a priest outside." More often, the workers and their families open the door, and the response of the workers is one of deep gratitude. Clergy, though, learn to reset their goals. Father Mike Walsh, who had done about a dozen home visits at the time of our interview, said initially, "I thought my job [was] to come in and make some kind of amazing change." His perspective changed over time. He related that on one occasion, he went to the home of a Filipina worker, where he noted a statue of the Sacred Heart. "I just got interested in the statue, of the Sacred Heart behind her, and asked her to tell me about it. And to talk to me about the love of Jesus." The woman had initially become a union activist but then had drifted away from the union. As she was talking about Jesus' love for people, Walsh said, "she could remember her original reason for caring about the union work. . . . You know, I didn't have that as a strategy in mind. I just remember thinking that this devotion to the Sacred Heart was a really big part of this lady's life, and that's why I asked her about it." The CLUE strategy was less about the clergy coming to twist the worker's arm and more about the clergy being there to hear the worker's point of view, allowing the worker to speak face-to-face with an ordained religious leader. "It varies," Salvatierra admitted, "but I think that on every visit, if the worker explains to the priest or the pastor or the rabbi about why he or she is involved, then that reaffirms their commitment."

These personal visits are also often powerfully transcendent for the clergy. Reverend Susan Craig, a Methodist minister, described going on visits to USC work sites during the Local 11 campaign to organize food service workers. A translator accompanied her because she did not speak Spanish, but this did not dampen her experience of transcendence. "It was a very powerful experience for me to be honored, to be taken into their lives," she said. "The fact that I was a pastor that was coming along and a woman—most of the workers were women—meant that there was a sense that they felt their spiritual needs were also being met, that we could pray with them in support." Not all clergy had the same experience, but Reverend Salvatierra, who organized the visits, concurred that most clergy were deeply moved by the visits. "Sometimes they have a lot of mixed feelings, but there is usually excitement, a sense of having been a part of something really important."

CLUE members are also involved in work site visits and in delegations that seek to meet face-to-face with management, and some of them have undertaken civil disobedience. All of these venues provide opportunities that blend faith and union struggles, religious belief and practice.

Neither all union members nor all CLUE members are expected to engage in civil disobedience, but some do. Accompanying the workers to jail is another way in which CLUE clergy offer support to the workers.

The union-led civil disobedience events are, as one CLUE member put it, "finely choreographed dances." Union organizers decide who will be arrested ahead of time, and names and identification are given to police so that the arrestees can be booked and then released. But on one occasion, things didn't go as planned, and Reverend Salvatierra related how she was able to offer her clerical and spiritual support, allowing immigrant workers to get through the experience. "The [union] organizer was trying to convince these worker leaders to participate in civil disobedience," she recalled. "None of [the workers] had ever done [it] before, and they were very frightened. And part of why they were frightened is a number of them are newly documented, or semidocumented, or, you know, come from countries where they've either been through terrible things from the authorities or they've known people intimately who have been tortured." At this point, CLUE was not planning to participate. But Salvatierra recalled that she just could not resist. "I was sitting in the meeting listening, and actually, I had never done civil disobedience before. I had actually organized civil disobedience, but for one reason or another, I had never done it," she said. "Then I just couldn't resist, and I said, 'You know, you are not alone in this. Not only is the union standing with you, but the community is standing with you. And the church is there. There are many pastors who would stand by you, and who will stand by you, who will even go to jail with you.'"

Although Salvatierra had only been with CLUE a few weeks, she wound up going to jail with about nine workers. "In jail," she said, "it was very important that I was a pastor. It was very important in this particular moment that a pastor got arrested with them. I held hands of people who were crying and terrified, and I could be there for them, and listen to them, and talk them through it." Not only did she offer spiritual support to the workers, but by virtue of her religious status, she was able to ensure better treatment for the workers. Here is where religious legitimacy and authority touched both the jailed workers and their jailers. "Part of the terrifying thing about being arrested is that the police treat you as a different kind of species, right? But when they saw my collar, then they started talking, and when the police became aware that it was a union thing, well, the police have a union. So suddenly, we're all friends, ya know, and they allowed us to stay together in one cell instead of getting in separate cells."

Chaplains on the Battlefield

The positioning of CLUE members as "chaplains on the battlefield" was a new concept that the organization embraced around 2001 but not a new practice. Salvatierra explained the military analogy this way: "This is a battlefield, and in battlefields, people have to deal with terror and grief. Grief for your fallen companions, and terror for your own life. And they need faith to help get them past that. Those who have religious faith are tremendously helped by chaplains who can help that religious faith flame up. So I have a chaplain core of all different kinds of pastors that are available to go to worker visits with organizers, to come to workers' sites where there's strikes going on, or where . . . actions [are] going to [be], and be with the workers." What did the chaplains do? "Sometimes," said Salvatierra, "chaplaincy is just a ministry of presence. It's just being there with your collar on, or your robes, or whatever [is] right by the workers, so the workers feel the support." In other words, just having the religious support and the moral authority and legitimacy of clergy helps the workers. Other times, this help required more skillful interventions, such as when clergy made home visits. And home visits required training, especially for dealing with their emotional aspects.

As the executive director of CLUE, Salvatierra was in charge of training and organizing clergy to make home visits. First, there were standard sorts of procedures: Participating clergy were required to read materials, such as a paper by Human Rights Watch on how workers' human rights are violated by employers who conduct antiunion campaigns. She conveyed to the clergy that "it's not an issue of forcing workers to join unions; it's the issue of the right to organize, the right to assemble, the right to self-expression." She also informed them of particular union and workplace campaigns. But Salvatierra was adamant that the skill of making a home visit cannot be learned in a

seminar or workshop format. Clergy needed to know about the particular worker *before* they went to the house. "Where does he or she come
from? What is their family situation?. . . Also, what are our goals?
What do we want to accomplish in this visit?" Beyond that, preparing
to make a home visit required an apprenticeship of sorts, which she
explained this way:

> It's really tricky. Not everybody can do it, and not everybody can do all
> that's needed. You know, almost any pastor can sit down with somebody
> who is from their denomination, active in the church, clear about their
> relationship with the union, and just needs a little encouragement. . . .
> But what does it take to sit down with somebody who is from a differ-
> ent religious tradition, who is so flipped out and so confused by the
> union busters, and, you know, the captive audience meetings that they
> don't know what's up or down anymore? They don't know whether
> to trust the union or not, and they are just terrified. That person might
> need ministry more than the other one, but not everyone can minister
> in that context.

Union organizers, she felt, did not always understand the religious
position of the clergy. She illustrated this point by relating that recently
she had trained a Spanish-speaking priest to do worker visits, a priest
with "a real heart for the workers, but he'd never done any activist
stuff." She pleaded with the organizers to give her "an easy one," meaning a worker who would not be overly fearful of the union visit. But during the week between making the arrangements and making the home
visit, the worker had, she said, "accepted the bribe and joined the union
busters, and suddenly this guy [the worker] went from being pretty
solid and just needing some encouragement to not being willing to let
me in the house. So he wouldn't open the door to the priest!" This was
precisely the kind of experience she had wished to avoid for the priest,
who was a newcomer to the home visits.

The chaplaincy program, like the Java for Justice events or the testimonials offered at the CLUE breakfast meetings, is an instance where
religion provides the tools for moral justification, movement resources,
public legitimacy, and ritual meaning. Yet these tools don't just drop
from a religious sky, and they don't just automatically appear wherever

clergy may be. These tools need to be sharpened and used with deliberation and planning. Even then, as we have seen with the chaplaincy program, there is no automatic guarantee that all will go as planned. "The process of chaplaincy," Salvatierra admitted, "still has a million bugs to work out. But when it works, which quite often it does, it's magical for everybody." In chapter 5, we'll see how CLUE uses religion to provide spiritual support to workers; how it deploys religious symbols and visuals in protests; and how members exercise their moral authority as clergy to advocate for immigrant worker justice.

FIVE Faith in the Union

The stranger who resides with you shall be to you as
one of your citizens; you shall love him [or her] as
yourself, for you were strangers in the land of Egypt.

Leviticus 19:34

"A new movement, an old commandment, or both?" This was the
question printed in big bold type on the envelope of a mass mailing from
the Interfaith Worker Justice (IWJ) during spring 2006, when millions of
people marched nationwide in massive rallies in support of immigrant
rights. The accompanying letter, sent to supporters nationwide, cited the
Leviticus quote that is reproduced above and informed readers that
many immigrant workers lost their jobs for participating in the marches.
It also listed the different ways in which IWJ participated in the "emerging social justice movement" for immigrant rights.[1] "We must stand with
all workers—both immigrant and native-born—when they fight for justice
in their workplaces," declared the letter, "we are called to do it through
all of our sacred traditions." CLUE did not come out with a similar mailing, but CLUE leaders also marched through the streets of Los Angeles

during spring 2006. Later that year, CLUE-CA and IWJ joined forces to help coordinate the new sanctuary movement to protect immigrant families facing orders of deportation. While CLUE continued to mobilize in favor of all low-wage workers, CLUE members also saw their mission as including immigrant workers because, as one member told me in an interview, Los Angeles "is a pretty immigrant-looking city."

Social movement unionism in Los Angeles, however, required multiracial unity. For that reason, some of the clergy approached the language of "immigrant rights" gingerly. Raising the banner of "immigrant worker rights" risked inflaming a city already rife with racial divisions and tensions, especially between black and brown workers. "If I'm going to build a coalition here, I'm not going to use the phrase 'immigrant workers,'" said one clergy member, who was raised Jewish but had converted to Christianity. "It is not going to help me build a coalition with African American leaders. So I'm just going to talk about workers. I am going to be honest—the vast majority are immigrants, but I'm not going to walk around using that phrase." By contrast, a black Baptist minister who worked with both the Southern Christian Leadership Conference and CLUE more openly embraced the concept of immigrant rights. "CLUE and the unions," he said, "helped us see where immigrants are, and they are at the bottom of the social ladder. . . . working without benefits." He expressed gratitude that "CLUE and labor have done a real service in terms of raising consciousness about immigrant rights."

Most fundamentally, the clergy leaders saw their support of low-wage workers, immigrant or U.S.-born, as a direct extension of their religious faith. "We don't see religion as isolated over here and handling one thing," explained Reverend William Campbell, a minister in an African American congregation. "We see it performing in all facets of life. Jesus clearly identified with the poor," he said, and clearly that is how he saw his mission as well. Regardless of whether they were Christian or Jewish, clergy saw their work in CLUE as rooted in scripture and ancient religious traditions. This chapter examines how faith and union politics mesh, and how CLUE participants used their faith in social action.

CLUE clergy did not fall into the tradition of religious leaders pursuing spiritual salvation by proselytizing in the slums and ghettos. They were not seeking converts or bodies to fill their temples and churches. When I first started this research, I had fully expected to find the clergy actively recruiting workers to become congregation members. That was not happening at all, although one Catholic priest, who, paradoxically, was already leading an overflow congregation of several thousand people, said that a few workers started attending his church after they met him during the Local 11 union campaign at USC. Most of the clergy active in CLUE shared the views of Dick Gillet, the retired minister whom we saw mustering the troops for the Holy Week–Passover Procession in the last chapter. "I do not see that we in the church are going to take Christ to [the workers]. I see that Christ is in them already."

The religious theme of suffering invited clergy to bring their theology to bear on the alleviation of economic suffering in Los Angeles. CLUE was primarily composed of Christians and Jews (with a few pagan, Buddhist, and, after 9/11, Muslim participants). Both Christian and Jewish clergy identified the amelioration of human suffering as the theological reason behind their economic justice work. Methodist reverend Susan Craig said, "Our faith calls for justice for those who are suffering the most," and Rabbi Steve Jacobs, a civic and political activist in many local and global causes, concurred that his entire biography of activism was rooted in his Jewish faith and motivated by the desire to end human suffering. For these clergy, religious life went beyond the pulpit to include the streets and public policy. CLUE activism provided a venue for ancient scriptures to come alive in the social landscape of contemporary Los Angeles. Working with CLUE made these clergy feel more religious, more authentic and in touch with the roots of their various faith traditions. "I find that when I am out on the front line, I meet reality," said Reverend Jarvis Johnson. "I find that reality is not far from the scriptures. Those same struggles that have taken place over two thousand years ago are still taking place." But how exactly did CLUE members bring religion to bear on these struggles? And how did their experience of social activism affect them religiously? This chapter answers these questions.

WORKING WITH THE UNIONS

CLUE members were unequivocal. All of them said they were fighting for workers' rights, including those of immigrant workers, and economic justice, and that unions were the central institution for promoting these goals. But churches and unions have different traditions and practices, and clergy and union leaders did not always mix easily. In fact, the executive director of CLUE suggested that they were so divergent in approach that clergy and organized labor represented "different universes." How do these universes work together without colliding and clashing?

The clergy adamantly underscored the autonomy of CLUE from the unions. "We are not on their payroll," they reiterated. "We believe in their work." They remained incensed at hotel management allegations that CLUE is the "handmaiden" of the unions. One Protestant minister went even further, insisting, "The job of the clergy is to educate the union folk as to our independence from them." When I asked her to explain, she related her experience at the USC campaign, where relatively young, inexperienced organizers had put clergy names on flyers and petitions before getting permission to do so. These organizers, she said, had to be instructed on how to relate to clergy. "It was small stuff," she admitted, "but I think it was caught." Her comments begin to hint at the delicate tensions that must be worked out between union organizers and clergy.

More than the volunteer members, it was the CLUE paid staff, who were also clergy, who had to deal with the rough edges in union-clergy coalition making. Reverend Jarvis Johnson, a CLUE staff organizer, complained about the "rent a clergy attitude" that some union organizers brought to the table. When I asked him to clarify this phrase, he said it referred to the union practice of just calling clergy to come to a rally. The chaplain project and the home visits were designed to avoid this add-on approach. Clergy wanted to be integrally involved in these struggles, not just come out ceremoniously in their robes for a rally. He also complained that in the past, the unions asked CLUE to mobilize clergy for direct actions, "and then only one clergy person is utilized! They [clergy] may have dropped everything that they had to come out, and it is kind of like the little boy who cried wolf." Fine lines distinguishing what clergy might legitimately do also had be to worked out. In another instance, SEIU had asked Reverend Johnson to provide clergy to go into a nursing home and conduct a survey. He did not comply with that request, as he saw it as an inappropriate use of clergy. "Clergy," he insisted, "are going in for counseling and comfort. They are going in as a pastor, not to deal with organizing work."

The evangelical Lutheran minister who served as executive director of CLUE, Alexia Salvatierra, had thought deeply about the problems and promises inherent in religious support for labor. She suggested that this kind of labor-clergy collaboration required meshing inherently different approaches. "The union thinks in weeks, and the church thinks in centuries," she explained. She saw the example of César Chávez and the UFW as an exception in this regard and as a template worth emulating. "Chávez's long-term perspective was actually extremely unusual, and most unions do not begin to do that."

Sometimes the urgency with which unions had to act made them pushy partners. "They [the union] want ten collars tomorrow. It was something that was decided last night," she recalled. "But you can't just call a priest and say, 'You have to be there tomorrow.' Once in a while, when it's absolutely urgent, of course you can, but not on a regular basis." Moreover, because they are in conflict with powerful opponents, unions often act with militaristic aggression. The unions, she said, "operate on a battlefield, and soldiers are not nice." Clergy may belong to hierarchical organizations, but they usually do not follow militaristic operations. Not only do they preach about love and compassion, but they try to exemplify these in their relationships, be they personal or organizational. "When you think in terms of centuries," Salvatierra reflected, "niceties in relationships are very important." CLUE exemplified "niceties in relationships," as we saw in the last chapter, by publicly honoring the hotel management who signed fair labor contracts. They exemplified these in the home visits with workers, where they provided spiritual support and counseling. More privately, CLUE participants kept relationships alive among themselves through the breakfast meetings, by sending thank-you notes or photos of individual clergy taken at protests, and by keeping clergy and laity informed of the different campaigns. Union organizers were more focused on the day-to-day urgencies of their campaigns, not in cultivating these kinds of relationships with the clergy.

Nevertheless, not all unions are alike. Unions are as different as denominations, each with their own set of beliefs and practices, and some unions are easier to work with than others. In this regard, Reverend Salvatierra saw the hotel workers' union, HERE, as a smooth fit with the clergy. "I am blessed with working with HERE because it is such a spiritual union," she said. "It's so much like Chávez's model," where prayer vigils, fasting, and processions formed core practices in the union's organizing efforts. By contrast, she said that SEIU, which represented the janitors and the nursing home workers, "is a very different animal. It is much harder to be a clergy organizer with SEIU than it is with HERE."

When I asked Salvatierra to explain what she meant about some of these statements—thinking in weeks versus centuries, and what it is to be a spiritual labor union—she emphasized the preference for developing the clergy's long-term organizing abilities, lasting social relationships, and commitments to a cause. CLUE strove, she said, to develop relationships not only among clergy, but also between clergy and workers. "We are always in the process of trying to deepen the capacity and commitment of clergy. That is why we call it 'clergy organizing'—not just 'clergy mobilization' or 'clergy recruitment' or 'clergy outreach,'" she said. "We are in a constant cultivation process of deepening people's capacity to serve this economic justice movement. . . . It is for me, fundamentally, a theological model that Chávez used."

For clergy, and for deeply religious laity, religion is fundamental to who they are. It is not ephemeral. This proves to be a big asset in organizing. As Kim Bobo put it, "The people who come out of the faith-based community are really engaged in this work. There's a longevity and a commitment to the work that just sustains people through the thick and thin." Thinking in centuries can help sustain activists through long, grueling, seemingly impossible-to-win struggles.[2]

So who is in charge, then, the unions or CLUE? Each person had a different idea. Salvatierra insisted that it was a "collaborating relationship," although she clarified that "of course the union is in charge of their strategy for unionizing workers, that's what they do. Our process is to support the workers." This meant that CLUE did not pick out the targets or sites of struggle, using faith as some kind of divination tool, but rather, as Reverend Miller said, "We wait for the union to say this is where we're going to concentrate now." Other clergy were more comfortable stating that they followed the workers, not the unions. Reverend Norman Johnson valued CLUE's willingness "to listen to the workers and to allow those stories to speak for themselves." This approach resonated with his ideas of faith-based activism as opposed to charity projects, where "you know, 'We're helping the poor.'" And Father Mike Walsh said that what he cherished most about his CLUE work was the ability to "walk with the workers," to be among them and offer spiritual support. They all agreed they worked in partnership with the unions, and that neither the unions nor CLUE could accomplish the goals of economic justice alone.

GIVE A MAN A FISH? TEACH A MAN TO FISH? OR GO UPSTREAM?

> I absolutely hate the soup kitchen . . . I do it
> because my pastor asked me to, but I hate the
> dynamics that get set up in the soup kitchen.
> The sort of rich white people coming into the city
> to serve, and the poor people of color receiving
> the food. It is just a structure of imbalance that
> is not good and healthy.
> Kim Bobo, executive director of IWJ

CLUE, as we have seen, is primarily involved in partnership with the unions to improve low-wage jobs. While members have organized food banks for striking workers, their focus is decidedly not on charity but on using religion to make lasting changes in workers' wages and working conditions. This is worth underscoring, because the recent historical

period has been one in which the federal government devolved responsibility for social welfare, transferring this to faith-based charities. Faith-
based, government-funded charitable organizations emerged as *the* face of
public religion during George W. Bush's regime. Moreover, congregations
in the United States have long traditions of charitable services. And even
soup kitchens that are run by ostensibly nonreligious organizations wind
up as spiritual and religious expressions of the volunteers' values, as the
sociologist Courtney Bender has shown in the book *Heaven's Kitchen*.

But many clergy and laity, as we see in Kim Bobo's quote above, grew
tired of the limited reach of charity and particularly with the ways in
which the dynamics of charity often wind up reproducing and under-
lining inequalities. The people in CLUE wanted their efforts to bring
about lasting social change. Service providing, said Reverend Jarvis
Johnson, was "like giving fish." You might feed a person for a day. By
contrast, "in advocacy," he said, "you are getting people to stand on
their own feet." The goal was not to feed workers but to get the workers
to feed themselves. "We have to give them the courage, and we speak on
their behalf, and we stand with them in the midst of their fight."

Reverend Salvatierra took it one step further. The workers—to continue the religious metaphor—were already fishing for themselves, but
they were still mired in poverty. "What if you go up the river and get
all the people who are taking the fish out of the river?" she asked. "I
think most people would like to attack things at their root causes. It's
important to have a theological basis that supports the change in the
paradigm shift."

Service providing was not, however, dismissed. In fact, many CLUE
clergy saw it as complementary to their labor advocacy work. Father
Mike Walsh, based in a large downtown Catholic congregation with
thousands of Latino immigrant workers, said that providing social services had helped him become aware of "the structural injustices that
keep people poor." "When you try to help people with rent and food,"
he said, "you become aware of the precariousness of their work" and
just how difficult it is for families to survive on low wages. Other clergy
who did not work directly with Latino immigrant workers discovered
through their CLUE activism the urgent need for services among these

communities. As an organization, CLUE began and continues with the focus on pushing for union contracts and worker-friendly legislation, but along the way, CLUE has also taken on service projects to advance social change. Most notably, after many hotel workers were laid off during the drop-off in post-9/11 tourism and travel, CLUE worked with the unions to establish emergency relief centers and food banks.

RELIGION AT WORK

CLUE participants used religion and their position as religious leaders to better the lives of low-wage immigrant workers. In this next section, I discuss three relevant CLUE activities: providing spiritual support to workers; deploying religious symbols in public spaces to underscore a labor struggle; and exercising moral voice and persuasion in favor of the unions.

CLUE participants offered spiritual support and strength to workers who were grappling with the risks that come with joining a labor union. As we saw in the last chapter, several CLUE institutions—such as the chaplain program, the home visits, and getting arrested and going to jail with protesting workers—allow the participating clergy to offer spiritual guidance, counseling, and consoling. Clergy are in a special position to offer spiritual strength and consolation; this is simply part of what they do in their profession. As Reverend Altagracia Perez related, "I was arrested twice and . . . leading prayer services. . . . trying to provide spiritual support and a community institution support for workers who are struggling for their rights." Not only workers but also union organizers needed spiritual guidance. Reverend Salvatierra was starting a spiritual reflection group for union organizers. She described it as a reading workshop, where the group would read about César Chávez and search for "lighter inspiration." The group, she hoped, would provide a place for spiritual reflection and a "light of the kingdom of God's struggle."

In contrast to these relatively quiet, private, face-to-face opportunities for spiritual reflection were the noisier, public, collective protests, processions, and direct actions. Here, the visual deployment of religious symbols was important. During the late 1980s and 1990s, the Latino immigrant unions in Los Angeles, such as SEIU Justice for Janitors and HERE Local 11, innovated protests that featured the dramatization of labor struggles in the streets. These involved using props like big papier-mâché figures, placing beds in the middle of a street protest to show how many beds hotel housekeepers must make in a shift, or having a person dressed as Scrooge represent a greedy employer. CLUE followed suit by boldly brandishing religious symbols far beyond the confines of their churches and temples. Material objects with roots in ancient scripture, such as stone tablets, bitter herbs, and milk and honey, played central roles in CLUE protests and processions.

Clerical dress was a key part of these public activities. For these public events, concerted organizational steps were taken to ensure that clergy arrived attired in ways that left little ambiguity about whether they were union people or ordained religious leaders. The flyer announcing the 2001 interfaith procession that occurred during Holy Week–Passover, for example, reminded the participants to bring appropriate symbols of their identities. The flyer said, "Religious Leaders: Wear Vestments; All Workers: Bring a Symbol of Your Work; and Congregations, Organizations: Bring a Banner." Procession participants complied with this request, and the outcome was visually stunning.

The participants were all costumed and carrying props, but these were not theatrical performances but rather enactments of verifiable identities and social locations. Reverend Bob Miller, a retired minister who became quite active in various union-led direct actions, recalled attending his first demonstration in support of the hotel and restaurant employees' union in 1997. There he saw a peaceful demonstration, where, he said, the workers were blocking traffic while "costumed according to whether they were a concierge, housekeeper, whatever." The idea of telegraphing one's identity, whether a worker or clergy member, appealed to him. "The workers received me so warmly," he recalled. "And I thought, Well, I'll have to buy some new shirts and collars and wear them because I want the hotel management to know that I wasn't just a union employee."

Religious garb was donned in the streets and in front of the luxury hotels, but it was not just theatrical costuming. It was used together with traditional religious practices, such as prayer, song, and scripture, and concrete, symbolic reminders of ancient texts. Together, this array of identifiably familiar practices and objects communicated the religious significance of these struggles. When the clergy offered blessings and prayers, they were momentarily transforming a secular site into a sacred place. Moments of Durkheimian collective effervescence ensued. When I asked Don Smith, a Presbyterian minister, to describe his experiences in the CLUE processions and protests, he recalled his experience at the first Holy Week–Passover events. "As you can imagine, it's a tremendous feeling of solidarity. You're there with all the workers, you're there with a whole bunch of clergy, . . . you're marching down Rodeo Drive, and . . . you're having an effect. People are stopping on the street, asking, 'What is this?'" Part of the excitement comes from breaking the norms of mundane social interaction, and part of the meaning comes from the religious rituals. As Reverend Smith put it, "There is the sense that this is not usually done. What are these religious people doing out here, dressed up? And that's what one has to do, to interrupt the status quo, to make a point." The marches, he said, were empowering and uplifting because they gave the "sense that you're making an impact."

In his analysis of social movements, the sociologist James M. Jasper focuses on "the art of moral protest." In fact, he convincingly argues that all protest is moral protest because it contains a critique of existent relations and implicit statements about what is right and wrong. It is the exercise of moral voice, he contends, that allows direct actions of protest to be so experientially satisfying. Protests, he writes, "give us an opportunity to plumb our moral sensibilities and convictions, and to articulate and elaborate them. And it is important to articulate them publicly and collectively."[3] This is exactly what CLUE was doing, and it had religious consequences for the CLUE participants.

Reverend Jarvis Johnson, a CLUE staffer and minister of his own Pasadena congregation, underscored this analytic point. He explained not only how the protests were imbued with prayer and faith but, in turn, how the entire experience of meshing protest and prayer and sharing the workers' struggles reverberated with biblical significance for him.

I refuse to get arrested, but in some of the [union campaign] struggles that we have on, I have gone to have prayer with workers. . . . I have been with them when we have been surrounded by the police, with the helicopters and the dogs and the full riot gear and the mounted police, seeing the fear that comes on people's faces. I have gone to workplaces where workers stopped us and asked us to have prayer and when we stopped to have prayer, the security was sent to kick us out. It reminded me of the New Testament in the Acts of the Apostles when the apostles were arrested and thrown in jail for witnessing for Jesus. What it does is reaffirm my own faith, and it renews me.

His description echoes those of activists in the civil rights movement protests of the 1950s and 1960s, who were also met with armed police and dogs. The simplicity of offering prayer in the face of fear and having the prayer forcibly stopped beckoned him to recall biblical precedents, reaffirming his religious faith. The act of articulating, through collective action, a religiously based moral position on a social issue provides an opportunity to deepen religious faith.

In all of these venues, such as the private home visits and the public processions and protests, the CLUE clergy were exercising moral voice. But part of their challenge was to use their religious authority to persuade others of the urgency of economic justice. CLUE's mission, as Reverend Perez summed up, involved "bringing moral pressure to bear, pressuring political leaders and working with unions, and pushing corporations and businesses to do the right thing." To be effective, they sought venues where they might direct their moral persuasion toward particular audiences. These included targeting the leaders at their own congregations, the owners and managers of the hotels, and their own congregation members. Clergy were well-suited to this task, as they are socially recognized as moral leaders, as experts in distinguishing right from wrong. Some of them felt that it was "not fair that clergy are respected more than the workers," but none of them failed to recognize the moral credibility which their positions afforded them.

The first audience that CLUE clergy confronted was themselves. Getting involved with CLUE and becoming educated about the living wage campaign and the various union campaigns showed clergy that they needed first to get their own houses of worship in order. They had to put their morality in practice by getting their churches and temples to comply with basic tenets of economic justice, such as paying living wages, not just minimum wages, to congregation staff, such as the janitors, cooks, and childcare workers. Wealthier congregations, of course, were better able to enact these changes than poorer ones.

The second targeted audience that CLUE clergy confronted was the corporate owners and managers of the unionizing workers. Here, CLUE clergy, usually wearing their clerical collars, joined delegations of workers and union organizers in visiting the offices of management. Sometimes they encountered resistance, with the executive management refusing to meet with them or claiming to be out of the office. In other instances, they met face-to-face with management to explain the predicament of the unionizing workers. In these meetings, they tried to match up clergy from the same denomination as the owner or manager. When CEOs and corporate managers resided and worked far away, CLUE used other tactics of persuasion. These included initiating letter-writing campaigns and enlisting the help of affiliated faith-based labor support groups.

A third audience that CLUE sought to address was the media and policy-makers. In this regard, CLUE's well-orchestrated public events such as the Holy Week–Passover Procession can be traced back to César Chávez's 1966 UFW pilgrimage from Delano to Sacramento. These events mesh religious notions of suffering and sacrifice to call attention to the plight of exploited workers. Religious activists in CLUE and IWJ use religious authority to call attention to the plight of immigrant workers, and they use the tool of moral authority to bring public shame to exploitative employers. As an article in a 2007 IWJ newsletter stated, religious leaders are effective activists because they are "trusted leaders" in the public sphere:

> Interfaith leaders have the capacity to make a unique contribution to the struggle for the human rights of immigrant workers and their families. Faith leaders are important guardians of the values and visions of our society. They have the capacity, with effective media support, to significantly influence public opinion. . . . Faith leaders can change the terms of the debate and create the conditions for comprehensive immigration reform.[4]

LABOR IN THE PULPIT

Last but not least, the CLUE clergy targeted the pews of their own congregations. Most of the clergy did not preach about economic justice on a weekly basis, but each Labor Day there was a concerted effort to do so. This is part of a national effort begun in 1996 and coordinated by IWJ and the AFL-CIO. On Labor Day weekend across the country, participating clergy are urged to speak to their congregations about the religious commitment to economic justice, tying the importance of unions today to biblical and scriptural readings. Union members are invited as guest speakers to discuss how they mesh their religious faith and union commitments.

During Labor Day weekend 2001, about one hundred Los Angeles–area congregations participated in this program, with guest speakers appearing at about fifty. I attended two services organized by CLUE clergy. Both featured special emphasis on immigrant worker rights and, in particular, Latino immigrant labor struggles. The two services were radically different, reflecting the different sizes of the congregations, the style of worship, and the congregations' demographic composition. Both, however, were unambiguously directed at the same cause: bringing religious communities and unions together to work for immigrant worker justice. Elsewhere, other religious services at predominantly black churches were focused on honoring the struggles of bus transit and airport security workers, many of whom are African American.[5]

The first Labor in the Pulpit service that I attended occurred at a relatively small Unitarian church in affluent Santa Monica. In this small church filled with natural light, about two hundred or two hundred fifty people, many of them elderly or middle-aged white folks, filled the pews. After welcoming remarks, the lighting of a candle within a chalice (with some difficulty because of a faulty lighter), and the singing of songs such as "This Little Light of Mine," a middle-aged congregation member hobbled to the altar. She revealed that she suffered from multiple sclerosis, and she read a beautifully rendered narrative of thanks to all of the workers who made her life possible—the taxi drivers, the concrete workers, the designers and builders of her motorized wheelchair, and the builders of ramps and rails. More songs ensued, and then small children entered with offerings of food for a food bank before gathering around the group Los Jornaleros del Norte. This is a band formed by Latino immigrant men who met in the day laborer organizing project of the Coalition for Humane Immigrant Rights in Los Angeles. Pablo Alvarado, an immigrant rights and day laborer organizer and member of the band, introduced them by saying, "All of us are immigrant workers and all of us are parents, too." And then he introduced Jose, one of the band members. With that, Jose took the microphone and explained, in Spanish and through a translator, that he was a single parent of six children in Mexico. "I would like to tell the children here," he said, directing himself to the kids who sat on the steps around the altar, "to thank God because they live with their parents. I would love to be with my children, but I cannot." While the band played one of their compositions about the plight of children "back home" with parents working in the United States, the audience bobbed their heads to the beat.

After the song, the Los Angeles–based immigrant rights activist and lawyer Victor Narro spoke. "Labor Day is an appropriate moment to recognize immigrant workers' contributions to the U.S. This should not be an exercise in guilt, but in appreciation of everything they do," he told the audience. "As consumers, we have a special relationship with immigrant workers who clean our homes and work as gardeners, roofers, and farmworkers who put food on our table." Notably, he did not focus on union workers, reflecting his position and sensitivity as an organizer for Latino immigrant informal sector workers, such as day laborers who work as gardeners, do construction, or perform odd jobs.

Members of the day laborers band spoke next. All of them were outfitted in crisply ironed white shirts, black pants, and black vests, looking not unlike Latino car valets at some of L.A.'s swankier spots. Their shiny and carefully pressed clothes and their brown faces provided quite a contrast to the wealthier congregation members' pale complexions and penchant for natural-dyed, crumpled cotton or linen clothing. Like the testimonials offered by union workers at the CLUE breakfast meetings, these were two different social worlds coming together. Speaking in Spanish through a translator, the first speaker said, "We day laborers use

this Labor Day to protest the exploitation of immigrant workers."
Another cited Leviticus and denounced abusive employers who violate
the laws of government and the laws of God. They played more songs,
ending with a lively rendition of "Sí Se Puede" on accordion, electric
piano, bass, and guitar, and the expressions on the band members' and
the congregation's faces suggested genuine warmth, appreciation, and
feelings of solidarity.

Next, Reverend Altagracia Perez, who was identified in the program
as "a rector at the Episcopal church of St. Philip the Evangelist in South
Central Los Angeles," came forward as the guest speaker and delivered
the sermon. She began by discussing her work with CLUE, and she
immediately drew an analogy with the lighter that would not light the
candle at the beginning of the service. "I thought it was interesting," she
said, "that the lighter wouldn't light the Chalice. Even those of us who
are committed sometimes have a hard time lighting that light of hope,"
alluding to the cynicism of progressives. "But if one lighter doesn't
work, another will! That's what the hotel workers have shown." She
then discussed the organizing campaigns in one industry, the hotel
industry, and in one place, the beachfront hotels in Santa Monica. In
deeply personal terms, she revealed that she had been going through an
emotional depression, a "spiritual sickness," one that plagued her until
she became involved with the labor struggle of the USC food service
workers. She confessed that she had initially signed up for the workers'
fast out of guilt but that she was ultimately moved by the workers. On
the second day of the fast, she said that she met Marisela Frutos, a USC
cafeteria worker and a single parent of five children, who was fasting for
five days on only water. Seeing committed workers like this prompted a
spiritual renewal in the pastor. "I woke up from my cynicism and I realized that God was busy," she said, "but that I hadn't been paying attention. I woke up from my cynicism. It was due to being with people who
didn't have the luxury of my cynicism, because they *had* to work, they
had to struggle."

Reverend Perez condemned hotel owners in Santa Monica who "make
millions of dollars in revenue yet refuse to pay living wages" to their
employees. She reminded the congregation that the Bible condemned

greed and idolatry, and she concluded with concrete actions that the congregation could undertake to help the cause of the hotel workers. She urged them to pray, to support their minister, Reverend Judith Meyers, in her work with CLUE, to volunteer to help a family, and "to create a buzz about justice wherever you go."

Compared to the deeply personalized and localized messages of clergy support for immigrant workers that I witnessed at the small Unitarian church in Santa Monica, the Labor in the Pulpit service that I attended the following day was quite different. This one was held at St. Vincent Catholic Church, near downtown Los Angeles, just a block away from USC. It was the most elaborately orchestrated Labor in the Pulpit event, written up in a large feature article in the Los Angeles Times, which estimated that sixteen hundred people were in attendance, a mostly Latino crowd.[6] When I arrived with my son, I found the ornate, cavernous church packed to the gills with not only families and elderly, but also with union members dressed in brightly colored T-shirts, clergy leaders, politicians, and journalists. Presiding and speaking at the two-hour Mass were some of the nation's major labor and spiritual leaders, including Cardinal Roger M. Mahoney and the president of the AFL-CIO, John Sweeney, visiting from Washington, D.C. In attendance also were California governor Gray Davis, Lieutenant Governor Cruz Bustamante, and many municipal officials.

The two-hour Mass began with a procession of union workers dressed in their work clothes, carrying the tools of their trade. Dozens of priests marched in with them, and then, finally, the cardinal, carrying a staff and wearing over his fine robes a vestment made from what looked like Mexican serape fabric. He was greeted with much applause and open admiration. Some Latina mothers held up their babies to touch him. Father Mike Walsh of the parish, also a CLUE participant, began the service by noting that St. Vincent Church is both an architectural treasure of Los Angeles and a spiritual landmark for immigrant workers, a place for them to find support for justice. He repeated this message in Spanish and English, and in his welcoming comments, he urged us to give thanks to all workers, but especially to immigrant workers.

After the liturgy from Genesis, Cardinal Mahoney read from the Gospel according to Luke, emphasizing Jesus' support for the poor and the marginal. He invoked Incarnation, saying that by taking on human flesh, Jesus served as a profound affirmation of human dignity. And with this, he segued into economic status and immigration status. "Organized labor and labor unions play a critical role in society, and in Los Angeles," he said. He reminded the audience that the families of minimum wage workers still live below the poverty line, and that unions seek to remedy this. He also talked about the plight of immigrant workers, saying that "their immigration status makes them vulnerable to different types of abuses at work." And then he named the occupations with the most lively organizing campaigns under way in Los Angeles, adding that "hotel workers, restaurant workers, home care workers, janitors, and farmworkers contribute" to the United States. He took this narrative one step further, telling those in attendance about the public campaigns to raise the minimum wage. Finally, the cardinal ended with a plea for compassionate and just immigration reform and legalization. "The Bush administration and Congress should find ways to reciprocate the contributions of immigrant workers by allowing workers to gain legal permanent residence and citizenship. The current focus on creating new guest worker programs should be viewed with extreme skepticism. . . . In upcoming months it will be critical for all of us to communicate with members of Congress." The cardinal concluded by reminding people to register to vote at tables outside of the church and to gather sample letters of what to write to Congress to call for the legalization of immigrant workers.

After Holy Communion, President John Sweeney of the AFL-CIO spoke. He began by discussing massive layoffs in manufacturing jobs, and he said that repairs were needed. "First on the list for the nation's repairs is amnesty legalization." He talked about his family's Irish immigrant roots, adding, "We're a nation of immigrants, yet we daily visit injustice upon new arrivals to our shores—a cruel irony not lost on those of us who share experiences as children of immigrants." He told those gathered that "at the AFL-CIO, we believe immigration reform should include legalization for millions of workers who lack legal status and basic benefits. . . . Labor laws should protect all workers, documented or not." President Bush and President Fox were, at that time, a few days before the 9/11 terrorist attacks, scheduled to meet to discuss immigration reform. It had been a hopeful moment, and Sweeney said, "I know all of you will offer prayers for reform."

It is significant that the president of the AFL-CIO chose to be in Los Angeles for Labor Day. "We see L.A. as a model for cities across the country," Sweeney reported to the *Los Angeles Times*.[7] Immigration and the pursuit of legalization for undocumented workers were clearly driving his choice of where to be on the most important labor holiday of the year. This confirms the idea that Los Angeles is an epicenter for organizing around immigrant worker rights, and that the clergy of Los Angeles play a significant part in this process.

DENOMINATIONAL DIFFERENCES?

CLUE and IWJ brought together clergy and laity from a variety of religious faiths and traditions, but when I asked if these denominational differences played out into conflicts, nearly everyone told me no. Reverend Don Smith, who had worked in numerous interfaith groups, including explicitly immigrant rights organizations, said, "In these social ministries, you'll never find the need to kind of say that, well, 'You're Catholic, I'm Jewish, and you're Episcopal.' There's this kind of innate understanding that all religions have in common, [which] is this need to address human pain, human suffering."

Just about everyone concurred. Political progressives were less likely to be mired in denominational differences. "The majority of those who will come into CLUE are your more progressive clergypersons anyway," said one clergyman, "and because they are more progressive, they are less likely to bring in denominational garbage." In fact, some clergy found this denominational diversity and shared understanding of social justice, theology, and social action to be particularly gratifying, giving them opportunities for clerical solidarity. Reverend Altagracia Perez, a youthful thirtyish female black and Latina pastor, said, for example, that she had tired of repeatedly explaining to other neighboring Episcopal pastors that she was not the youth minister or the pastor's wife. She said she had more in common with a particular Lutheran minister (and co-CLUE participant) who pastored in the same Central Los Angeles neighborhood and was similarly bound up with problems of poverty and worker injustice than she did with pastors in suburban Episcopal churches. "We have the same kind of population, we're serving the same neighborhood, and we have a lot of the same issues," she said of the Lutheran minister. "We share a common theology." In fact, she went even further, stating, "I think that the priests, ministers, and religious leaders that see themselves as part of the call to social justice feel more connected to each other than they do to people within their own denomination." A ministry focused on social and economic justice brought diverse clergy together in ways that being ordained in the same denomination did not.

Denominational differences did come up when CLUE planned liturgical programming. During the plans for the Journey toward Justice march in Santa Monica, there was some dispute over the incorporation of Wiccans from Santa Monica. A couple of CLUE clergy felt that an interfaith organization needed to be open and inclusive. In fact, during the discussions, these two people said that even having "clergy and laity" in the name of the organization was regressive and exclusive, as some religions, such as Buddhism, do not have ordained clergy. Other clergy disagreed, including one clergy member who anticipated that if pagan rituals were included in the interfaith blessings, Latina women in the union would fear becoming involved with anything that smacked of brujeria, or witchcraft. Another person told me that union organizers had asked, "How's it going to look if we invite a witch?" Big theological discussions ensued within CLUE, with some clergy arguing that pagan traditions were part of indigenous religion and at the root of Christianity and other faith traditions while other clergy were still opposed. The resulting program reflected something of a compromise, with blessings to the four directions included in the liturgy. In general, in efforts to be inclusive, the CLUE liturgies walked a fine line, avoiding overtly Christ-centered ceremonies and yet remaining true to ancient faith traditions of the major religions, principally those of Christianity and Judaism.

CLUE and IWJ define themselves as expressly interfaith organizations, but particular denominations remain absent. Most notably absent were evangelicals and Pentecostals. Reverend Salvatierra said she had plans to recruit them, although she realized it would take considerable effort. Evangelicals and Pentecostals are thought by some to have "otherworldly" beliefs, more focused on spiritual attainment after death than on social justice on earth. Their theologies do not seem to lend themselves to social action campaigns, although, as some of the interviewees noted and as has been noted in *Streets of Glory* by Omar McRoberts, this is not the case for African American evangelical Christian churches. This may be changing for Latino evangelicals, too. Although Latino Pentecostal and evangelical clergy were not participatory in CLUE, they too formed their own alliances to seek justice regarding immigration reform issues in 2006.[8] Muslim leaders did not seem to be very prominent in CLUE and IWJ until after September 11, 2001, when Muslim American organizations, as I detail in chapter 2, made a concerted effort to work together in coalitions with other progressive and racial-ethnic minority groups. At that point, Hussan Ayloush, the executive director of the CAIR in Orange County, joined the board of IWJ, and Maher Hathout of MPAC got involved with CLUE.

When it comes to denominational participation in CLUE, I was always struck by the relatively slim representation of Catholic clergy at the CLUE breakfast meetings or on the smaller organizing committees. During a moment when CLUE was primarily backing the union organizing efforts of Latino immigrant workers, a group well-known to be predominantly and deeply Catholic, this seemed odd. Moreover, regardless of the workers' religious traditions, the theological basis of Catholic social teachings would seem to predict greater Catholic participation. Where were the Catholics?

Three factors account for the limited Catholic clergy participation in CLUE. First, many Catholic clergy in Los Angeles find themselves consumed and overwhelmed with their parish obligations. Many of them, especially those serving Latino immigrant congregations, lead large, needy congregations that require sacraments, such as baptisms, communions, funeral services, and so on, as well as social service programs.

St. Vincent Church, where the central Labor in the Pulpit Mass occurred on Labor Day, had twelve hundred registered families and about five thousand people attending Mass every Sunday. Multiple social programs, which included an elementary school, catechism classes, Bible study, a youth ministry program, and courses to prepare for baptisms, marriages, and *quinceaneras,* were all run through the St. Vincent parish. The priests presided over all of this as well as daily Mass (seven on weekends) and confession. Three priests and a small handful of staff kept all of these parish activities afloat. Among them, Father Mike Walsh had become active in CLUE through his work with the campaign at USC, which was just across the block from his church. But rather than putting more energy into CLUE, he was hoping to better integrate CLUE activities into his congregation.

As the hub of sacraments, social service programs, and activities, and because it was so large, St. Vincent Catholic Church contrasted with the much smaller churches and temples that other CLUE clergy headed. Reverend Altagracia Perez, for example, headed up a poor congregation, St. Philip's Episcopal Church, located not far from St. Vincent Church. There were social programs there, too, and she had to confront the ambivalence, and sometimes the hostility, that long-standing African American members expressed toward the new Latino immigrants attending the services, but the church was much smaller. Three services were held on an average Sunday, and when my research assistant, Kara Lemma, attended one of them, she reported about sixty people in attendance.

Other CLUE clergy led affluent congregations in the suburbs, or they did not pastor in churches at all. A number of them were retired or held special peace and justice positions in their respective religious organizations. Don Smith, for example, did not minister at a church but worked with the Presbyterian synod of Southern California and Hawaii, a post that allowed him to become active in CLUE and the statewide Interfaith Coalition for Immigrant Rights. When Dick Gillet retired from ministering a congregation, the Episcopal bishop appointed him as the minister of social justice for the Episcopal archdiocese, affording him similar opportunities. Reverend Miller was retired and hence enjoyed a flexible schedule that, as we saw earlier, allowed him to attend direct actions during work hours. Consequently, he was called very often to visit workplaces and make home visits. To be sure, these were all busy and active people, but none of the clergy leaders seemed as overwhelmed with congregational duties as the Catholics. As retired clergy, as leaders in social justice missions, or as leaders of small congregations, other Christian and Jewish clergy seemed to have more time and energy for CLUE activities than did the Catholic priests.

The organizational structure of denominations was also a factor in constraining or enabling clergy participation in CLUE. Catholics were constrained by a rigidly hierarchical structure, one that reflects Catholicism's roots as a medieval, pre-Reformation religion, and one that today requires clergy to follow orders from their superiors. At one of the direct actions I attended, a union organizer with a petition in hand approached a Catholic bishop. He asked for his signature of support, but the bishop, although clearly there to support the cause of the hotel workers, shook his head and explained that he could not sign without permission from his superiors. In another instance, when CLUE was seeking endorsements, the Catholic archdiocese representative had insisted on changing a few words before signing on to the document. In still another example of this kind of hesitancy, the CLUE director told me that Catholics would come to the processions but not the planning meetings, because "once you come to a planning meeting, it's uncomfortably close to being responsible for the organization, which they are not allowed to do." Mandates from the cardinal, the U.S. Conference of Catholic Bishops, and the pope may be necessary to sanction priests' public activities.

Order priests enjoyed a bit more autonomy than diocesan priests, as they were able to fit their work into their particular missions or respective orders. The Scalabrinians, for example, are dedicated to working with immigrants; the Vincentians, with the urban poor; and the Franciscans, with the poor. But even order priests were somewhat stuck. One of the order priests who was involved in CLUE told me of frank internal conversations that he had with other priests. "Sometimes we're in our meeting, which is [with] the local churches—we're about twenty churches in this area—and at one of our meetings, we kind of criticized ourselves, saying, 'Why we do wait for some kind of sign from the cardinal?'" he said, referring to the cardinal's decision to attend the AFL-CIO-sponsored event at the Los Angeles Sports Arena calling for immigration reform. The cardinal had participated in the event and, hence, so had many Catholic churches. Rather than a top-down process, he suggested, "it should be the other way around; we should be bringing issues to the archdiocese and saying that we have a strong commitment about this, and we want you to be on board, too." It was disappointing to him that "Catholic parishes are not more involved in worker rights, especially in immigrant labor," but he remained hopeful that support might be growing.

Again, the contrast to other mainline religions is striking. Rabbi Steve Jacobs, who participated in numerous progressive activist causes, underscored his autonomy. "Being an independent agent, I don't have to worry about following the bishop or the archbishop," he said. "In Judaism you don't have that," and that absence of hierarchical authority facilitated his support of CLUE. In fact, he saw his mandate as a religious and moral leader to be something of a rabble-rouser. "The great movements have always been established by the pulpit and by the masses in the street. The politician has to compromise," he said, "a preacher doesn't have to compromise." He presided over a relatively affluent, Jewish, suburban temple where the congregation was disconnected from contemporary work and union struggles, and he faced the potential of leading two opposing constituencies, but the mandate of being an autonomous moral leader seemed to outweigh potential class conflict. During our interview at his office in the Woodland Hills temple where he presided, he quoted from a plaque on the wall that spoke to this mandate: "A rabbi whose congregation does not want to drive him out of town isn't a rabbi, and if they do drive him out, he isn't a man."

A third and final reason that explains the relative paucity of Catholic clergy in CLUE organizing activities is that many of the Catholic clergy were directing their activism toward LA Metro, an Industrial Areas Foundation (IAF) affiliate that organized communities and was sanctioned by the Catholic Church. This also goes back to the hierarchical nature of Catholicism, as one person (not a Catholic) told me: "The archdiocese baptized the IAF. . . . The archdiocese [said to clergy], 'You will work with the IAF.'" Additionally, regional and spatial factors were operative here. Often, the Catholics were working in different geographical regions of Los Angeles, in neighborhoods closer to where their parishes were located. CLUE organizing focused on the Westside or in downtown, while the Catholics were involved in community activism on the Eastside of Los Angeles or in the San Gabriel or San Fernando Valleys. Additionally, one priest told me that there were competing extra-parish Catholic activities. "We [Catholics] are caught up in our own infrastructure fighting," he said. As a Mexican American priest, the Hispanic Priest Association had invited him to meetings, but when he told them that he had competing CLUE meetings, they responded by telling him, "Well, you need to be with your brothers." With that statement, they were telling him he should prioritize Catholic activities over ecumenical ones. Catholic clergy did participate in CLUE-sponsored interfaith processions and direct action, but with the exception of a few clergy, most of them were not among those who were doing the core CLUE organizing work.

SPIRITUAL RENEWAL

"CLUE doesn't realize it, but I needed them just as much as they need me." These are the words of Reverend Jarvis Johnson, and they speak to the deep gratification that many of the clergy derived from their participation with CLUE. In the struggle for economic justice and for the rights of Latino immigrant workers in Los Angeles, we have seen how important the integration of religion and religious moral voice has proven to be. Religion is critical to this burgeoning social movement, but so, too, many of the clergy said that CLUE activism was a way for them to reaffirm their faith.

No one was more effusive in this regard than Reverend Altagracia Perez, who found her CLUE involvement to be deeply transformative. She had been experiencing something of an emotional and spiritual crisis, but she was newly revitalized and inspired when she met the workers through CLUE. These mostly Latino immigrant workers "were taking risks and making sacrifices—and not just doing it, but doing it willingly and joyfully," she recalled. "And I, who had all this privilege, was doing everything begrudgingly. . . . It really shamed me. . . . It was a conversion experience for me to see that, and it invited my involvement." Although she had been active in community organizing around youth and HIV in the Bronx, she had never really experienced a seamless fit of faith and action. Becoming a faith-based activist in CLUE, she said, was "what I always dreamed of when I was in seminary. I had studied liberation theology, and . . . I was finally doing it!"

Similarly, Reverend Dick Gillet, a veteran of religiously inspired economic justice activism, also found a sort of redemption in his CLUE work. He had worked with factory workers in Puerto Rico in the 1970s, then in Los Angeles in the 1980s as part of "a very small but quite effective coalition to address massive plant closures in Los Angeles" and high unemployment.[9] But it "was not right for a massive protest at that time, and the religious community, well, there was just a handful of us that were involved in that." As a retired clergy, he felt renewed through CLUE, which had provided him with new experiences. "I find that in my late sixties I am learning, and I'm kind of in awe that I can learn, and I feel myself developing skills. I feel myself really rooted in this higher plane, and so it's an exciting time."

PART III Faith *sin Fronteras*

six Enacting Christian Antiborderism

It's the third Saturday in December, just days before Christmas, and several hundred people have gathered at a desolate spot in San Ysidro, California, where the fence dividing the United States from Mexico extends into the Pacific Ocean. Like a razor, *la línea* cuts sharply through hilly, rocky terrain and parts the sea. The fence, however, lacks biblical legitimacy, and it's a big, ugly thing. But on a chilly December evening, the beachfront sunset panorama, with its pink and lavender skies and silvery blue slice of ocean, is among the most beautiful I have ever seen. This is a relatively gentle spot along the border, one of the few places in the San Diego area, a woman tells me, where you can actually stick your wrists through to touch people on the other side, as we'll do later that evening as part of the ceremony. In other areas along the U.S.-Mexico border, thick air-landing mats from the Gulf War (the government's idea of recycling) now block visual and human access.

We're here for the annual Posada sin Fronteras, an interfaith, predominantly Christian celebration of cross-border unity and protest against the social injustice of U.S. border policies. People from as far away as Los Angeles and Northern California, but mostly from San Diego County, have driven down freeways and then a windy, bumpy dirt road to Border Field State Park, an antiseptic-looking grassy field scattered with a few picnic tables. This is a site of surveillance, a park where two lone Border Patrol agents are typically the only people present to enjoy the seaside vistas. Peering through the fence, we can see people gathered on the Mexican side, where homes in the affluent middle-class neighborhood of Playas de Tijuana straddle up next to the bullring and the lighthouse. When I arrive with my students at 3 P.M., there are only about thirty people, but by sunset, a diverse group of about three hundred have congregated on either side of the fence.

A posada is a traditional Catholic Latin American procession which reenacts Joseph and Mary's search for shelter in Bethlehem. It's a familiar cultural tradition in Mexico and in parts of Latin America, the Caribbean, and the U.S. Southwest.[1] During the Advent season, just before Christmas, a group carrying a doll, which symbolizes the Christ child, spends eight or nine evenings processing through neighborhoods, stopping at previously selected homes to ask for lodging. Sometimes adults or children are dressed as Mary and Joseph, and they reenact their being rejected before they are met with hospitality. It's a joyous occasion. Participants sing special posada songs, read scriptures, and end the evening with refreshments.

The Posada sin Fronteras, sponsored by various faith-based and immigrant rights groups, readapts the traditional posada procession to commemorate the plight of migrant families traveling from the south to the north in what has become one of most dangerous border regions in the world.[2] The event is more than a commemoration—it is a call to welcome the migrants and to protest border policies that kill people. I see it as an expression of Christian antiborderism—although most of the participants and organizers do not intend to erase nation-state borders.

Rather, they challenge border policies that promote the suffering and deaths of undocumented migrants in transit. They posit Christian kinship as an alternative to this injustice. Every year, but especially since the fortification of the U.S.-Mexico border with Operation Gatekeeper in 1994, hundreds of people die as they attempt to cross the U.S.-Mexico border. Thousands have died in the last decade seeking less-regulated border-crossing spots. Just as Mary and Joseph sought hospitality in a foreign, inhospitable land, so too, faith-based organizers tell us, are Mexican and Central American migrants from the south seeking hospitality in the north. They insist that Joseph and Mary, carrying Jesus, were among the first undocumented border crossers.

At the 2002 Posada sin Fronteras, Reverend Art Cribbs served as the emcee and began by getting us to think about the event's central theme. "Why are we here?" he rhetorically asked of the crowd, which included, by late afternoon, about a dozen clergy in collars, several Franciscan brothers wearing robes and sandals, and families with children as well as Christian youth groups. "We're here," he explained in his booming voice, with sharp enunciation and dramatic cadence, "to experience hospitality and inhospitality. We're here to know what it means to be friends and strangers." Finally, he proclaimed to the attentive audience gathered on either side of the fence, "there is a spirit that transcends the border." While not all the participants would agree that religious spirituality trumps nation-state borders, this declaration invited reflection and cast a spell of silence over the people gathered.

RELIGIOUS RITUAL AND REENACTMENT AT THE BORDER

The Posada sin Fronteras is only one expression of Christian antiborderism. Religious-based activists have creatively adopted and embraced a liturgical calendar based on Catholic and Mexican traditions to underscore the connection between faith and commitment to social justice along the U.S.-Mexico border. The Posada sin Fronteras, Via Crucis del Migrante Jesus, and Día de los Muertos are now celebrated at multiple points along the U.S.-Mexico border by ecumenical, faith-based, binational groups and in some spots in the interior (a Posada sin Fronteras, for example, was held in Washington, D.C.).[3] Since Vatican II, Euro-American Catholics celebrate ritualistic devotions less while Mexican American and Mexican immigrant Catholics have expanded these collective rituals and devotions, fortifying community solidarity and belonging.[4] Some of these public rituals incorporate critiques of social injustices, as has been noted with Día de los Muertos celebrations in Los Angeles, Guadeloupean devotions in San Antonio, and Via Crucis Good Friday enactments in the Pilsen neighborhood of Chicago.[5] But something special is happening with these at the border—the rituals are expanding beyond Mexican Catholics to include participants of neither Mexican nor Catholic heritage. These collective reenactments, usually conducted in situ, in strategic sites along the border fence, constitute part of an expressive religious culture of Christian antiborderism. This culture is used to denounce government immigration and border policies that have killed thousands of migrants, to commemorate the migrants, and to refresh activists' commitments to faith-based social justice work. In the process, symbolic racial-ethnic and denominational borders are crossed.

The Posada sin Fronteras, celebrated now for over ten years at the Tijuana–San Ysidro border, appears to be the grandmother of these hybrid events. Its site and the number who attend change each year, but typically a few hundred people gather on both sides of the fence to sing songs, read aloud the names of those who died while crossing the border, and reenact the seeking of hospitality and sharing across borders. Together with a small group of students, I attended the Posada sin Fronteras from 2001 to 2004, and we interviewed the people who started it as well as the current organizers and some of the participants.[6]

The organizers say the event allows people to see immigration and border issues through a religious lens and that it offers hope and faith that the border divisions and policies will change. The physical place where it occurs is critical. Brother Gioacchino Campese of the Scalabrini Order, a key organizer of the posada during the seven years he spent ministering in the Tijuana shelter for migrants, Casa del Migrante, said that the border site evokes religious expression and reflection. "I don't think there is any place in the world," he said, "where the message [of Jesus] is more striking because [the border] is the place . . . you see just the opposite of that hospitality. There is a wall that divides two nations." Art Cribbs, the Lutheran minister of a largely African American congregation who emceed the Posada sin Fronteras for several years in a row, emphatically agreed that the visceral combination of the site and the opportunity for personal connection made for a very moving experience of solidarity. "There is a drama associated when you go to the border, and you are at the fence, and people can't cross the fence, and you can't cross the fence, and yet you are standing together." Francisco Herrerra, one of two singer-musicians who regularly performs at the Posada sin Fronteras, emphasized the spiritual authenticity of it. "We are not celebrating a commercialistic, dead ritual . . . our faith is about receiving people who are really going through the experience that Joseph and Mary went through when they were moving." And Rosemary Johnson, one of the key organizers of the event, concurred, "It's such an obvious metaphor for the whole immigration issue in terms of Joseph and Mary going from place to place, seeking shelter and being turned away." The ultimate rejoicing that occurs when an innkeeper finally welcomes them into a stable is critical, she felt. "To hold that vision in our minds in the midst of all this xenophobia is very important, and what's so neat is that we celebrate with the people of Tijuana at the border fence."

Due to rain and border fence reconstruction projects, the Posada sin Fronteras is not always held in the same spot, but each time I attended, I experienced a multisensory happening with rich visual, audio, and symbolic elements. Participants do not passively stand but are urged to sing, stand, process with lighted candles, and share in simple ceremonial rituals such as singing Christmas carols and a special migrant pilgrimage song. Popular songs that everyone seems to know, like "Come All Ye Faithful," are sung in Spanish and English along with the special posada song. Participants on the U.S. side throw candy—one year it was fleece scarves—across the fence to those congregated on the other side to symbolize sharing. At sunset, church ladies always light hundreds of luminarias, lunch-sized paper bags with candles and sand inside, allowing the crowd to see that each bag illuminates the name of a person who died trying to cross the border. Bags bearing names such as "Juan Carlos" or "Andres" are usually interspersed with bags that simply read "no olvidado" (not forgotten) and "no identificado" (not identified). This is one of the many haunting images that stayed with me after I left the posada and the border fence.

In this chapter, using ethnographic observations and interviews with organizers and participants, I examine how this particularly Catholic Latino religious ritual has become a key tool of social activism in responding to border policies. I discuss changes in border policies that explain why the Posada sin Fronteras emerged in 1994, and I report on other faith-based actions that have emerged as an important dimension of Christian mobilizations for migrant rights and antiborderism. I suggest that the sanctuary movement of the 1980s provides the primary historical precedent—although other strong influences include the activities of and values espoused by the UFW, liberation theology, and the Catholic Left of the 1960s. With the focus on the border and migrant rights, there is a direct legacy between the sanctuary movement and both the instrumental and expressive faith-based activism that we see today at the border.

DEATH AT THE BORDER

Violence and death at the U.S.-Mexico border are not new. The border was born in violence with the conclusion of the Mexican-American War in 1848, but violence and migrant deaths have escalated as new policies have gone into effect in recent years. As we saw in chapter 1, the anti-immigrant uproar of California's Proposition 187 had several national-level repercussions. Operation Gatekeeper—which stepped up enforcement at the San Diego–Tijuana crossing point—was inaugurated the same year as Proposition 187, 1994. Both initiatives were political responses to the public perception that illegal immigrants, namely from Mexico and Central America, must be prevented from entering the United States. Political advertisements and media coverage fanned these flames of public discontent and outrage. Newspaper editorials bemoaned the "loss of control" at the border, and politicians scapegoated Mexican immigrants for a host of social and economic ills. Illegal border crossing and drug smuggling were cited as evidence that the United States had lost nation-state sovereignty and that anarchistic, chaotic regimes prevailed along the southern border. Among the most memorable television ads of 1994 was the one developed by Pete Wilson's gubernatorial reelection campaign. It showed Mexican migrants flagrantly running across the world's busiest border checkpoint in broad daylight while the voice-over warned of invasion.

All of this led to new federal investments in fortifying the border against illegal migrant crossings. The results? The INS budget tripled in six years during the 1990s, and the number of Border Patrol agents ballooned.[7] By 2002 there were more than ten thousand Border Patrol officers, and the Border Patrol office itself had an annual budget of $1 billion, making it the nation's largest armed police force in the immediate post-9/11 era.[8] The government also deployed militarylike operations—complete with ground sensors, military helicopters, and stadium lights—at a number of key crossing points.[9] After September 11, 2001, fears of border-crossing terrorists and bombs fueled new efforts at controlling the U.S.-Mexico border, which were directed by the newly created Department of Homeland Security. Never mind that Mohammed Atta and the other attackers of 9/11 had entered through the U.S.-Canada border, with documents.

As a direct consequence, more migrants, the vast majority of them Mexicans and Central Americans, began dying in transit. New enforcement efforts prompted smugglers and migrants to create dangerous new crossing points, most of which they devised in precarious mountain and desert terrain. Scholars at the University of Houston and observers such as Human Rights Watch and the American Friends Service Committee's Immigration Law Enforcement Monitoring Project compiled evidence of increasing numbers of deaths and grotesque human and civil rights violations—rape, sexual extortion, murder—committed by actors who included law enforcement agents, gang members, and thieves who roam both sides of the border. Law enforcement officials from both the United States and

Mexico have engaged in illegal searches, physical and psychological abuse, deprivation of food and needed medical attention, and even assault, battery, and murder of migrants.[10] As enforcement efforts and media attention focused on the U.S.-Mexico border, armed private ranchers and civilian militia groups also came on the scene.

Survey researchers and demographers tell us that the new enforcement measures have not deterred illegal migrant crossing.[11] Rather, the crossing points have shifted to more dangerous terrain, redirecting migrants away from older, more established crossing points near San Diego and El Paso and toward new more environmentally treacherous crossing points in Arizona, New Mexico, and Texas. Dehydration in the desert, drowning in the river, suffocation and heatstroke in locked auto or rail compartments, and hypothermia in freezing mountains are common causes of death. Precisely estimating how many migrants die is difficult because no one knows how many bodies are never found, but the estimates now run in the thousands.[12]

The increased enforcement and fortification of the U.S.-Mexico border drew public approval and became, momentarily at least, politically successful in affirming an image of U.S. national sovereignty. In this regard, the political scientist Peter Andreas (2000) observed that border enforcement policies of this era constituted a political success and yet, because they did not stop migration, a policy failure. After 9/11, anxieties about foreigners increased, and as it became apparent that these policies were not deterring illegal migration and that the undocumented immigrant population had grown to about 10 million by 2005, many Americans began to feel that more severe measures were necessary. As media attention and populist sentiment against continued illegal border crossings increased, the extent to which border militarization strategies could be deemed a policy success diminished. In spring 2005, a right-wing populist armed group calling itself the Minutemen Project emerged in the media spotlight, vowing to blockade the Arizona border. Although they pledged over one thousand volunteers, journalist Marc Cooper counted no more than one hundred thirty-five at their opening day rallies—but the Minutemen received an inordinate amount of media attention.[13]

In fact, the media played a central role in whipping up public fears and anxieties about the dangers of permeable borders. About seven hundred thousand people illegally entered the United States in any given year from 1995 to 2005 (Passel 2005), and proliferating media stories of this period generally discussed neither the causes nor the consequences of illegal immigration but highlighted instead the social problems associated with illegal border crossings. Those cast as bad guys included not only migrant border crossers but drug smugglers, human traffickers, rapists, gang members, and finally the potential terrorists lurking at the perimeters of the nation. Invasion metaphors abounded. The media in this period also focused on the discovery of underground tunnels developed by smugglers, while the governors of western states continued to pressure the federal government for ever-tougher border enforcement.[14] The death tolls continued to grow. In response to human rights violations and deaths, various groups mobilized to protest U.S. border policies and to assist migrants on their journey. People acting out of Christian faith emerged as a highly visible segment of this sector.

FAITH-BASED PROJECTS AGAINST BORDER VIOLENCE AND MIGRANT DEATH

Clergy and religiously inspired activists from different denominations have initiated important projects to challenge the new status quo of violence and deaths of undocumented migrants along the U.S. border.[15] Among the most institutionalized of these responses is the network of migrant shelters established by the Scalabrini Order of Catholic priests. This order, established in 1866 by an Italian bishop who ministered to Italian immigrants, is dedicated to the mission of serving migrants and immigrants, and it now claims over six hundred priests in more than twenty countries. Along the U.S.-Mexico and Mexico-Guatemala borders, the Scalabrinians operate a network of migrant shelters that provide spiritual, religious, and practical support for undocumented migrants in transit.[16] The first Casa del Migrante (house of the migrant) was built in Tijuana in 1987, and when I visited in May 2005, I found a substantial four-story building. At the entrance was a big sign that read "Yo fui extranjero y tu me acojiste," a biblical quote which translates as "I was a stranger, and you took me in." Inside, a staff of Scalabrinian laity and clergy kept the operation going. In the kitchen, three female volunteers were cooking industrial-sized vats of sausage, chili, and nopalitos, but only ninety-five men would be eating there that night. The numbers of migrants that the Casa del Migrante in Tijuana accommodated in 2005, I learned, had declined from a high of about two hundred daily during the late 1980s and early 1990s, before the San Diego–Tijuana crossing point had become so difficult to trespass.[17] At the Scalabrinian migrant women's and children's shelter, Casa Madre Assunta, that I visited just down the street, I also found that numbers were down. Beginning in the 1990s, the major crossing points and sites of migrant crisis had shifted to Arizona.

The Mexican and U.S. Conference of Catholic Bishops in 2003 issued a major statement against border policies that kill with their joint pastoral statement, "Strangers No Longer." As we saw in chapter 1, this statement declared the rights of sovereign nations to control their borders, but it challenged the morality of enforcing border sovereignty in ways that cause death or violate human rights and dignity. The statement declared, "Persons have a right to migrate to support their families," and "Government policies that respect the basic human needs of the undocumented are necessary."[18] Meanwhile, a plethora of faith-based direct action and emergency assistance programs have emerged at the U.S.-Mexico border.

Religious activists of various denominations, most of them Christian, are now using this proclamation to aid the poor and downtrodden as a springboard for mounting innovative projects of emergency assistance to migrants along the U.S.-Mexico border. Most of these projects have sprung up around the Arizona desert, where a new cluster of treacherous crossing points emerged in the late 1990s, and many of these projects were started by Presbyterians. Humane Borders has emerged a major force in this faith-based response. Founded in 2000 by Reverend Robin Hoover of Tucson's First Christian Church, it is a binational, religious nonprofit organization, composed of Protestants and Catholics, that offers emergency assistance to migrants in transit along the Arizona-Mexico border. By 2006 members claimed to have constructed more than seventy water stations, some of them large enough to include a half-dozen barrels dispensing hundreds of gallons of water as well as first aid kits and food.[19] Hundreds of volunteers, including forty trained drivers, maintain the water stations in the desert of the Arizona borderlands. A similar but smaller project arose in the San Diego area with Border Angels, founded by Enrique Morones, a longtime Mexican American activist who cites religion as his motivation for setting up stations of food, water, and clothing in the desert hills east of San Diego.[20]

In 2003 a project called Samaritan Patrol was initiated by Reverend John Fife, a former moderator of the General Assembly of the Presbyterian Church (USA) and well-known founder of the U.S. sanctuary movement of the 1980s. Together with nurses and doctors, he started this new interfaith project, putting water stations on wheels. Trained volunteers now roam the desert in jeeps and vans from daybreak to nightfall, looking for migrants in distress.[21] In spring 2004, the No More Deaths campaign began. This too is a binational, interfaith group, one that uses the biblical ark of the covenant to establish emergency aid camps for illegal migrants in the desert. Another faith-based group operating in the Arizona area is BorderLinks, an ecumenical organization founded in 1987 by Presbyterian minister Rick Ufford-Chase. It offers experiential education and border tours for U.S. citizens, as it seeks to provide a theological understanding of conflicts and inequalities at the U.S.-Mexico border. In 2005 more than nine hundred people from Canada and the United States participated in one of their programs.[22] One of their board members and author of the book *Border Theology*, Jerry Gil, has stated, "If God calls us to cross borders and break down barriers, it is not a vague or impossible mission."[23] The American Friends Service Committee, an ecumenical organization of the Quakers, has also had a strong presence through the U.S.-Mexico Border Program in California's San Diego and Imperial Counties, offering migrant advocacy, information, outreach, and referrals through the Immigration Law Enforcement Monitoring Project, started in 1987 in Texas to challenge violence at the border.[24]

These projects constitute a new civil society of biblically inspired social action groups at the U.S.-Mexico border. They combine advocacy, service providing, and civil disobedience. Most of these projects arose in the mid-1990s, but the actions and some of the principal actors are direct heirs of what happened in the sanctuary movement of the 1980s. The section below revisits that moment.

THE 1980S: THE SANCTUARY MOVEMENT

The sanctuary movement began in 1981 with the kind of basic service provision that is common among American clergy. As the civil wars in Central American intensified, thousands of refugees, primarily Guatemalans and Salvadorans, fled to the United States, where they were denied legal status as officially sanctioned refugees or authorized immigrants. In Arizona, a small group of Catholic, Quaker, Presbyterian, and Jewish clergy formed the Tucson Ecumenical Council Task Force on Central America, and they began helping undocumented Guatemalans and Salvadorans who had been detained by the Immigration and Naturalization Service at the border zone. They posted bond, offered legal assistance with INS deportation hearings, and prepared asylum applications. During two weeks in the early 1980s, faith-based volunteers freed, on bail, ninety Central Americans.[25] Still, the clergy and faith-based activists felt frustrated with the small number of people they were able to help and particularly with the practices of U.S. foreign policy and asylum granting.

Tucson clergy and church workers quickly discovered that U.S. immigration authorities, in spite of the then recently passed Refugee Act of 1980, were not granting political asylum status to Central Americans fleeing their war-torn countries. The 1980 Refugee Act, signed into law by then president Jimmy Carter, was intended to detach refugee policy from cold war policy and to ensure political asylum in the United States to all people fleeing persecution due to their race, religion, or political beliefs—regardless of political orientation. But cold war politics trumped refugee legislation, and those fleeing right-wing government or military persecution were generally denied refugee or asylum status. In Tucson, clergy observed this hypocrisy when they saw Salvadorans and Guatemalans routinely forced to sign "voluntary departure" forms, in effect deporting them back to Central America. As news of U.S. military complicity with the war atrocities in Central America—such as the persecution of those deported—reached those in the incipient sanctuary movement, members decided to act with more defiance. Frustrated with their best legal service efforts, sanctuary tactics escalated into what some observers have called "evasion services."[26] Clergy and congregation members along the U.S.-Mexico border began sheltering Central Americans in their homes and churches. Eventually, they formed what became known as "the new underground railroad" to transport and shelter Central Americans on their trek northward.

The sanctuary movement started small, under the leadership of Jim Corbett, a lay Quaker and Harvard-educated rancher, and the Tucson Ecumenical Council, but it quickly mushroomed. A major turning point occurred in March 1982, with a public declaration from Reverend John Fife of Southside Presbyterian church in Tucson. Five San Francisco Bay Area churches did likewise, publicly declaring themselves co-sanctuary churches. Reverend Fife sent a letter to the U.S. attorney general that read:

> We are writing to inform you that Southside United Presbyterian Church will publicly violate the Immigration and Nationality Act, Section 274 (A). We have declared our church as a "sanctuary" for undocumented refugees from Central America. . . . We believe that justice and mercy require that people of conscience actively assert our God-given right to aid anyone fleeing from persecution and murder. The current administration of U.S. law prohibits us from sheltering these refugees from Central America. Therefore we believe the administration of the law to be immoral, as well as illegal. . . . Obedience to God requires this of all of us.[27]

At that moment, sanctuary movement participants shifted away from secret evasion of immigration authorities to defiance of U.S. government authorities and public pronouncement of sanctuary spaces. They did this to bring public attention to U.S. government policies. As Jim Corbett put it, "By keeping the operation clandestine, we were doing exactly what the government wanted us to do—keeping it hidden, keeping the issue out of public view."[28]

Suddenly middle-class, church-going, law-abiding homemakers, congregation members, and clergy leaders were deliberately challenging U.S. federal laws by harboring illegal aliens, and they were using biblical passages to justify their actions. As one such woman reported to sociologist Robin Lorentzen, "I don't see that we have any choice. Clearly these people are being persecuted. The U.S. is clearly in violation of international law. We have a higher law that we must obey."[29] Spare rooms and basements in churches, temples, and homes were converted into temporary way stations for Central American refugees migrating to San Francisco, Chicago, Boston, Los Angeles, Seattle, and New York. In the United States, harboring or transporting an illegal alien is a federal felony. Acting out of religious conscience and moral obligation, thousands of religious leaders and congregation members broke the law and put themselves at risk. Although it is difficult to precisely count how many people and congregations participated, participation took root across the country and across denominations.[30]

Biblical authority and sacred texts served as the primary justification for breaking the law, trumping government authority or cold war rationale. The religious activists were not shy about declaring their religious motivations. After Fife sent his letter to U.S. attorney general William French Smith, declaring, "We believe the administration of the law to be immoral," he raised two banners in his church. One read, "This is a sanctuary for the oppressed of Central America," while the other proclaimed, "Immigration: do not profane the sanctuary of God."[31] Similarly, David Napier, a biblical scholar and participant in sanctuary, cited the Hebrew Bible as justification for the sanctuary movement's defiance of U.S. law. He wrote, "Hear the Hebrew Bible: 'Never mind what *they* tell you to do: your peers, the electorate, your governmental prophets and priests. What God requires of you is the doing of justice.'"[32]

Once the sanctuary movement openly defied federal law, the government engaged in surveillance and wiretapping of movement members and indicted sixteen sanctuary workers in Tucson, eventually convicting eight of them.[33] As predicted by many participants, government prosecution backfired and won the sanctuary movement more media publicity and public sympathy. Sanctuary members used their public platform to openly criticize the implementation of federal immigration policies and the trajectory of U.S. foreign policy in Central America. While the government painted the religious activists as "alien smugglers," the movement participants portrayed themselves as religious Americans acting out of biblically based morality and religious conscience.

The majority of clergy and laity in the sanctuary movement did not minister to or worship with Latino immigrants. So how did they come to champion refugee rights? Public testimonials given by Central American refugees conveyed personal, eyewitness accounts of some of the atrocities of the civil wars, and these evoked strong emotions among listeners. The social movement literature has acknowledged the critical role of personal narratives and "movement stories" in solidifying faith-based mobilizations.[34] In the transnational solidarity movement with Central America, which was closely connected to the sanctuary movement, progressive U.S. Christians built ties with progressive Central American churches. Stories couched in Christian faith and rituals facilitated this process, as sociologist Nepstad has underscored.[35] As we see below, personal face-to-face testimonials from Central American refugees, rendered in ritualistic, religious settings, were key to sanctuary movement mobilizations.

Among sanctuary movement participants, the testimonies were dramatic. The content of the testimonials centered on chilling descriptions of military torture, rape, and the murder of friends and family, and many times, the Central Americans refugees had arrived in the U.S. cities where they spoke only a few hours or days before. Adding to the drama and the sense of urgency, they wore bandanas to hide their identities. Robin Lorentzen, who conducted an ethnography of women's participation in the sanctuary movement in eight sites in Chicago, rendered this vibrant description of these encounters:

> The refugees' arrival is usually accompanied by much fanfare and publicity, with processions of cars traveling to meet them and public speakouts along the way. Refugees frequently "give witness" at formal declaration ceremonies where they meet members of the congregation and describe in moving detail their torture or imprisonment by

government agents at home. . . . First contact with the refugees is a highly charged, impelling experience that stimulates the subsequent activism and commitment of newcomers to sanctuary. Meeting the refugees and hearing their stories often represents a cathartic high point, a moment of "collective feeling" that produces dedication to the tasks ahead.[36]

These testimonials were the sanctuary movement's key mechanism for recruiting new members.

Why did these testimonials prove to be so effective in mobilizing clergy and faith-based advocates? Certainly the grotesque nature of the war atrocities was a motivating force, but the context in which these were related was also critical. The face-to-face nature of the testimonials made these venues for transmitting information and events. Witnessing became an active way of expressing Christianity. The fact that the stories conveyed were personally rendered experiences deepened the sense of urgency. As one Tucson minister told researcher Susan Coutin, "Once you spend time with the people who are coming here, once you have heard their stories, then there's no turning back."[37] Another sanctuary participant told Lorentzen this: "It was very disturbing to see people with bandanas on their faces. . . . They talked about what was happening in El Salvador—what the government was doing, and why they had to leave. They were pleading with us to please do something. They really had me then, putting those refugees in front of me. All of a sudden I felt responsible for our government's actions."[38]

Sanctuary members developed a political analysis of U.S. involvement in Central America and extended their advocacy work beyond charity. In 1985 a group of churches filed suit against the U.S. federal government for illegally and selectively applying asylum law.[39] By this point, it was undeniable: Faith-based service providing had clearly moved to direct actions and contestations of government authority. Religious beliefs and testimonies and the emotional responses to those testimonies formed the basis for developing a political analysis and response to the crisis at the border. This constitutes part of a legacy that has developed into contemporary expressive religious activities that advocates have innovated at the U.S.-Mexico border. In the next chapter,

I offer an analysis of the Posada sin Fronteras and an examination of the meanings that participants attribute to it.

The posada, we must remember, is only one of the religious responses to the challenges and injustices faced by migrants at the border.

THE NEW SANCTUARY MOVEMENT

"Who would Jesus deport?" So reads the T-shirt of the highly photographed Mexican woman, undocumented immigrant Elvira Arrellano, who sought refuge in a Chicago church in August 2006, thereby sparking a new interfaith sanctuary movement around the country.[40] The new sanctuary movement arose in response to immigration raids that occurred around the country in spring and summer 2006. It gained some traction in 2006 and 2007 in Los Angeles and surrounding Southern California communities, coordinated by CLUE in Los Angeles, IWJ in Chicago, and the New York Sanctuary Coalition/Association Tepayac, but it never became as massively adopted, or as publicized, as the sanctuary movement of the 1980s.[41]

The new sanctuary movement also walked a legal tightrope, inviting congregations to participate in "prophetic hospitality" in various ways, one of which involved hosting an immigrant family under order of deportation for three months. But participating in the new sanctuary movement did not require participating congregations to break immigration laws. Rather, it invited congregations to show support by offering legal assistance, financial support, and witnessing at day labor pickup sites or other workplaces where immigrants face challenges. As Bishop Gabino Zavala explained when I interviewed him during spring 2007, "We're dealing with people who are already in the system, with people whose names are out and public, so we're not really putting anybody in jeopardy in that regard." The new interfaith sanctuary movement posed less risk and was also formed to raise awareness about immigration injustices among American congregations. As the bishop said, "I think that that's the way it's different. Apart from letting these people know that they are not alone. . . . it also informs the congregation so that the congregation has more of a consciousness."

Participants and organizers of the Posada sin Fronteras share much in common with prior supporters of the 1980s sanctuary movement. Their actions are all religiously motivated, and they frequently cite Christian scripture to justify their actions and to challenge U.S. borders and boundaries of exclusion. They both rely on biblical texts that say to welcome the stranger and to love one's neighbor. In the case of the 1980s sanctuary movement, activists broke the law by "harboring illegal aliens" and risked going to jail, but they insisted they were acting morally and in accordance with "a higher law." The posada organizers and participants also appeal to religious morality, but they make their statement while following state laws. (They have even taken out permits to hold the event at Border Field State Park.) While organizers and participants in the contemporary Posada sin Fronteras rely on religious resources, mostly religious social networks, to mobilize, they are perhaps most distinguished from their sanctuary predecessors and contemporaries by their embrace of religious ritual. In fact, they use Mexican, Catholic religious ritual and reenactment to create a momentarily sacred space that symbolically violates the divisions imposed by nation-state borders.

SEVEN

Jesus Would Stand at the Border
and Would Not Accept It

The Posada sin Fronteras symbolically enacts Christian antiborderism both across the U.S.-Mexico border and across the boundaries of race and ethnicity. It is not solely a political or a religious event but is a hybrid, combining political protest and religious ritual. Protestors rely on symbols, ideas, and beliefs that resonate with participants, and religion and ethnicity provide fertile soil for these symbolic and ideological resources. In the section below, I underscore how symbols and rituals from distinctively Mexican and Catholic traditions mesh with interdenominational Christian beliefs to galvanize moral voice against U.S. border policies.

Perhaps this posada's most striking sociological feature is this: It is a Mexican, Catholic cultural form that is enthusiastically embraced by many people, including those who are neither Catholic nor Latino. The Mexican and Catholic elements are palpable and immediately observable.

These include procession, pageantry, reenactment, songs and poems in Spanish, and luminarias. As such, it provides an indicator of how Mexican immigration has led both to the proliferation of Mexican cultural practices in the United States and to new crises and contestations over the governance of immigration and the border. The appeal of public, religious authenticity combined with the social action message allows persons with diverse identities—Anglos and Mexicans, Catholics and Protestants, sacred and secular—to coalesce. The posada provides an experience of symbolic border crossing, and through it, participants find spiritual, religious transcendence *and* social, political relevance.

The organizers of the Posada sin Fronteras take a creative approach, so the ceremony is a little different each year. Musicians Javier Herrera and Rosa Marta Zarate, however, are mainstays, animating the event with meaningful songs, and clergy usually serve as emcees. The commemoration usually begins with a familiar, routinized format of speakers and song, and clergy and laity from both the U.S. side and the Mexican side of the fence gather to speak out against the injustices. While the sanctuary movement used witness and refugee testimonials, here that would require first-person testimonies from the dead. Instead, speakers tell stories of those who died in transit, and participants engage in reenactments and processions to commemorate the dead. The organizers always devise new, creative ways to personalize these stories, allowing for new connections among groups that might otherwise remain apart. There are usually moments for spiritual reflection and collective expression of emotions. One year, in 2002, the posada hit an emotional crescendo with a theater skit that dramatized particular border death tragedies.

A church youth group from Escondido, which is located near San Diego, performed a skit based on a grim true story. Eleven migrants had boarded a U.S.-bound freight car in Mexico, expecting to disembark in Houston. The train's destination was changed, and four months later, in October 2002, the train car was found in Iowa with eleven badly decomposed bodies.[1]

This border tragedy was reenacted at the Posada sin Fronteras. Using only two by fours draped with plastic tarps and sheets, the youth group constructed a railroad car. The youth performed the play in Spanish, and a Franciscan brother, clad in his brown robes and sandals, translated into English. Most people in the crowd sat on the ground cross-legged, and others stood behind them. The skit opened with an actor playing a coyote talking on a cell phone. Next, a group, including a young child, ran across the makeshift stage holding hands. That was the last we, the audience, saw of them. They disappeared into the makeshift railroad car, and throughout the duration of the skit we could not see them—the audience only heard their conversations and cries through a microphone. The actors playing the migrants began with simple, hopeful conversations about their American dreams. They talked about the jobs awaiting them, and a child innocently asked his mother what language he would need to speak in school in *el norte.* As the days passed without the coyote coming for them, the young actors dramatized the agony that the migrant captives must have suffered. There were loud, audible cries of hunger, howls of desperation, a mother pleading to her child that she had no water and only one piece of bread to share. The sheet served as an effective prop when the actors inside the tentlike structure clawed their hands up and down. The audience saw only the ripples on the sheet and heard the agonizing and amplified cries. The cries of the child were very realistic. A narrator informed us that on the fourth day, temperatures hit 105 degrees. We heard loud sobbing, more cries, and then the anguish of a mother when she discovered her son was no longer breathing. More cries followed, and then finally silence.

At the conclusion, the audience remained frozen. My students and I were deeply moved by the skit. We stopped jotting down field notes, because it seemed inappropriate, and when we looked around, expressions of sorrow and sympathy appeared on the faces of most of those in attendance. One young woman, from Europe we later learned, watched with a deeply mournful expression and tears streaming down her cheeks. The drama ended with these words: "Many never make it. Many leave their dreams at the border itself."

After the dramatization, two young Mexican adults read a poem in Spanish critical of the Mexican government, and then the crowd, led by the two singers, one of whom provided accompaniment on acoustic guitar, sang a song imploring everyone to help their *paisanos*. Then the crowd turned to hear a priest from the Mexican side of the border. From Border Field State Park, on the U.S. side, where we stood, we could see him through the chain-link fence. In heavily accented Spanish, he urged the crowd to have open hearts to receive brothers and sisters crossing from the south, and he decried the shootings of migrants in Arizona by both the Border Patrol and armed militias. This was followed by a teenager, also speaking from the Mexican side of the border, but this time in Spanglish. This was 2002, and he read a poem about terrorism and the terrorism that migrants experience with U.S. border control strategies. After the poem, small, woven bracelets that said "no olvidado," or "not forgotten," were passed out to the crowd on the U.S. side, and we were instructed to tie them on the wrists of those congregated on the Mexican side of the fence. We watched the panoramic sunset, and along the shoreline wall, we could see the luminarias lit up across the backdrop of the crashing waves. A chilly ocean mist moved onshore; people shivered, but no one seemed to complain of the cold.

As it grew dark, candles were passed out for the principal part of the posada ritual, the procession. The crowd of several hundred, mostly on the U.S. side but with growing numbers on the Mexican side, marched eastward along the chain-link fence. It was dark, and the ground was uneven. Along the chain-link fence, organizers had placed cardboard placards with the names of the principal states where migrants cross. Rather than going to a house seeking shelter, as we might in a traditional posada, we marched to the different points that symbolized the states where migrants seek shelter, beginning with California. Through a portable microphone and amplifier, individuals on both sides of the fence took turns reciting the names of those who had died this past year while trying to cross into those states. After each name was read, the crowd chanted "presente," or "here," to signify the remembrance of that person. The group reenacted migrants' rejection and acceptance at various state crossing points. According to theologian Virgilio Elizondo, the posada's two key experiences—the rejection of the poor from an inferior land and the joy of welcoming "God's chosen ones"—reflect key Gospel proclamations.[2]

Song was a key element. While walking to the different stations, the crowd sang—in Spanish, but observing the English translation in our brochure—the special song, "Las Posadas del Barrio," that Rosa Martha Zarate and Francisco Javier Herrera had adapted from the traditional posada song.[3] Like the traditional posada song, it represents a dialogue between those seeking shelter and those rejecting them. The adapted lyrics, instead of reflecting an exchange between Joseph and the innkeeper, tell of an exchange between a would-be migrant and an inhospitable person—who was apparently an earlier migrant.

En el nombre de la justicia	In the name of justice
Busco apoyo solidario	I am looking for some help
Cruce la línea de noche	I crossed the border at night
Ando de indocumentado/a	And I don't have papers yet
No vengas con tu miseria	Don't come to me with your poverty
Ni vengas a molestar	Don't come here bother me
Te voy a echar la migra	I am going to call the Migra
Pa' que te mande a volar	And get you out of here quick
Paisana/o soy de tu tierra	Hey, countryman, I'm from your land
Como tú vine a buscar	As you did, I came to look
Con mi familia el trabajo	For work to support my family
Mira mi necesidad	Notice how needy we are
No me interesa quién seas	I don't care who you are
Deja yá de mendigar	So stop your begging
Yo ya soy cuidadana(o)	I am a citizen already
Y te voy a reportar	And I'm going to report you

The song continues until a third voice enters with this:

Yá no les siga rogando	Do not beg them anymore
Venga a la comunidad	Come with us to our community
Donde juntos trabajamos	Where we all work together
Por justicia y dignidad.	For justice and dignity.

In total, there are nine stanzas and also a posada chorus, which ends the song with the promise that justice, like a star, will shine in the barrio.

At the conclusion of the posada, the crowd threw handfuls of candy across the chain-link fence in both directions and sang the final chorus of "Las Posadas del Barrio." It was a joyful, spirited moment.

MULTIPLE PARTICIPANTS, MULTIPLE RESPONSES

How do the participants experience the Posada sin Fronteras? Why do they participate, and what meaning do they create out of their experience? Equipped with our cassette recorders, my students and I fanned out among the crowd immediately after the theater skit, before the procession began, to find answers to these questions. The responses varied, and we quickly discovered that for many participants, there were multiple meanings and motives.

Christian Faith and Religion

Religion, especially the promise of fulfilling the dictates of Christian kinship and morality, emerged as the central theme. Many people said that faith-based convictions drew them to the remotely located posada on a busy Saturday and that Christian religious beliefs prompted them to question border policies. This is no surprise, as the posada, as already noted, was sponsored by various faith-based organizations, and the reenactment, the procession based on Mary and Joseph's search for shelter, is perhaps the world's best-known Bible story. What is striking among the participants whose words are represented below is the extent to which their Christian identities and beliefs indicate inclusion, equality, and hospitality. Their statements suggest that religious identities and beliefs supersede government-established definitions about who should be accepted into the United States as a migrant or refugee. Consider these declarations:

> I'm a Catholic Christian, and I believe in inclusivity. I believe all people are equal in worth as human beings. And I don't like the idea of refugees not being able to come into our country. (older white woman)

I am a Christian. . . . We're all, I guess, illegal here in some way, so we want to be together. (middle-aged white woman, accompanied by four children)

It's important, as a Christian, to be what they were talking about . . . there shouldn't be borders, and we're all one people. (young white woman)

I think Jesus would stand at the border and would not accept it. (young European woman)

Several respondents invoked the idea that people on both sides of the border are children of God, suggesting that nation-state borders violate the notion of a common humanity and a higher law of nature and spirituality. One older white woman said, "It [the U.S.-Mexico border] goes out into the ocean; it's just like a sin against the planet, and against God's earth. . . . Surely there is room for everyone on God's earth. . . . It belongs to all of his children." Two female college students, one white and one Asian American, who were attending the event with a Christian youth group, also stressed the theme of a common humanity and noted that differences in race and nation should not divide. "We're all children of God," observed one of them. "We're all here. We breathe the same air." Her friend concurred: "It doesn't matter what country you're from or what color skin you are because we all have the same blood running through our veins. We all still need the same things."

With the exception of this one Asian American college student, all of the respondents who emphasized *only* faith-based convictions and rationales were white. We did not ask them to name their racial-ethnic identities, but they appeared to us to be white and, with the exception of two European women, they all seemed to be American. For this group, Christian religious ideals and morals served as a bridge that enabled them not only to identify with "alien others" but to stand alongside Latino immigrants in their struggle for human rights and equality. Faith provided them with a moral blueprint for criticizing unjust government border policies directed against people of color, primarily Mexicans and Central Americans, and for reimagining these policies. Faith, and in particular the example of Jesus' compassion for the poor and downtrodden, and the idea that people on both sides of the border are children of God allowed them to challenge injustices that they themselves have not experienced.

The act of participating in the Posada sin Fronteras and challenging social injustice became, for these participants, an act of religious affirmation. As one young man reflected, "It's directly motivated by our commitment to find what it means to be Christian—my commitment to find what it means to be Christian in the context of gross disparities in income and in the context of racism." As he continued with his own self-inquiry, he suggested that moral questioning of societal injustice and divisions constitutes a key part of his religious quest: "I think part of what it means to be Christian is to cross borders that normally aren't crossed intentionally and with the intention of being reconciled. So I think those are deeply Christian themes." Here, redemption is brought about through social action. Christian identities are reaffirmed not only through identification with disadvantaged others but also by questioning secular rules and regulations.

One man, perhaps in his sixties, voiced his concern for alien others more strongly. For him, Christian faith prescribed not only identification with the suffering of migrants but also a biblical duty to help them. He said: "I just feel compelled by the dictates of my religion, which is Christian, to help these people. [I believe in] this injunction in the Bible, such as, 'Remember you were an alien yourself in Egypt.' And you have to help the aliens. This is spread out throughout the Bible. And I feel just a duty, really, a religious duty to try to ease the burden of some of these people. . . . I do what I can to try to help." Another interviewee, also a middle-aged white man, told us of his recent trip to help migrants in the desert. Here, the theme of Christian redemption through social action was expressed more strongly:

I visited a water tank a couple weeks ago in the Arizona desert, and I talked to more immigrants and helped them make contact through the use of the cell phone. . . . I was embraced with tears and great gratitude. It was a very tender moment. [To witness] the struggle in the desert is to be humbled. It is just horrific. It is so shameful there. Tax dollars are going to that. Just to meet someone who is walking to cross the desert is a very poignant moment, so it is very special to be here.

The experience of actually setting out to help migrants in the desert provided this man with spiritual transcendence and political awareness.

Certainly not all of the participants at the posada were ready to call for a radical reconfiguration of U.S. immigration and border policies, nor were they necessarily ready to roam the desert and maintain water stations for undocumented migrants in transit. One college-aged woman echoed the strong notions of Christian unity but voiced skepticism about completely reconfiguring U.S. immigration policies. "I have faith that as Christians, we are supposed to open our hearts and open our doors to people," she offered. She also acknowledged that "maybe we can't accept all the Mexican immigrants into our country, but at least we can be open-minded and open our hearts and see them as people from other countries who don't have a lot of money; maybe [they] aren't the same as us, but [they] still have human rights." The event draws many people who rely on faith-based ideals to challenge government immigration and border policies, but there does not appear to be a shared plan for how this should be accomplished. Some of the participants were full-time social activists working around issues of migrant rights, migrant health, and the environment at the border, but many participants told us they were also attending the posada as a learning experience. For this latter group, the information they receive at the posada helps them to formulate their emergent critiques. Family, community, and religious groups had brought them to the posada, but many of those gathered were still in the early stages of learning about the implications of border policies.

Religious faith and morality enable alliances and challenges to government immigration and border policies to emerge. Notions of Christian kinship, inclusivity, and a moral duty to take action against injustice allow white Americans to participate in the posada. They simultaneously embrace Mexican and Catholic cultural forms (singing songs in Spanish, processing, etc.), *and,* importantly, they loudly reject the current U.S. government immigration and border enforcement policies. The singer Rosa Martha Zarate, who came to the United States as a nun from Mexico, found this kind of cross-group solidarity to be inspirational. As she said in her interview with me, conducted in Spanish,

"To be with people who are not Mexican or Latino but who are other faithful who believe in justice *[personas creentes de la justicia]*, well, it is a great motivation."

Religious-Ethnic Identities

Latino respondents said they attended the posada as both a religious and an ethnic event that connected them to Mexico and to their sense of "Mexican-ness." Participation in the posada reaffirmed their religious identities as Catholics, and their ethnic identities as Mexicans. It made them feel closer to Mexico and brought out strong emotions about family connections.

Family figured heavily in the narratives we collected from Latino respondents. Mexican and Latino parents reported that the Posada sin Fronteras was a way to connect their children to the past and the present. One Latina mother, with her two young children in tow, spoke emotionally, almost tearfully, about the posada both as a tradition that she wanted to pass on to her children and as a religious morality lesson about international borders and divisions. In this instance, the political lesson about border policies and the negotiation of difference was also a big part of the way this mother was teaching her kids about religion and ethnicity. "La Posada is something that is traditional within the Mexican/Latino culture. But it has a special meaning. . . . How do we look at people who are different? What are the barriers that we put [in place]? Like Joseph and Mary, they were denied lodging, love, and acceptance because they were poor, because of the way they looked, [because] they were from another country, another area. . . . I bring my children because I want to teach them as well." For this woman, family participation in the Posada sin Fronteras helped to connect the children to the past through an important cultural tradition, but it also served as an opportune pedagogical moment. It provided a way to teach her children about the ways in which the doors to the United States are closed for some people due to race, class, and citizenship. The border fence site provided her with a particularly effective instructional moment. "I can tell them [the children] about the way things are all day long," she said, "but to bring them here to the border and for them to see the people on the other side of this border and for them to learn firsthand that these border patrolmen are here to keep them out does so much more."

Some parents also hoped the posada would serve a disciplinary function for their children, serving to remind them that they enjoy U.S. citizen privileges that others lack. One woman, speaking in Spanish, suggested that the posada helped to instill ethnic pride in her children: "Well, for me it's really beautiful to bring them [the children] here, to teach them so they know how to value everything that's happening day after day. As Mexicans, right, so that they know we come to the United States to try to make something of ourselves, to do good things" (my translation).

Unlike the white participants, many of the Latino interviewees had personally experienced painful separations from family members due to the U.S.-Mexico border. For them, affirmations of religious faith and ethnic identity were consolidated through the ritual of the posada, but the event also held special meaning. In one way or another, they had lived through what the clergy, speakers, and songs related during the ceremony. They had experienced the pain of border separations, and some had even crossed illegally. They were now celebrating the hope of unity across borders, but for them this held real meaning and familial consequences. A young Latino man said that the posada helped him commemorate and heal prior family separations. The posada, in his words, was "related with Mexico . . . exactly what the Bible says—one people, one land. And I want to experience that. I want to feel that . . . I was born in Mexico. . . . I used to see my dad crossing the border and all I [could] see was a border between my dad and I."

An older woman, perhaps in her seventies, began by enthusing that she was attending the posada because it was a tradition among all Latinos, Mexicans, and Catholics. For her, the posada was a way of collectively expressing ethnic and religious identity. "Llevamos todos los Mexicanos, los Latinos. . . . All of us Mexicans, Latinos carry the case of las posadas of Jose and Maria! It's a tradition that we have, and we do it every year, and it's very important to all of us." She also echoed the experience of having her own family life transformed by border policies. She related how easy it had once been to cross the line, when she herself had lived on the Mexican side but crossed over to work in the fields and in a packing plant in San Ysidro. Pointing to the luminarias she had just been lighting, she drew the contrast with today's regime: "Todas estas bolsas. . . . Each one of those bags represents a dead person." When she saw the theater skit, she said couldn't stop crying because she knew those who suffered were her *paisanos*. "Since they are my *paisanos*, that was more reason to feel very badly about it. I couldn't believe it. When I saw the roles the youth were playing, well, it pleased me. . . . but I couldn't stop crying!" Her friend, another elderly Latina woman who had been lighting the luminaria candles with her, also recalled how easy it had once been to cross the border to work in the fields and in the packing plant in San Ysidro: "There was just a wire. We would cross, work, leave tired from working and we would cross back on foot because there was no other way." She decried the changes that had come about, saying, "Well, it's sad—all of our brothers who have died with this battle. Before it wasn't so difficult" (my translation).

Another Mexican woman, perhaps in her thirties, who was attending the posada with her husband and a friend, spoke animatedly about family separations caused and prolonged by border militarization. She emphasized that the border enforcement not only presented particular dangers to U.S.-bound migrants but also trapped undocumented immigrants in the United States. "Some can't cross and some can't leave," she said, affirming research that shows that border militarization has led to prolonged settlement by undocumented immigrants who are now less likely to return to visit their families in Mexico or Central America because of the increased dangers and costs associated with migration.[4]

> I come to support my fellow countrymen in this posada. It means a lot for me to be participating in this. There are many people who cannot cross and they cannot be seen. There are also those who can't leave [the United States], and this is an opportunity for us to see each other. We can greet each other and seek shelter. . . . So now this border divides us, but it's only a fence. But with the Christmas spirit and heart, we are *paisanos*, and that's why we are here supporting them. (my translation)

Her husband and her friend echoed her sentiments, but they emphasized the dangers of crossing. Her husband said:

> Well, for me this means something really big, because *paisanos* suffer a
> lot when they cross the border. They risk their lives [and must confront]
> people who try to cheat them. . . . Other people steal from them, and
> they are left without money, without anything! So to use this as a mes-
> sage so that. . . . people can look at their families and have more hope. . . .
> We are all brothers, all children of God. (my translation)

His wife also suggested that this was part of a larger prayer, a specific
supplication to God to change immigration policies so that family members might be able to gain legal permanent residency and thus be
reunited with loved ones. "Here we are asking God to allow many people to get [their papers] fixed so they can leave and go see their families
and so that others can come and see a new future." As interviewers, we
did not ask respondents about their own migration histories and documentation status, but it is likely that she was praying for legal papers for
herself as well. As she explained, "We always look for greater hope for
the family and a better future."

The couple's friend, a middle-aged Mexican woman who also spoke
only Spanish, echoed the theme of legal rights and asking God for help
with legal papers. "I think that everybody has a right. It hurts me to see
so many deaths—there are so many! So we have to unite and dedicate
ourselves to God and our brothers for support because we all need it. We
all need support and a permit to work or whatever for the glory of God,
and so that we can stop so many deaths" (my translation).

Regardless of whether they themselves had felt the pain of family
separation or the precariousness of working in the United States without
authorization, all of the Latino and Mexican respondents said the
posada reaffirmed their ethnic and religious identities. One young man
put it this way:

> We're all aware of the implications that this border has—namely, that
> it is dividing a lot of people. It's categorizing people as "illegal," some-
> how different from who we are. And I think that really undermines just
> the whole concept of human dignity, and my needs are no more important

than the people and their needs across the border. I think for me also as a Catholic, and being a Hispanic myself, this is just a way for me to maintain that connection with my native land. . . . I think the unity for me is what brings me to it every time.

Another young Latino man who appeared to be in his twenties said that the posada allowed him to show solidarity with others on both sides of the border. "Being here for me is really important to be able to establish, not only to the people who are here in the U.S., but people who are across the border in Mexico and Tijuana, . . . a solidarity between the faith traditions that are represented here. But also [I am reminded of] the struggle in the lives of migrants who attempt to cross the border and have died as a result of unjust policy implemented by the U.S. . . . It's really important for me to be here and to show solidarity on both sides."

Transcendence

The participants find meaning, transcendence, and affirmation in the Posada sin Fronteras. The collective gathering, the stories that are shared, and the reenactment not only allow them to call for the end of border divisions, but allow them to momentarily experience a world without border divisions. For many of the participants, this was a sublime, transcendent moment, one that was predicated on extending the hospitality of the posada story. In this collective venue, structured with religious ritual and symbolism of shared humanity, they experienced a sacred, spiritual moment, together with their friends and loved ones and with many strangers. Joy and unity, rather than grief, defined the way this made the participants feel. These emotions uplifted them with a sense of hope about the future.

It is very sad but at the same time it is really wonderful because people are trying to do something about this line. . . . Like they have been saying all afternoon, we are just one people . . . one, one, we are just one! Like he [God] wants us to be. (Mexican immigrant woman)

I love the feeling that we are one people without borders. You know it is one of the few times that people on both sides of the border can reach

across and express their humanity without the confines of human-created
boundaries. . . . This is probably the eighth or ninth year that I've been
a part of this. It is always an inspiration. (white middle-aged man)

This is my first posada. . . . I am a faith-based person. . . . The gathering
of people with so [many] different values has a great deal of significance to me, and to act a simple story in this context is a very important
way for us to reach deep into the history of humanity. . . . So it is very
special to be here. (white middle-aged man, quoted earlier regarding his
experience of helping migrants in the desert)

For me I think it's like other songs. You know, once in the United States
they make these songs bilingual, like it is something that really gets
you in your heart because I mean it just, it just moves you right there
[motions for heart]. I mean because when it's bilingual . . . we sing on
this side, and they sing on that side; it's like an answer. It's like an invitation that we answer. But everything goes for me, like with my faith,
all the prayer goes . . . to heaven! (young Latino man, quoted earlier
regarding how the border once separated him from his father in the
United States)

While it would be easy to dismiss the Posada sin Fronteras as ephemeral,
the many repeat attendees suggest otherwise. And Pastor Art Cribbs
said that the spiritual feelings of transcendence and unity are sustained
long after the event, bringing out profound personal and collective
transformations. "When we go to the fence, when we go to the border, it
doesn't end when we get in our cars and drive away. That experience is
now part of the definition of our being. And it comes back because we
have ingested the history, the story, the suffering of others who prior to
that moment we may not have known. They become part of our community. It is Martin Luther's 'I am thou' experience."

A striking feature of Western modernity, noted by many observers, is
the movement toward secularization and personal spirituality. The
philosopher Charles Taylor (2002), revisiting William James's *The Varieties
of Religious Experience*, noted that many people privilege the primacy of
individual religious experience and feelings as the most authentic form
of worship and reject "church."[5] Many people, for instance, claim they
are spiritual but not religious. Here, personal devotion and inward inher-
ence to Christ are superior to collective ritual. The distinction is important,

but in the instance at hand, the opposite is occurring. At the posada, both white Christians and Catholics of Mexican origin alike relish the authenticity of the collective enactment and gathering. They experience it as a moment of transcendence, of finding enchantment and joy in the enactment of unity across racial, ethnic, citizenship, and national borders.

The Posada sin Fronteras, both participants and organizers concur, *feels* special, connecting people beyond borders and different traditions. And as we have seen, it does so through collective ritual. Emile Durkheim's observation about the power of rituals to coalesce community and obtain collective effervescence is apt. The singing, processing, and collective ritual enactment create solidarity, feelings of unison, and joy. Rather than personal spirituality, the participants realize a politicized spirituality, one that is realized collectively in a public venue and is directed at a social and political issue but yet resonates with religious beliefs. The symbolism and enactment drawn from Mexican-Catholic traditions may also lend an exotic whiff of Orientalism for the white Americans, further deepening the feelings of authenticity. The posada feels more "real" and participatory than a routinized, staid Sunday church service.

That the Posada sin Fronteras occurs at the U.S.-Mexico border is important for both political articulation and religious expression. Political protest, as James Jasper has noted, often relies on the symbolism of place. Protestors commonly assemble at monuments or seats of government where they can "visit, touch, and smell these sites, and somehow be persuaded of the reality of history through the reality of the physical objects and places."[6]

The U.S.-Mexico border is the site where rejection, death, and border enforcement occur on a daily basis, *and* it is the site where redemption, a postborder world of hospitality, and the sharing of shelter can be imagined and even experienced for a few moments. The site, then, contributes to the articulation of a political statement that simultaneously symbolizes the reality of border enforcement and deaths and yet transgresses and transcends it. As one Latina woman who helped organize the event explained: "Just having this is almost like it makes it [the border] invisible just for this couple of hours that we are here. We are able to talk to people. We know the people on the other side, so it can get pretty emotional."

Pastor Cribbs agreed that the personalized connections and the place were critical. "We hear voices, see faces, read names," he said. In this context, the loss of life is "no longer an abstract occurrence that takes place in the desert or mountains away from here." And Roberto Martinez, one of the original founders of the event, concurred that the realism of the site was critical. "The border patrol is right there, like centurions watching us, but that is what draws people too—the whole location, the [border patrol] agents." Religiosity and place allow for dramatization of something that might otherwise seem abstract and distant.

Traveling to the site also contributes to feelings of religious authenticity, as the event occurs outside of institutionalized churches or temples, which might be seen as mandatory sites of inauthentic worship. It becomes both a political and a sacred pilgrimage. To participate in the posada, people must give up a Saturday afternoon and evening before Christmas and drive freeways and then a rocky, windy, sandy road to convene at Border Field State Park in San Ysidro. Traveling to the posada in families, groups of friends, or religious-based youth groups involves a modest outlay of time and effort, but unlike traditional sites of pilgrimage, the border fence is a profane, secular place. The Posada sin Fronteras transforms an offensive place, for a few hours, into a sacred space. The posada participants made sacred what is otherwise a site of separation, surveillance, violence, and death. And it is through the sacred lens that participants affirm their resistance to U.S. border policies that result in death.

The annual Posada sin Fronteras is mainly a Christian-based expression of antiborderism, but it is many things to many people. It encompasses performance and participation, and it provides participants with a didactic experience, an opportunity to learn about the consequences of U.S. border enforcement policies as well as an opportunity to reaffirm and consolidate identities based on faith and ethnicity. It offers a poetic, Mexican, Catholic ritual experience that is simultaneously aesthetic and inclusive of sacred elements—encompassing candles and luminarias, songs and hymns, a procession, and so forth—and it is an action of protest that temporarily mobilizes civil society. The posada is a moment for remembering and reenacting past injustices as well as for collectively imagining and calling for a more just future. As such, it is a political action and an ethnic religious event.

But it is a very particular way of blending religion and politics. Unlike the sanctuary movement, which used civil disobedience and religious discourse to articulate specific demands of the government, and unlike the Muslim American immigrants, who use mainstream methods to communicate their civil rights demands to the government and the media, the Posada sin Fronteras does not put forth a specific agenda. It is not a baldly instrumental action. In this regard, we can see the Posada sin Fronteras as an expressive social movement event—but it is not constituted by a social movement organization that speaks with a singular voice or in favor of a uniform platform.

Listening to the multiple voices at the Posada sin Fronteras underscores the multivocality of meaning and resistance to current U.S. border policies. Different subjects are grounded in different experiences and identities. Some are exclusively faith based, some combine faith and ethnicity, and still others are rooted in more secular notions of morality. Religion and ethnicity are particularly powerful sources for drawing diverse groups to these collective actions. Similarly, the posada participants include longtime faith-based activists who work with nonprofit organizations and specific campaigns, such as the American Friends Service Committee or Border Angels, as well as newcomers who are just beginning to learn about the situation at the U.S.-Mexico border. For the former, the posada refreshes commitments that run the risk of burnout, and, for the latter, it serves as an important didactic moment. And the posada draws people who hold various opinions, some in favor of open borders and others in favor of less-aggressive regulations. Some observers might see this lack of unanimity as a weakness of the resistance, but it might alternately be seen as a source of strength. Lisa Lowe, discussing the possibility for coalition building across national boundaries, believes that this process "entails processes of learning, translation and transformation of perspective."[7]

People of different voices and social locations come together in the Posada sin Fronteras, and for a moment they imagine themselves with a collective identity. They are united in their belief, as one participant said, "that we are one." An imagined identity of oneness that transgresses nation-state borders prevails. Nation-state borders are seen as inauthentic, and a notion that God unites all people across borders takes hold. The participants enact a utopian vision of antiborderism, one that requires a postnational unity of humanity. This is both a political and a religious act. As Noreen Sullivan, one of the posada founders, wrote to me prior to our interview: "There is no spirituality without the political, [and] the border/immigration situation is completely political and we must speak out and act in order to change things. And that speaking/acting is the highest form of a true spirituality rooted in justice."

In this regard, faith-based ideals and rituals offer promising routes both for challenging unilateral nation-state immigration and border policies and for reaffirming unity and diverse identities. Difference and distinct social locations among the participants at the posada may help build a more powerful coalition of resistance than one that is constituted by homogeneity. A shared collective identity—whether it be religious or ethnic—is not necessary for protest, nor is it a necessary or perhaps even a desirable outcome.

EIGHT Religious Rule or Religious Voices?

Should religion rule? To what extent should religion and faith-based morality and resources inform public policies and decisions? Societies around the globe are grappling with these questions. In the late twentieth and early twenty-first centuries, religion has emerged as a force with which governments must contend. Regardless of whatever beliefs we may hold, secular sociologists and intellectuals can no longer pretend to live in a godless world, for as the early Chicago school sociologist W. I. Thomas observed, once we "define our situation as real, they are real in their consequences." The United States is defined daily as a God-saturated world, and there are real consequences for immigration policies and practices.

Until now, the proliferation of various strains of Islamic and Christian fundamentalism has fueled debates about the extent to which religion should be decisive in establishing the rules by which people live.[1] This book has focused on a different story line of contemporary politics and religion. It is about how Christian, Islamic, and Jewish believers use flexible, nonfundamentalist forms of religion to exert a humanistic influence on immigration practices and policies. They do so in different ways, as we have seen, and they act in different arenas. To better understand this story, my research has examined the goals and activities of religious activists and organizations working for immigrant civil rights, labor rights, and border rights as well as the manner in which they use religious tools to achieve these goals. In this chapter, I revisit these issues and sketch some of the implications of how religion can be used in immigration matters, both in tandem and sometimes against market and state forces. Central to my analysis is the recognition that the historical moment in which all of this unfolds is characterized by the re-Christianization of the United States; a deepening distrust of religious interventions in politics; and a now-constant hostility toward new immigrants and others perceived to be beyond national borders.

The familiar markers of re-Christianization include the rise of the Christian Right in the 1980s and, later, the important role of right-wing evangelicals in electing George W. Bush; the proliferation of televangelists; and the post-9/11 U.S. military invasions accompanied by declarations of Christian righteousness. During this era, saying "Happy Holidays" was perceived as an anti-Christian attack, and Christian fundamentalists cried out for the replacement of public school science curricula and sex education with teachings of "intelligent design" and premarital sexual abstinence. The boundaries of marriage, sexuality, and reproduction (including stem-cell research and abortion rights) became the targets of Christian political mobilization.

What are we to make of this re-Christianization? First, it is important to recognize that re-Christianization is not a totalizing process. The United States is not a theocracy, and religious uniformity is not imposed from above. Neither liberals nor all conservatives or Republicans agreed with the turn toward conservative, evangelical politics.[2] In fact, as I suggest in chapter 1, there is a kind of religious dualism in the United States. As the U.S. war in Iraq dragged on, as the excesses of Islamic fundamentalist violence intensified, and as conservative fundamentalist Christians continued their vociferous calls for Christian regulation of social life while simultaneously being exposed as moral hypocrites, many Americans grew wary of religion ruling public life. The United States, after all, was founded on the ideals of church-state separation. While Christianity prevails as the dominant religion, most Americans do not want state policies and practices to be dictated by fundamentalist Christianity or by any other religious platform.

At the same time, we have seen an explicit disconnect between the movements of re-Christianization and immigrant restrictionism. As I have noted elsewhere, the Christian Right has *not* taken up the anti-immigrant cause as a rallying point.[3] This has created an opportunity for progressive religion and activists who are concerned with the social issues of immigration.

Looking at what faith-based persons are doing to promote immigrant rights reveals diverse activities on multiple fronts. As this book has shown, these faith-based activists are pursuing different immigrant rights issues, and they use different religious tools. In this chapter, I analyze how these activists and their organizations use four religious tools of mobilization to make claims and pursue immigrant rights. These tools include moral justification and motivation for action, religious resources, religious legitimacy, and religious rituals and cultural symbols. I also address how these activists' political, racial, and religious identities relate to the processes of collective mobilizations, and I hazard an analysis of how well these activists did in reaching their goals. Finally, I offer my own views on how we should approach religion in public life and what form immigration rights and progressive immigration reform might take in the future.

WHERE IS THE RELIGION IN FAITH-BASED ACTIVISM FOR IMMIGRANT RIGHTS?

We have seen how Muslim American immigrants and their affiliates responded to the post-9/11 attacks on their civil rights by engaging in established, institutional politics. They use nonconfrontational, nonviolent means to advocate for their communities. This involves press conferences, public forums, conventions, town hall meetings, lobbying efforts, and old-fashioned American civic engagement, such as teaching community members to serve as media and community spokespersons and as letter writers to elected officials and for newspaper columns. These organizations favor institutional measures as they seek civil rights for their communities. It is important to note what they do not do. They do not march in the street and stop traffic. They do not usually raise their voices and yell to persuade their opponents. They do not wave the Quran in the faces of their opponents. While they are fighting for the right to a particular American religious identity, religion remains somewhat hidden in their mobilizations for Muslim American immigrant civil rights. We see instead a type of action that favors secular, institutional, and professional mechanisms.

The Muslim American immigrant activists and their affiliates use religion sparingly in their struggle to protect civil rights for their communities. Their main leaders are indubitably people of faith, but they are neither imans nor recognized religious leaders who use religious moral authority to convince others of the merits of their struggle. The participants in organizations such as MPAC and CAIR are of course Muslim, and they participate in those organizations out of shared religious identity and faith. In this sense, religion motivates them. They do not, however, cite sacred Islamic scripture but rather the American Constitution, and the protections it offers citizens, as their main authoritative text. American civil religion seems to guide them in their efforts to set things right, although it is possible that as we move further away from the heightened, alarmist Islamophobia of the immediate post-9/11 period, these groups will be freer to hold up the Quran as a moral document guiding politics. That was suggested to me at the December 2006 MPAC convention, where Quranic interpretation was used to justify a moderate political path.

Religious resources *are* used by these groups. These include concrete resources, such as money that is donated by people of shared religious faith, and more abstract ones, such as Muslim American social networks, both within and across organizations, and skills and talents within their religious-ethnic communities. For this group, which includes highly educated, relatively cosmopolitan, affluent professionals, these are rich resources. Members of their communities have deep pockets and well-honed public and professional talents.

Notably, appeals to religious legitimacy and rituals and symbols are not integrated into Muslim American civic and political activism. These are certainly not prohibited, but they appear only subtly, such as in the use of prayer rooms—always optional—made available to conference attendees, or perhaps a brief Quranic passage read at the outset of a meeting. The Muslim immigrant groups, then, do not really rely on Islamic traditions to provide moral justification, public legitimacy, or rituals to be used in public and civic engagements. Why is this?

Between the backdrop of the re-Christianization of the United States and the post-9/11 American fear and suspicion of Islam, Muslim Americans are caught between a rock and a hard place. In the post-9/11 United States, moral justifications for civil rights based in Islam and any appeal to legitimacy of their cause based on religion are strictly verboten. Muslim American immigrant groups and their affiliates, Arab Americans and South Asian American immigrants, navigate this tension, as we have seen, by working hard to disassociate themselves from the Islamic revivalist movements, but they are also operating in a national terrain where Christianity and nationalism coincide. While the current time is celebrated as an age of multiculturalism and religious pluralism, they are operating in a historical moment when U.S. nationalism and imperial projects rely not only on the re-Christianization of the nation, but also on the demonization of Islam. Clearly, this polarization makes it hard for them to use religion in their pursuit of immigrant civil rights.

By contrast, we have seen how a group of clergy, most of them from Christian and Jewish traditions, use religious tools more freely to promote the labor rights of Latino immigrant workers in the service industries. These clergy, many of them influenced by the strategies and experiences of clergy in the civil rights movement and of César Chávez and the UFW, enjoy access to a well-stocked religious tool box. First, they not only come to their social activism motivated by their religious beliefs, but they are frequently verbally reasserting this to one another in meetings and forums.

The clergy members in particular are motivated by faith, and they profess it on a daily basis. When I asked why they do what they do for the immigrant workers, they frequently invoked scripture, and they spoke of the importance of faith-based sacrifice for the good of others. They said their activism around economic justice was a way to express and practice their faith. For these clerical leaders, this activism goes to the core of what it means to be a religious person.

Second, they rely on the concrete religious resources at their disposal to organize protests, meetings, and lobbying visits to the homes of workers or the offices of hotel managers and employers. Important religious-based resources include the well-honed oratory skills and charismatic talents of many of the clergy and the mundane but vital resources of church meeting halls, folding chairs, and office equipment. While their social networks extend to the unions, community leaders, and other activist clergy and laity, their social networks do not reach into the obvious ripe source for mobilization: their own congregations. I am not entirely sure what explains this, but I have some hunches. Some of the CLUE clergy, as noted earlier in the book, are in fact not in charge of leading congregations but rather hold other religious posts, as directors of projects or as denominational administrators. For those who do actively lead congregations, I believe some of the recalcitrance about activating their congregational membership has to do with the notion that direct congregational recruitment may cross the boundaries of religion and politics. They may be reluctant to impose their own political views on their congregations.

These clergy and laity, however, are not at all shy about using their religious authority and moral legitimacy for the cause. At this, they excel. They engage in civil disobedience, direct actions, and street protests when necessary. They are committed to nonviolence, but they will shut down the streets and avenues of Los Angeles, if necessary, and they freely use religious symbols and morality in these activities.[4] They also use religion to directly pressure and persuade employers and managers to negotiate in good faith with the unions. In this regard, they employ more established methods of lobbying and appealing to elected officials and private employers, and they meet face-to-face with private and public sector authorities clad in their religious vestments. They use a combination of methods and institutional politics as well as the more disruptive and directly confrontational tactics of civil disobedience, and they weave religion into both sets of activities. In both lobbying activities and direct actions, they act as moral specialists.

Why do these people use religion forcefully in their projects? As mainline Christians and even Jews, their religions are acceptable in the public sphere. They do not encounter the fear, hatred, and suspicion of their religions as Muslims do. Not only are their religions acceptable, but they are respected, revered, and can be used strategically to garner moral legitimacy and authority. They know this and use this knowledge.

CLUE members and the unions they support are media savvy and telegenic. As modern clergy, they do not wear collars and robes on all days of the week, but when doing their political work, they deliberately wear the clerical garb with the intent to persuade others with their moral authority. In this regard, there is a very modern quality to their protest that can be traced to César Chávez and the UFW and that also takes inspiration from the contemporary labor organizing in Los Angeles that accompanies CLUE efforts.

These religious activists are also cognizant of the need to respect religious pluralism and multiculturalism against the backdrop of re-Christianization. Therefore, they include religious rituals drawn from their various religious traditions in protests, being careful not to get too denominational or exclusive. In the process, they make secular spaces momentarily sacred and imbue their movement for social change with collective corporeal activities that invoke ancient religious connections with the past.

In chapters 6 and 7 of this book, we saw how a group of largely Christian-based activists are responding to the migrant deaths and state-supported violence at the U.S.-Mexico border by providing direct services that can save lives, such as medical assistance and water. The Christian border activists who gather to reenact the Posada sin Fronteras also engage religious ritual to sustain themselves as activists and to spread the word of what is happening to other Christians and local community people. Unlike the other cases, they collectively engage in neither institutional politics nor confrontational direct actions. Rather, they seek to deepen their own spiritual commitment by creating a temporal sacred space that allows them to religiously express their condemnation of immigration policies that lead to death. They use the most important and heavily commercialized Christian holiday, the commemoration of Christ's birth, as an emblem of the stranger's struggle to find hospitality and shelter. This serves as a spiritual guide for how new immigrants should be treated. The means are both corporeal and spiritual, as through the ritualized enactment they seek to create a socially and politically relevant enchanted space. The participants eschew the familiar tactics of politics, using neither lobbying nor conventions, neither megaphones nor street protests. Instead, they favor collective, prayerful gathering for spiritual replenishment and social change.

Here, we see that religious faith guides the activists' commitment to ending death at the border and to participating in a shared religious ritual. As a largely lay group of people, they act less as "moral specialists" than do the pro-labor clergy, but Christianity clearly animates their activities. When asked why they do what they do, they invoke scripture as well as Christian parables of hospitality and the biblical idea of welcoming the stranger or the alien. Religion gives them moral justification and incentives for providing direct services and engaging in religious reenactment. It provides a conduit for a spiritual type of educational outreach and consciousness raising about border violence.

Religious resources are at work here, too. The concrete religious resources participants bring together for this event are modest, garnered from pastoral donations and from the San Diego Catholic Archdiocese, the American Friends Service Committee, the Scalabrini Center in Tijuana, and a few other organizations. Relying more on church-based networks and religious infrastructure, they spread the word about the event through flyers and announcements made in churches and at Christian youth groups. Here, religious social resources are important.

While participants claim religious legitimacy, they signal this more to each other than to the outside world. Religious authenticity, as expressed in prayerful gathering and in the enactment of collective religious ritual, is what counts the most for them. Here is where the distrust of religion in politics comes into play. Some of the organizers recalled the early days of the Posada sin Fronteras, when reporters and television cameras came to cover the event. This, they felt, was somewhat sacrilegious and took away from the deeply spiritual quality of the event. Overt politics and the media seemed to dirty an otherwise spiritually pure commemoration of the deaths at the border. Dissenting views regarding this issue, to be sure, were held by some of the other posada organizers who wanted more overt political action.

IDENTITIES IN MOVEMENT

All of the actors examined in this study identify themselves as religious. They turned to some form of social activism, joined organizations, and decided to participate in particular collective groups because of their identities as religious people. That much they have in common. But when we consider how their religious identities are involved in the pursuit of their goals, we see differences. How do their identities inform the mobilizations, and, in turn, how are their identities transformed in the process?

Identities, we know, are not static but are situationally and relationally defined and constantly in flux. One Italian theorist of social movements, Alberto Melucci, emphasizes that social movements are processes of identity formation. Individuals come to know and define each other through repeated interactions as they attempt to organize for social change. In the process, they form new identities and new visions of what might be.

Some social movements appear to be largely about gaining acceptance for new social identities, such as gays, greens, or people living with HIV. These are sometimes termed "new social movements" because they use expressive cultural strategies to gain recognition for new postindustrial identities that are not well-accepted in society.[5] New social movements are thought to be distinct from traditional citizenship or class-based social movements, which are usually about gaining rights for some excluded category of people, such as workers, peasants, women, or

African Americans. The case of Muslim American immigrants strug-gling for their social rights tears apart this binary. In this instance, peo-ple are mobilizing both to gain inclusion and civil rights and to end discrimination and harassment, as a traditional citizenship social move-ment would. But they are also devoted to a discursive project. They are constructing an identity for themselves as Americans who are Islamic, forging the right to exercise a Muslim American identity. This identity is still under construction, and while all members of the community may not agree on the content, the principal leaders have defined the content in such a way that it relegates religion to the private sphere. This means exercising a collective identity that avoids overt forms of piety in politi-cal and civic engagements yet defines Islam as integral to individual and collective identities. They seek to strengthen Muslim collective identity in the United States and to gain the right to exercise religion in daily life—to fast during Ramadan or to pray daily at the workplace—but they are also committed to solving problems without referring to Islamic texts.

It is tempting to suggest that Muslim American civil rights actors are simply reformist, moderate "model minorities." That would be a mistake. As I see it, their project is a radical one—and I mean that in a positive, progressive way. Although they rely on institutional political tactics, they are engaged in a profound social change project, one that is in line with the highest democratic ideals of integration and inclusion but one that also threatens the idea of a singularly Anglo-Saxon Protestant nation. They seek nothing less than to create a space for themselves as Muslim Americans, and so this is a project of identity and inclusion. Their tactics may be different, but their goals are similar to the black power, Chicano, and gay rights movements, which sought to create pride in previously disparaged social locations.

The clergy activists fighting for the rights of Latino immigrant workers already enter the picture with firmly established, socially accepted, and revered identities. They are clergy from Lutheran, Methodist, Jewish, or other mainline denominations. Becoming involved in the economic justice movement and in advocacy for exploited immigrant workers exerts a powerful pull on their religious identities. They come to see their acts of protest and lobbying as sacred acts. Coming together in mobilizations,

gathering regularly with other like-minded clergy from different denominations, and developing working relationships feed their identities as
religious activists. As one minister explained, "Faith is what you do." For
her and for other clergy, CLUE activism made their faith come alive.

Through discussions that take place as they hear testimonials in
church halls or when in strategy-planning meetings, CLUE members
reflect with other clergy on their role as moral leaders. They build an
interfaith community among themselves as progressives and leaders,
sharing an understanding and vision of the world that some perceive is
lacking among clergy from their own denominations. This process,
based on collective gathering, discussion, reflection, and action, exerts a
powerful force on their religious identities. One clergy member,
Reverend Jarvis Johnson, said that he needed CLUE as much as CLUE
needed him. He spoke of the satisfaction of meshing politics and prayer
and said that his CLUE participation deepened his religious faith: "What
it does is reaffirm my own faith and it renews me." Reverend Altagracia
Perez reported that the CLUE work had cured her of her "spiritual sickness" and allowed her to finally realize the kind of clerical and spiritual
life she had idealistically imagined when she was in seminary. These
clergy and others saw their religious identities intensified and made
more satisfyingly authentic through their CLUE activism.

The Christians who participate in the Posada sin Fronteras to make a
statement about border violence experience a different kind of identity.
These people come from diverse racial-ethnic, religious, and national
origin backgrounds. No preexisting identity brings them together, nor
are they deliberately working to promote or advance a singular identity.
Some undoubtedly see themselves as Christian antiborder activists, but
not all of them. Rather, their actions are defined by polyvocality and
multiple subjectivities as they gather to denounce what they see as a
shared problem. Faith draws them to speak out against state-promoted
violence at the border. They speak quietly, signaling to one another in
multiple voices, expressing a reverent, Christian antiborderism. They
use their religious identities less strategically than the clergy labor
advocates, and, unlike the Muslim Americans, forging and gaining
acceptance for a particular American religious identity is not their goal.

They embrace an identity as people of faith who cross borders of religion, ethnicity, and national origins to join together in denouncing something that they see as immoral. In this regard, they embrace, at least momentarily, a shared identity as border crossers.

The religious tools the activists use to mobilize are shaped by their identities. In turn, their religious identities are strengthened in the process. These are neither static nor organized solely around religion, as identities and alliances organized around race and gender are also at play in these movements.

WHERE IS GENDER?

While I have constructed this project in such a way that gender dynamics are not the principal dynamic, they are not absent. In fact, gender relations are a constitutive feature of the processes discussed in this book. First, it is notable that women play an important part in all three of the sites of faith-based activism discussed in this book. This is stunning because Islam, Judaism, and Christianity all exhibit strong patriarchal orientations and legacies. The feminist critiques of these religions are well-known. The Abrahamic religions of the book traditionally exclude women or relegate women to subordinate positions and roles. Yet not only have women been included in the faith-based organizations and mobilizations examined in this book, they are often at the helm.

Both CLUE and its national umbrella group, IWJ, are headed by charismatic women. CLUE's leader is the evangelical Lutheran reverend Alexia Salvatierra, and many of the other prominent spokespeople and leaders in CLUE are also female clergy. IWJ was founded by and remains headed by a woman, Kim Bobo. My own eyes, trained under pre–Vatican II Catholicism, initially had a hard time adjusting to the presence of women in clerical collars and positions of religious leadership in CLUE meetings. These women were also, in many instances, leaders of their own congregations.

Among the Muslim, Arab, and South Asian organizations that I studied, women were not usually at the helm (the only exception was the explicitly female-identified group, the Palestinian American Women's Association). Nevertheless, they were critical spokespersons and seemed to play strong supporting roles in the organizations. Both CAIR in Orange County and MPAC featured young women as their principal spokespersons. Most of the women involved in these organizations were relatively young, in their twenties and thirties. It seems likely that as these organizations mature and cultivate a second generation of leaders educated in the United States, they will have more young women leaders coming into prominence.

Some of these changes are already happening. In 2006 members of the largest Muslim organization on the continent, the Islamic Society of North America, elected a woman as president. Ingrid Mattson, the new president, is a white, Canadian, former Catholic who converted to Islam and holds a PhD in Islamic studies from the University of Chicago. The *Los Angeles Times* described her as, among other things, "soft-spoken and quick to smile. . . . [and] a suburban soccer mom."[6] As such, she is intended to provide a soft, friendly face, one no doubt intended to deter American Islamophobia and fear of angry, bearded, foreign Muslim men. Her election to the post confirms Muslim Americans' desire to refute stereotypes about their communities and to show their mainstream modernity on gender issues.

At the U.S.-Mexico border, I found that women were the key organizers of the Posada sin Fronteras, yet they were mostly not the featured speakers or identifiable hosts of the event. They did the invisible backstage work of organizing the posada, such as selecting the songs to be sung, deciding on and gathering the items to be thrown across the fence, and getting the park permit. This is an old, familiar story—male leaders featured in front and women working behind the scenes. When I noted that women were doing all the work during my interview with one of these women, she simply chuckled and said, "Yes, only the women are left. All too true." These women did not seem to be clamoring for the spotlight or leadership roles. Among the Christian antiborder activists, the principal actors were lay religious leaders, people who were deeply religious and tightly affiliated with religious institutions yet who had experienced deep dissatisfaction with Catholic religious hierarchies.

NEW RACIAL IDENTITIES AND ALLIANCES

Like gender dynamics, racial dynamics and racialization processes have not been at the forefront of this study, but I would be remiss to ignore the unexpected ways in which race plays out in these three instances of religious mobilizations for immigrant rights. Among the Muslim American immigrants, the racialization of religious identity is irrefutable and well-known. In fact, the mobilization of Muslim American immigrants is a direct response to the racialization of religious identity, which has included the targeting of Middle Eastern men by name and phenotype, airport profiling, governmental surveillance, and hate crimes and the scrutiny of and government crackdowns on Muslim charity organizations.

Less well-recognized, however, are three processes of race that accompany the mobilization. These include (1) a new process of racial diversification of religious identity; (2) exacerbated conflicts and distance between immigrant American Muslims and black American Muslims; and (3) new alliances forged by the Muslim American immigrant Muslims with other racial-ethnic minority civil rights groups.

Muslims in the United States have always been multiracial, but in the post-9/11 period, many Muslim organizations have actively represented themselves as multiracial. While the membership of CAIR hails largely from South Asian and Middle Eastern origins, the public relations spokesperson for Orange County CAIR is a white woman convert, as is the new president of the Islamic Society of North America. CAIR also worked to promote this multiracial image through the billboard released in the post-9/11 months that featured the caption reading "Even a Smile Is Charity" alongside smiling multiracial faces, not unlike the old Benetton advertisements. In a similar way, the persecution of Muslims in the United States has extended beyond only foreign-born Middle Eastern or South Asian Muslims. José Padilla, a U.S.-born Latino who converted to Islam and whose photo appeared widely in newspapers, has become perhaps the most widely publicized terrorist suspect of non–Middle Eastern origin. The entertainment media also promoted multiracial Islam, as seen in the Showtime television show *Cell*, which represented Muslim terrorists of diverse racial backgrounds. Finally, hate crimes committed against Muslim targets were extended to other ethnic groups, as perpetrators usually got the racial-ethnic identities wrong. So here we see contradictory developments, with the racialization of Muslim Americans of Middle Eastern origins alongside the simultaneous racial diversity emphasized by civil rights organizations, by media representations of suspected terrorists, and among victims of persecution.

Second, conflicts and distance between black American Muslims and immigrant Muslims have grown in the post-9/11 period. African American Muslims make up about one-third of the Muslim population in the United States, yet at all of the public forums, town hall meetings, and conventions that I attended in Southern California, blacks were scarcely present, and I can recall only three occasions where African Americans were featured as prominent speakers.[7] As Karen Leonard, an expert on American Muslims, has noted, the different class and racial locations of African American Muslims and immigrant Muslims have led to divides between the two, and the post-9/11 backlash and mobilizations have exacerbated these divides. Many African American Muslim scholars subscribe to more radical interpretations of Islamic law, interpretations which they see as congruent with the race, class, and gender injustices facing poor African American communities.[8] Meanwhile, as we have seen, the more middle-class and professional-class immigrant Muslims are turning to the American legal system to safeguard their civil rights.

Finally, the process of post-9/11 mobilizations for civil rights has brought Muslim American immigrant activists and organizations into new alliances with racial-ethnic minority groups who are also working for civil rights. These new partners include the Mexican American Legal Defense Fund, Japanese American Nikkei groups that have organized for retributions, and prominent African American civil rights attorneys and social justice–oriented clergy. Speakers such as Reverend James Lawson, a veteran leader of the civil rights movement, and the African American civil rights attorney Connie Rice have been featured at MPAC conventions. Muslim American immigrants have also organized new alliances with white Christians and Jews, many of them working through interfaith dialogue or in civil liberties organizations such as the

ACLU and the National Lawyers Guild. In all of these new alliances, Muslim American immigrant activists are positioning themselves as a minority that has faced persecution and discrimination. As they do so, they walk a tightrope, aligning themselves as a minority group and as "good Muslims." Even if an American minority group is by definition on the margins, it is still within the perimeter of the nation, unlike outsider "bad Muslims" (terrorists).

In the case of the clergy who organize on behalf of Latino immigrant hotel and restaurant workers, the most stunning observation is this: There is a racial difference between the activists and the workers. CLUE activists are mostly white and African American, while most of the workers in these industries are Latino immigrants. There are many Latino and Asian American clergy in Los Angeles, but with a few exceptions, they were largely missing in CLUE. Here, I can detect three possible explanations for this racial disconnect. First, many Asian American clergy are in fact Korean Protestants, and they tend not to adopt progressive political platforms. Second, many Latino clergy are Catholic, and as Catholic priests, they are constrained by a restrictive organizational hierarchy and consumed by servicing large congregations. Third, other Latino clergy are Pentecostal storefront preachers, and although they lead Latino immigrant worker congregations, they are not well-integrated into a denominational structure. Moreover, their theology is not one that has prioritized social justice activities, although this was beginning to change in 2006 with the mobilization of Latino evangelical pastors for immigration reform under the leadership of Pastor Samuel Rodriguez. The absence of Latino and Korean clergy in immigrant worker justice actions, however, is explained more by the structure of various denominations rather than by racial distancing. What keeps the African American and white clergy and laity engaged with immigrant worker justice campaigns? It is part of the tradition of mainstream Judeo-Christian religions to work for social justice, and the mechanisms that allow them to connect across communities and languages are testimonials, as was the case with the sanctuary movement in the 1980s.

At the Posada sin Fronteras, long-standing divisions between whites and Mexicans become an opportunity for symbolic racial border crossing.

Anglo-American, English-speaking Christians come together with Mexican Americans and Spanish-speaking Mexican immigrants to reimagine a world without the borders of nation-states and without the borders of race. Here, Anglo Protestants and Catholics show a remarkable openness to embracing Mexican-Catholic traditions. One of the key organizers of the event, the now-deceased Franciscan brother Ed Dunn, told me that this racial bridging was reminiscent of the cross-racial and cross-religious support received by the UFW. "I think there's that same thing with the posada," he said. "There [in the UFW] was this great respect that [non-Mexican, non-Catholic] people brought and said, 'We understand this is part of the tradition, and we want to learn from it.'"

Among scholars of religion and civic engagement, there is much discussion about the extent to which charity extended by well-to-do white congregations can help poorer, minority communities. Most of this literature suggests that the much-anticipated bridging and bonding capital fails to materialize in these situations. In the case of the Posada sin Fronteras, I am not able to assess the extent to which long-term relations form between different racial and religious communities at the border, but at the event itself, unity rather than distance is the normative shared experience.

The experience of unity and the momentary blurring of religious and racial borders occurs, I believe, because the Posada sin Fronteras does not represent a top-down act of charity or a giving from the rich to the poor (like the soup kitchen). Instead, it is a shared reenactment. More important still, at the Posada sin Fronteras, Anglo Protestant religious culture takes a backseat to Mexican Catholicism.

The Mexican-ness of the posada is irrefutable. The Mexican organizers of the Posada sin Fronteras whom I interviewed emphasized that it drew from Mexican religious folk traditions and from Latin American and Latino forms of socially committed religiosity. These include the legacy of the UFW, liberation theology, and the Chicano movement. As Rosa Marta Zarate, a former nun and singer-songwriter who has released a CD called *Posada sin Fronteras* with her musical collaborator, said: "When I'm asked why I do what I do, I say it's because of my *cultural herencia* [cultural heritage]. . . . The Chicano movement was vindicating my cultural roots of origin, of our indigenousness."[9] Maria Lourdes Arias Trujillo, who helped organize the Posada sin Fronteras when she was a lay Scalabrinian worker at the Casa del Migrante in Tijuana, said that she found inspiration in the spiritual images and the sharing with gringos on the other side: "To see people on the other side who were deeply hurt by what was happening, who were in solidarity with us, and who weren't necessarily Mexican but rather gringos and Americans strengthened our resolve. . . . One day, this wall will disappear."

SUCCESS OR FAILURE?

"Success is an elusive idea." This statement certainly applies to many arenas of social life, and it is offered by social movement scholar William A. Gamson in his discussion of defining movement success.[10] What metric are we to use? Is movement success determined by the achievement of concrete advantages for the group's intended benefici- ary, or is it defined by the challenging group's acceptance as a legiti- mate entity? As Gamson indicates, these are two very different ways of assessing movement success. Alternatively, we might define movement success by organizations' ability to raise and expand political con- sciousness within others about what is wrong. Along these lines, social movement scholars Verta Taylor and Leila Rupp have emphasized that long-term consequences of organizers' efforts may not be readily appar- ent for many years or even decades.[11] In this view, social change activists may be planting seeds that may take decades or generations before bearing social change results. James Jasper further complicates the picture by reminding us that protestors may pursue multiple goals simultaneously, winning some battles and losing others.[12] And then again, many social movements simply fail on all counts. With these caveats in mind, I will attempt to address the question through several metrics, gauging how effective the faith-based activists have been in winning advantages for immigrant beneficiaries; in achieving organiza- tional longevity and legitimacy; and in planting the seeds for later social change.

On all counts, I see the clergy labor advocates as the most successful in provoking the desired outcomes. CLUE and its national organization, IWJ, have achieved many of their goals. Union contracts offering fair wages and benefits have been signed between the unions representing Latino immigrant workers and large employers; a living-wage ordinance was passed in Los Angeles; and, increasingly, service workers' union demands are seen as legitimate. In fact, the Local 11 union leader who was so instrumental in the founding of CLUE, Maria Elena Durazo, was elected in 2006 to direct the Los Angeles County Federation of Labor, and she is widely recognized as a civic and civil rights leader. Reverend Salvatierra, the director of CLUE, is now co-chair of a statewide alliance of interfaith worker justice groups. So beneficiaries have seen some real benefits, and the faith-based supporters have gained voice and consolidated leadership. But judging CLUE and IWJ by benefits that have accrued to low-wage immigrant workers is tricky, since CLUE and IWJ are affiliated supporters of a much larger union and economic justice movement. CLUE and IWJ are autonomous, labor-supporting religious organizations, but they work in tandem with organized labor and other labor supporters. In fact, in Los Angeles alone, organized labor has cultivated an entire organizational infrastructure that allows these activists to coordinate their work for economic justice.[13] Not all wins can be attributed to the clergy and laity.

Assessing their activities using the second criterion of having established legitimacy, we see that CLUE and IWJ have grown in size and strength. When I started studying CLUE in 2000, it claimed two hundred fifty members, but by 2006, it claimed over six hundred fifty members. IWJ also has grown in size, going from forty-one affiliated groups around the country to about sixty in 2006, and it has successfully launched outreach projects such as Seminary Summer, recruiting thirty-five to fifty future religious leaders to participate in a paid internship devoted to worker justice. IWJ has expanded membership beyond Christian and Jewish clergy and laity to include Hindu, Muslim, and Buddhist participants (the board of directors of the IWJ now includes Muslim civil rights leader Hussan Ayloush). In this regard, both groups seem to be establishing legitimacy beyond Christian and Jewish circles.

How well they are establishing legitimacy with employers and managers is something I cannot definitively assess.

The Muslim American immigrant civil rights organizations and their affiliates continue to face a hostile climate. It is especially difficult to assess the extent to which they have leveraged civil liberties for members of their community. These organizations have certainly grown in members and in the number of people they reach. CAIR, for example, had only eight offices in September 2001, but by the end of 2006, it boasted thirty-two offices spread throughout the country. The measurable achievements of these organizations seem modest, but perhaps the level of hostility and repression directed at Muslim, Arab, and South Asian American immigrants—the hate crimes, deportations, and racial profiling at airports—would have been much more severe without the public voice and interventions of organizations such as CAIR and MPAC.

How well have these groups been accepted as legitimate political and civic actors? Although the organizational longevity of these groups is not in question, they have not received acceptance as valid spokespersons from all sides. While organizations such as CAIR and MPAC have established secure, stable working partnerships with civil rights groups and with many interfaith, primarily Christian and Jewish, groups, they are still vilified by Zionist Jewish groups and accused of being terrorist sympathizers. The power that Zionist individuals and groups wield in the U.S. political sphere means that the Muslim Americans face an uphill battle on the road to full acceptance as Americans. When the Los Angeles County Commission on Human Relations honored Maher Hathout, chairman of the Islamic Center of Southern California and one of the directing visionaries of MPAC, with a major human relations award, the Zionists protested. Once again, the Muslim leaders had to struggle for civic voice, inclusion, and legitimacy.[14] A nearly identical instance unfolded when the liberal California senator Barbara Boxer rescinded an award she gave to Basim Elkarra, director of CAIR's Sacramento offices, after a website posted unsubstantiated accusations that the award recipient had ties to Hezbollah and Hamas.[15] When Los Angeles mayor Antonio Villaraigosa and California governor Arnold Schwarzenegger spoke at an event in support of Israel, Muslim leaders held a news conference to complain that they had been excluded and ignored.[16]

Clearly, Muslim leaders are still fighting for inclusion in American political and civic spheres at the local, statewide, and national levels. They have made some progress. As we saw, these groups have established working relations with units of federal and local government, such as the FBI, the INS, and, later, the Department of Homeland Security and the sheriff's office. Their leaders are invited to *iftaar* dinners at the White House to celebrate the end of Ramadan. But there is a long way to go. As Muslim Americans, they want not only to stop the violations of civil liberties but also to be accepted as Muslims and Americans. They want to see Muslims represented in politics and in city, state, and national positions of authority. They want to end Islamophobia and discrimination against Muslims. They would like to see Muslim Americans in Congress and the Senate. The first Muslim was elected to the U.S. House of Representatives in November 2006, and this was hailed as a great success and as an indicator that Islamophobia was diminishing. But these groups are still struggling to find representation and to be seen and included as legitimate political and civic actors.

These Muslim American organizations know they must cultivate the second generation. Through internships and organizational programs, they are encouraging Muslim American youth to choose careers in political science, journalism, and media. They are trying to increase political and civic involvement and strong Muslim identities among the youth. To do this, the organizations sponsor youth groups, councils, and retreats. Through careful cultivation and preparation of talent among the youth and the second generation, the Muslim American organizations are trying to ensure that their efforts will lead to greater inclusion for Muslim Americans in the future.

Judged by the criteria of benefits for border-crossing beneficiaries, the Christian organizers and participants working at the U.S.-Mexico border have shown little progress toward diminishing death, violence, or fortified walls. After more than a dozen years of gatherings, the Posada sin Fronteras—and the related activities—has not put an end to border militarization. In fact, border enforcement and expenditures have increased and so have the deaths. In 2006, just months after the nation witnessed the largest immigrant rights marches in the country, the House and the Senate agreed to build a triple fence across seven hundred miles of the U.S.-Mexico border. In spite of the prayerful gatherings, religious reenactments, and emergency services provided to border crossers, the wall has been strengthened, not torn down. Yet there is organizational continuity. Through their involvement in the posada, participants are learning about border policies and collectively sharing and signaling a faith-based challenge to national policies that they interpret as immoral and unjust. To whom are they signaling? It is to themselves. As I have emphasized, they do so from different perspectives and social locations—some more heavily drawn by faith, others more heavily drawn by ethnicity, and others drawn by an amalgam of politics, religion, and ethnicity. In this time of post-9/11 hypernationalism and militarization, when concrete and symbolic boundaries are accentuated, the counterhegemonic vision promoted by events such as the Posada sin Fronteras and the bringing together of diverse groups should not be underestimated.

From many vantage points, the Posada sin Fronteras is impressive—but prayerful gatherings and religious reenactments are not bringing the wall down. Other borders, however, may be eroding. The religious, moral impulse against border militarization and the strong Mexican cultural presence in the U.S.-Mexico border area—heightened during the last thirty years of immigration—allow participants who are neither Mexican nor Catholic to embrace Mexican-Catholic ritual forms. In particular, white Protestants and Catholics are embracing forms of Latin American popular religiosity in noncommercial ways—they're not just buying the votive candles or decorative Día de los Muertos brooches. This is the opposite of what assimilation theory would have predicted. And that is one type of border erosion. This kind of religio-cultural expansion and border crossing appeals to participants because it provides not only social and political relevance but deep spiritual meaning and transcendence. The collective, public, and highly ritualistic elements of the event and the site itself yield feelings of hope. As Pastor Cribbs offered, "I have to believe that every time we come together, the wall comes down slightly. And I believe that one day, it will come down completely." Religious symbols strengthen moral beliefs and postnational political positions. These people are driven to action by faith and moral conviction more than by calculated chances of bringing an end to current border policies. This strong culture would seem to bode well for continuing to galvanize supporters.

Since mine is not a longitudinal study, it is difficult to assess the extent to which these faith-based activists are sowing the seeds for future social change movements. But it is easy to see how they take inspiration from religious activists of the past. The Posada sin Fronteras organizers draw from traditions as diverse as the sanctuary movement; Latin American liberation theology, with its "preference for the poor"; the Catholic Left of the 1960s, which brought Catholic symbols and rituals to the streets for antiwar efforts; the United Farm Workers movement, where César Chávez's organizing projects for migrant workers incorporated religious leaders of various faiths as well as pilgrimages, fasts, rituals, and symbols with decidedly Mexican-Catholic origins; and the solidarity movement's focus on witnessing in Central America. This movement culture is largely U.S. based, but it reflects the history of United States' involvement in Latin America throughout the twentieth century and the subsequent legacies of U.S.-bound Latino migration organized around labor needs. Religious people who were inspired by movements from other times and places, either vicariously or through hands-on involvement, brought together these traditions to create and sustain the Posada sin Fronteras, and today these serve to sustain a religious denouncement of death and violence at the U.S.-Mexico border.[17] In the same way, people who are involved in the Christian antiborderism movements of today may go on to fuel future social change efforts. As Rosemary Johnson, one of the key organizers of the posada, reflected, "We have to plant the seeds. . . . I can't say that this is going to change immigration policy, but you know it's going to change some minds and make people rethink or think twice about the prevailing sentiment." As she said this to me, she reached under her writing pad and drew out inspirational quotes from Archbishop Romero and Dorothy Day. She read these to me aloud. "Romero says that we cannot do everything, and there's a sense of liberation in realizing that," she said. "This enables us to do something and do it very well. It may be incomplete, but it is a beginning. . . . an opportunity for the Lord's grace to enter and do the rest. We may never see the end results, but that is the difference between the master builder and the worker."

Why have these smart, talented, and dedicated faith-based activists not seen greater success in achieving immigrant rights? The answer has less to do with their efforts, strategies, and use of religion and more to do with the tenor of the times. We are living during a period, in the United States and in other postindustrial nations, of hardened xenophobia. Restrictionist sentiment once ebbed and flowed with capitalist economic cycles, predictably rising with economic downturns and recessions and quieting during boom times. That pattern no longer holds. From the 1990s until now, institutionalized restrictionism and a new nationalism based on exclusion have prevailed in the United States and elsewhere. Consequently, there are few political opportunities for those promoting immigrant rights, integration, and social cohesion.

Yet international migration is now the way of the world, and liberal democratic states must grapple with these issues in ways that foster integration and social justice. Two hundred million people live in countries other than the one they were born in. There are about 34 million foreign-born people in the United States, an estimated 12 million of them without authorized permission to live and work here. As many commentators have pointed out, and I would agree, the U.S. immigration system of laws and regulations is not working. So what is the place of religion in this state of affairs?

I don't believe that religion should rule, nor that religion alone can fix the United States' immigration dilemmas. I do believe, however, that the religious actors and activists featured in this book offer an important voice to which we should listen. The Muslim, Jewish, and Christian leaders and activists that I interviewed are deeply religious people who have found meaningful ways of living their religion outside of churches and temples. They see the tenets of their religious beliefs not as rigid dictates that should be imposed on others but as guidelines for interpreting the social world and for acting to bring about social justice.

There are multiple ways of being Christian, Jewish, and Muslim, and the activists within those monotheistic religions represented here are all engaged in cosmopolitan, inclusive religion. They are not interested in imposing their religious beliefs or ways of life on others. Rather, they use their religious ideals to help make a society that transcends the limitations of the modernist, rigid imagination of the nation-state. In this way, progressive religion can contribute to democracy and pluralism.

Without these voices, we are largely left with an immigration regime ruled by what I have come to think of as market fundamentalism and state fundamentalism. When it comes to immigration, market fundamentalism is the idea that labor market concerns should drive immigration policy. This is neoliberalism, and it winds up justifying the conditions of bad, low-wage immigrant jobs, the recruitment of immigrant scientists and technicians, and informing proposals for new guest worker programs. Any scholar or casual observer of immigration knows that there is no such thing as temporary worker visa programs. Regardless of the intentions of policy makers or migrants, these types of programs necessarily lead to permanent settlement and continued migration flows, as we saw with the Bracero Program in the United States and the postwar guest worker programs in Western Europe. Moreover, guest worker programs are based on creating a subordinate, second-class group of workers, a goal that would appear to be in conflict with the ideals of a liberal democracy and a capitalist system of free wage labor.

State fundamentalism is the idea that a nation-state's immigration laws must be strictly obeyed, regardless of how outmoded they may be or how out of sync with global processes. It is based on the absolutist belief in state sovereignty and nation-state power to unilaterally decide on immigration. It takes the form of people putting faith and reverence into laws that are essentially illegal and unconstitutional, such as the USA Patriot Act, or the myriad of municipal and state immigration restrictions that we have seen enacted in the last decade. (Immigration is supposed to be a federal matter.) It is exemplified by the belief that nation-state borders should be policed, that existent immigration laws must be rigidly respected, and that there are black-and-white, fixed forms to the categories of "illegal" and "legal." Progressive religion, as I have outlined in this book, encourages critical thinking about these issues. And we cannot afford to ignore critical thinking, which will be necessary to devise viable options to the neoliberal market and state fundamentalism that currently informs immigration laws.

The solution will also eventually require us to rethink the institutions where immigration rules and regulations are made. In the current moment, we are using an old nation-state system to deal with an issue that is global and that necessarily involves more than one nation-state. A unilateral system of immigration policy will no longer work and is likely to continue the ineffectual and undemocratic fortress building of the United States—albeit with some backdoors held open by particular employers and advocates of market fundamentalism.

I believe that to remedy many of our immigration problems and dilemmas, we must begin by building bilateral or multilateral policy-making institutions to help govern immigration matters. It is, after all, the era of NAFTA and the European Union, when free trade agreements governing capital and goods are decided upon multilaterally. The world, at least the world I see around me, is not yet ready for this sort of arrangement when it comes to people and labor. For example, the United Nations and other supranational bodies frequently ratify conventions and agreements on human rights. But while nations sign on to these agreements, they often disregard the implementation. Still, the whole idea of multilateral decision making is not as far-fetched as it sounds. While constituencies are not presently clamoring for a supranational or multilateral policy-making body, in ten or twenty years we may see such a model implemented. And when it is, it will need to reflect multiple voices, perspectives, and bodies of knowledge. This body might include representatives from labor and business and from religious and secular sectors, health and education providers and administrators, and economists, sociologists, and philosophers.

Religious groups should not be at the helm, nor am I advocating the erasure of church-state divisions. Religious activists, however, offer an important voice in our immigration discussions. Why? The United States is a multicultural, multiracial society that is deeply religious. Most immigrants to the United States are deeply religious. Finally, and perhaps most important, religion can help temper the troubling manifestations of unreflective, exclusionist affirmations of nationhood that we see exemplified in inflammatory talk radio shows and vigilante groups patrolling the border. If religious groups such as those examined in this book come to have a greater say in immigration, I think that it will advance the project of immigrant integration, not immigrant exclusion. Such a process might help us understand how immigrants become "us," and how the United States is becoming, once again, a nation of immigrants.

APPENDIX Research Methods

I conducted the research sequentially, beginning in 2000. From the start, I knew that I was interested in how religion fuels immigrant rights activism, how religion gets used in this process, and, in turn, how the whole process affects people, but the cases I would study were not immediately apparent. These unfolded over time and reflected historical circumstances, the regional locality of Southern California, and some degree of serendipity. Several University of Southern California students, both undergraduates and graduates, served as research assistants in key parts of the research, and in my description of the research, I wish to recognize them and their particular contributions.

During spring 2000, with the support of a small grant from the PEW-sponsored Center for Religion and Civic Culture at USC and through conversations and collaborations with then undergraduate student

Kara Lemma, I began the research on CLUE. A small grant from the American Sociological Association fund for innovative projects allowed Kara Lemma to work on this project as both research assistant and CLUE volunteer during the summer of 2000.[1] Her preternatural social skills served the project well, so that by the time I attended my first CLUE meeting in July 2000, I found her already working a registration table, just before I was taken aback by someone from a microphone publicly welcoming the arrival of "Kara's professor from USC." We collaborated on this project over the course of the next year. This part of the research involved the study of one organization, CLUE, through face-to-face, audio-recorded, guided interviews and participant observation at the CLUE breakfast meetings and at various public protests. Kara Lemma's contributions were substantive, as she conducted many of the interviews on her own, she participated in the smaller CLUE planning meetings that I did not attend, and, during spring 2001, she even took a part-time paid job with CLUE. After all events and meetings we wrote detailed field notes, and we also collected documents produced by CLUE and other related organizations. Based on our observation at CLUE meetings, we identified the principal leaders who then formed the hub of CLUE, and we approached them for interviews. Only three of the twenty-one clergy and lay CLUE participants that we approached for interviews proved to be too elusive or too busy to comply with our requests. A total of eighteen interviews were conducted with CLUE participants, and, later, I conducted an additional four interviews with key staff in the Chicago offices of IWJ, the national umbrella organization which helps to coordinate organizations such as CLUE. All of these interviews were conducted in person, tape-recorded, transcribed, and coded for relevant themes. When direct quotes are used from the interviews, they reflect verbatim transcription segments, but when testimonial segments from meetings are included, they are drawn from field notes that I initially wrote by hand on the spot and later typed up. Chapters 4 and 5 are based on research with CLUE and the IWJ.

On the morning of September 11, 2001, I heard a radio news report as I was pulling out of the driveway around 7:30 A.M. The magnitude of what had happened did not convince me of the merits of staying home, so I went to the scheduled CLUE breakfast meeting at Holman United Church in Central Los Angeles, where the mood was somber but where they continued with that day's agenda of honoring particular clergy. As the days and weeks passed, it became apparent there were many repercussions from the terrorist attacks of what became known as 9/11. Among these was the realization that Muslim immigrant communities in the United States were being deeply affected, and not always positively. Racial profiling at airports, massive roundups, and detentions by the FBI and the INS filled the news. I began discussing these unfolding events in my sociology of immigration classes, formulating what would become the next phase of research.

During fall and winter 2001, I began reading about Muslim and Arab American immigration history and current immigrant communities, and I recruited two very capable USC undergraduate students, Sharene Irsane and Margaret Perez-Clark, to read and discuss this literature with me. With a small grant from a USC initiative designed to incorporate undergraduate students in professors' research projects, I employed these students as research assistants to do bibliographic research, transcribing, and field work. This was a time when there were a lot of meetings and public forums dedicated to urgent issues of concern in the Muslim, Arab, and South Asian communities of Southern California. During this period, we attended the numerous public forums, town hall meetings, conventions, and conferences that sprouted up all over Los Angeles and Orange Counties. These were sponsored by various organizations where I wound up conducting interviews. These organizations included the MPAC, CAIR, SAN, both the Los Angeles and Orange County Commissions on Human Relations, the American Arab Anti-discrimination Committee, the Palestinian American Women's Association, and an organization with which I had long-established ties, the Coalition for Humane Immigrant Rights in Los Angeles. At these public forums, my students and I collected and studied the materials produced by the organizations, and we wrote and analyzed field notes based on what we had seen and heard. I conducted seventeen interviews with key organizers working around faith-based responses to the post-9/11 backlash, and Sharene Irsane conducted an additional one. We began field work in January 2002 and continued through spring 2003, but all of the interviews were conducted in 2002. Later, when other obligations precluded me from attending important conferences or meetings, I sent graduate student research assistants Lata Murti and Sarah Stohlman to observe and write up field notes with particular themes in mind. The materials collected for this part of this study are presented in chapters 2 and 3.

Chapters 5 and 6 focus on efforts at the U.S.-Mexico border and are largely informed by an analysis of an annual event, the Posada sin Fronteras, which occurs at the U.S.-Mexico border during Advent season. I first attended this event in 2000 with Kara Lemma, and we photographed the event, participated in it, and wrote field notes while my son Miles videotaped it. I attended the posada in subsequent years with small teams of student research assistants. In 2002, with USC graduate students Genelle Gaudinez, and Hector Lara and with undergraduate student Maeve St. Leger, I conducted brief onsite interviews with forty-seven participants, trying to discern the meaning the event held for them and how border politics connected to their religious values and sensibilities. Later, in 2003, with Genelle Gaudinez and Hector Lara, I conducted guided, audio-taped interviews with twenty religious people, including the key organizers who started this event and the key people who keep it going today. This involved conducting interviews mostly in San Diego and Tijuana but also in Los Angeles, Chicago, and San Francisco. Later, I interviewed Reverend Ricardo Moreno, a Presbyterian pastor who is involved in social justice activism for Latinos and immigrants. Much later, after I had written a draft of this manuscript, I conducted an additional interview with Bishop Gabino Zavala, someone who has been deeply involved in immigrant social justice in the Catholic Church. All of the in-depth interviews for this project were conducted in person, with the approval of the USC Institutional Review Board and with full consent from the interviewees.

I also collected a good deal of data that I have judiciously decided not to use in this book.[2] There was simply too much to include. While the data informing this book is substantial, there are some limitations. First, the portraits I sketch here are based on snapshots taken at a certain time. Although I have tried to stay up-to-date on new developments, this is not a longitudinal study. Second, all research is partial and situated by social location. I was neither a religious nor activist insider in any of the groups I studied, and I was certainly not privy to everything said and every planned strategy. If you read the preface to the book, you will know that although I had a traditional religious upbringing, I am not a religious person, but I am sympathetic to the causes and goals pursued by these activists. Finally, I wish to anticipate the criticisms of scholars working from a more disciplined historical comparative methodological tradition, one that demands evenly parallel cases for comparison. While the rigor of this kind of research is admirable, this kind of approach remains best suited for historical study or experimental designs. The social world does not present itself to us in neat little packages, with evenly distributed cases and characteristics, and so it is that I have come to include in this book three different instances of how religion comes to the service of immigrant rights.

While I am deeply grateful to all of the research assistance I received from USC students, it should be clear to readers that all errors of fact, representation, or interpretation remain my own. I have tried to represent organizations and people and their words with integrity. I retain tremendous respect for the social actors featured in this book, and in my effort to balance generalizations against particularity, I may have tilted toward the latter. If an overnuanced portrait emerges, complicating the general picture of a coherent, seamless narrative, that is the reason.

Notes

1. Spanish-language radio personalities played a big role in urging protestors to march and to carry American flags, lest there be any confusion about immigrants and their national loyalties. During the immigrant rights marches against Proposition 187 in 1994, many protestors carried Mexican flags in the streets, fueling popular outcries that they were unpatriotic Americans. For a description and analysis of the mobilization for the spring 2006 immigrant rights marches and the ways in which Spanish-language radio DJs emerged as leaders, see Hondagneu-Sotelo and Salas 2008.

2. Speaking of the House bill, Cardinal Roger M. Mahony said, "If you take this to its logical, ludicrous extreme, every single person who comes up to receive Holy Communion, you have to ask them to show papers" (Watanabe 2006:A1). This was not a hyperbolic statement. A few months later the Los Angeles archdiocese revised a policy to root out pedophiles by mandating that

all church volunteers be fingerprinted and present photo IDs. In Los Angeles and Orange Counties, where there are many Latino immigrant parishes, this would have excluded many immigrant volunteers. As Orange County auxiliary bishop Jaime Soto explained, "We are doing this because these people [immigrants] want to participate, they want to serve their church, and we want to welcome them" (Delson 2006:B3). Soto wanted to make sure that the fingerprinting policies would not scare off immigrant parishioners.

3.   Just as immigrant populations that once concentrated in California have fanned out to other states, so too have anti-immigrant backlash movements and initiatives. Proposition 187, which California voters approved in 1994 to exclude services to undocumented immigrants and their children, went on to inspire the federal 1996 Illegal Immigrant Reform and Immigrant Responsibility Act (IIRIRA). Pro-immigrant rights organizers working out of Los Angeles seem to have a disproportionate influence on the national scene too. The AFL-CIO's shift in policy—embracing the organization of immigrant workers and sponsoring the Immigrant Workers Freedom Ride of 2002—began with ideas hatched by Maria Elena Durazo, the Local 11 leader in Los Angeles. Similarly, religious and secular activists and leaders meeting at Los Angeles' Our Lady Queen of Angels Church, informally known as La Placita Church, proved important in organizing the national immigrant rights marches of 2006, which were mightily publicized through the efforts of Spanish-language DJs based in Los Angeles but broadcast to other U.S. cities (Hondagneu-Sotelo and Salas 2008). For books examining the recent surge of labor and immigrant workers' rights activism in Los Angeles, see Ruth Milkman's *L.A. Story* (2006) and Karen Brodkin's *Making Democracy Matter* (2007).

4.   Nominally and in popular discourse, the United States is often referred to as a Judeo-Christian country. Yet Judaism remains a minority religion and is perhaps accepted more as a cultural identity than a religious orientation parallel with Christianity's dominance in the United States. I thank Micole Siegel for this insight.

5.   The term "re-Christianization" was first used by Francois Burgat in an article referring to the situation in Western Europe. He suggests, "Western societies are in fact, strictly speaking, not so much 'secular' as 'de-Christianized'" (2003:23), but he also refers to "born-again" evangelical Christianity as a re-Christianization form of fundamentalism. In the analysis developed here, I am conceptualizing the re-Christianization of the United States in broader terms, as a process permeating national identity.

6.   Christopher Hitchens's 2007 polemical book, *God Is Not Great: How Religion Poisons Everything*, led the pack of atheist denouncements of religion, claiming that all religious belief promotes intolerance, tyranny, and violence. The philosopher Martha C. Nussbaum published a more measured look at religion.

In *The Clash Within: Democracy, Religious Violence, and India's Future* (2007), she argues that religious nationalism provides the biggest danger to democracy in the world today. Here, the argument is not against religion per se but against the religious domination of others. And the sociologist Mark Juergensmeyer, in *Terror in the Mind of God* (2000), shows the connection between religious moral justification and acts of violent terrorism perpetrated by members of just about every major religion, also casting doubt on the positive impacts of religion.

7. In 1986 immigrant rights coalitions were formed in Los Angeles, San Francisco, New York State, Massachusetts, Chicago, and Texas (personal communication, Angelica Salas, executive director of the Coalition for Humane Immigrant Rights in Los Angeles, November 6, 2006). These coalitions were loosely tied together through the National Network for Immigrant and Refugee Rights and Services, which maintains offices in Oakland, California. The marches of spring 2006 were organized by many groups, including the Coalition for Comprehensive Immigration Reform (CCIR), a coalition that includes the labor unions SEIU and UNITE HERE! as well as immigrant rights coalitions from Los Angeles, New York, and Illinois and law centers and policy groups such as the Asian American Justice Center and the National Council of La Raza. The CCIR launched the New American Opportunity Campaign (NAOC) to ensure comprehensive—not just punitive or restrictionist—immigration reform. The NAOC received participation from organized labor, community-based organizations, and religious groups.

8. Many immigrant worker rights organizations emerged in Los Angeles during the 1990s to address the needs of immigrant workers employed in occupations that are not easily unionized. These include KIWA, the Korean Immigrant Workers Alliance, which initially targeted Korean immigrant workers before expanding to include Latino immigrant workers, who constitute the majority of the low-wage workforce in Los Angeles' Koreatown; the Domestic Workers Association (DWA) and the Day Laborers Project, which both came out of the Coalition for Humane Immigrant Rights in Los Angeles; the Pilipino Workers' Center (PWC); the Association of Latin American Gardeners of Los Angeles (ALAGLA); and the Garment Workers Center (GWC). Many of these groups united under the title of the Multi-ethnic Immigrant Workers Organizing Network (MIWON).

9. Christianity and Roman republicanism are the main traditions influencing American civil religion, according to Robert Bellah. These traditions allow Americans to interpret the nation's history through a religious lens (Bellah 1970).

10. Casanova 1994:5.

11. The classic statement on religion's role in American assimilation is Will Herberg's 1960 book *Prostestant, Catholic, Jew*. In this book, Herberg also argued that it was the Russian Jewish and Italian Catholic immigrants of the early

twentieth century that helped to eventually transform the United States from a Protestant to a Judeo-Christian nation. More recently, a plethora of scholarship emphasizes the role of religion in providing social capital for immigrant incorporation and in facilitating ethnic identities, adaptations, and hybridity. See Leonard et al. 2005; Ebaugh and Chafetz 2000, 2002; Eck 2001; Miller, Miller, and Dyrness 2001; and Warner and Wittner 1998.

12.   On religion enabling border crossings, see Hagan 2007. For analysis of the ameliorative effect of religion on anomic immigrant life, see Menjívar 2003 and Stohlman 2007. For analysis of the transnational dimensions of immigrant religion, see Levitt 2001 and 2007 and also Vasquez and Marquardt 2003. For an analysis of the diverse ways in which Christianity allows people in Latin America and in Latino immigrant communities in the United States to face the challenges of globalization, see Peterson, Vasquez, and Williams 2001.

13.   Freeman 1995:121.

14.   Freeman 1995; Hollifield 1992, 1995.

15.   Joppke 2005:49.

16.   Hondagneu-Sotelo 1995.

17.   Widely recognized by legal scholars as one of the most draconian acts of immigration legislation, the IIRIRA funded increased border enforcement and introduced new grounds for exclusion and deportation, stricter criminal alien laws, and new restrictions on public welfare eligibility.

18.   Marchevsky and Theoharis 2006; Fujiwara 2005.

19.   Kretsedemas 2008.

20.   Matomoro 2006:B8.

21.   Ngai 2004.

22.   Writing about the situation in France, the scholar Etienne Balibar contends that the racism directed toward new immigrants, who are largely Algerian and Muslim, is centered on the idea of cultural difference, not biological difference. It is a framework, he argues, of "racism without races," which, "at first sight, does not postulate the superiority of certain groups or peoples in relation to others but 'only' the harmfulness of abolishing frontiers, the incompatibility of life-styles and traditions" (1991:21).

23.   Cornelius, Hollifield, and Martin 2003.

24.   Espiritu 2003:47.

25.   See Coutin 2000 and Menjívar 2006.

26.   "Welcoming the Stranger among Us: Unity in Diversity," a pastoral statement from the U.S. Conference of Catholic Bishops, November 15, 2000, www.usccb.org/mrs/welcome.shtml, accessed January 10, 2003.

27.   "Stranger No Longer: Together on a Journey of Hope," a pastoral letter concerning migration from the Catholic bishops of Mexico and the United States,

issued by the U.S. Conference of Catholic Bishops, January 22, 2003, www.usccb.org/mrs/stranger.shtml#1, accessed June 27, 2006.

28. On November 14, 2006, in his message on the 93rd World Day of Migrants and Refugees, Pope Benedict XVI spoke out in favor of migrant family rights, drawing parallels to Mary and Joseph fleeing from Nazareth to Egypt. He called on all governments to ratify "the international legal instruments that aim to defend the rights of migrants, refugees and their families." Zenit News Services, http://www.zenit.org, accessed November 14, 2006.

29. Like the Catholic statement but perhaps worded more strongly, the statement issued by the Lutheran Church–Missouri Synod states, "We recognize and affirm the responsibility of the government to regulate immigration," but then it goes on to acknowledge that many people migrate illegally because they have no other recourse. The declaration is backed up with citations to many biblical passages, such as "And you are to love those who are aliens, for you yourselves were aliens in Egypt" (Deuteronomy 10:18–19); and "Do not forget to entertain strangers, for by so doing some people have entertained angels without knowing it" (Hebrews 13:2). "Joint Statement Regarding Immigration Concerns," issued by Dr. Gerald B. Kieschnick and Reverend Matthew Harrison to the Lutheran Church–Missouri Synod, June 2, 2006, www.lcms.org/pages/internal.asp?NavID = 10023, accessed June 28, 2006.

30. The presiding bishop of the Episcopal Church in the United States came out in support of legalization opportunities and against blatantly restrictionist measures, underscoring that "as Christians, we are called to remember the Gospel mandate to extend hospitality to the stranger." Episcopal News Service, March 27, 2006, www.ecusa.anglican.org/3577_73170_ENG_Print.html, accessed June 28, 2006.

31. See Nawyn 2007.

32. See Wood 2002 and Palacios 2007.

33. Demerath 2003; Kurien 2004; Williams 2002; Smith 1996a; Wuthnow and Evans 2002; Wood 2002.

34. Williams 2002:249–250.

35. Nepstad 2004:23.

36. According to sociologist Christian Smith, a particularly worldly cause may be perceived through "the ultimacy and sacredness associated with God's will, eternal truth, and the absolute moral structure of the universe" (1996b:9).

37. Morris 1984:23.

38. For the classic statement on the importance of resource mobilization in social movements, see McCarthy and Zald 1977.

39. On religious resources fueling the civil rights movement, see Morris 1984. On the role of religious resources in the United Farm Workers movement, see Dalton 2003.

40. For a discussion of how churches and religious organizations served as "movement midwives" for the Central America peace movement of the 1980s, see Smith 1996b. Neither Morris nor Smith prioritize existent social networks as the most crucial factor in fueling social movements, as they both acknowledge the important role of religious moral norms and values in the respective movements.

41. Casanova 1994.

42. Jasper 1997:184, italics in original.

43. Nepstad 2004.

44. A fuller description is included in the appendix.

CHAPTER 2

1. The USA PATRIOT Act is a complicated and far-reaching piece of legislation that made changes in criminal, banking, immigration, and intelligence and surveillance law. While U.S. citizens are affected by these changes, USA PATRIOT subjects noncitizens to new double standards, defining terrorist activity or support much more expansively for immigrants than for U.S.-born citizens and allowing for secret searches without probable cause for both citizens and noncitizens. See Cole 2003:57–71 for a discussion of these differences.

2. For analyses of U.S. government violations of civil rights and liberties, see Cole 2003; Elaasar 2004; Hagopian 2004; and Murray 2004.

3. To put this event into context, it is important to underline that the speech at the MPAC convention occurred only one month after the U.S. government inaugurated a special registration program requiring male noncitizens from twenty-five Arab and Muslim countries to register with immigration authorities. According to immigration law scholar Bill Ong Hing, about eighty-three thousand men presented themselves to the INS and nearly thirteen thousand were put into deportation hearings (Hing 2006:148). No one, he reports, was charged with terrorism crimes.

4. The FBI probed the murder of Adel Karas, originally from Egypt, as a hate crime, but because no evidence of "hate" (such as graffiti or notes) was found, investigators concluded it was a robbery—even though they found nothing stolen, or evidence of attempted robbery. Post-9/11 murder victims that were the likely results of hate crimes include Balbir Singh Sodhi, killed outside his gas station in Mesa, Arizona, on September 15, 2001.

5. In their volume *Muslim Minorities in the West*, Haddad and Smith (2002:v) argue convincingly that "Muslims are a permanent and growing element in the populations of nearly all Western nations," including not only Canada, the United States, and Western Europe but also South Africa, New Zealand, and Australia.

6. Eck 2001:228; Haddad and Smith 2002:v.

7. Haddad and Smith 2002.

8. Eck 2001; Leonard 2007.

9. Leonard 2003.

10. Salam Al-Marayati, for example, was born in Baghdad, Iraq, moved to the United States at age four, and received a bachelor's degree in biochemistry from UCLA and an MBA from the University of California, Irvine. He initially worked as a chemical engineer before becoming active in Muslim community civic engagement. He eventually became one of the founders and the executive director of MPAC. Omar Ahmad, the founder and chair of the Board of Directors of CAIR, holds BS and MS degrees in computer engineering and is also president and CEO of a Silicon Valley software company.

11. Leonard 2003; Saeed 2002.

12. The American Muslim Political Coordination Council (AMPCC) formed in 1999 as an umbrella group representing the American Muslim Alliance, MPAC, CAIR, and the American Muslim Council. The AMPCC formed, according to Professor Agha Saeed, because of the lack of unity among Muslim American organizations. Until the 1990s, Saeed writes, these groups were "lacking an institutional mechanism for mutual consultation and decision making" (2002:50). The AMPCC endorsed George W. Bush for president in 2000, believing that he would repeal the Secret Evidence Act, which had been signed into effect in 1996 after the Oklahoma City bombings. I asked my interviewees if this endorsement was also driven by the fact that a Jewish candidate, Joseph Lieberman, ran on the opposing ticket or by the fact that Muslim Americans, as an affluent group, concurred with Republican policies on taxation and government. My interviewees said no and said that the reason was because they had been persuaded by Bush's promises to repeal the Antiterrorism and Effective Death Penalty Act of 1995, signed by Clinton in 1996, which allowed the government to try non-U.S. citizens with secret evidence that is not shared with the accused. Saeed (2002:51) cites evidence suggesting that as many as 2.3 million Muslims voted for Bush in 2000.

13. It is important to note that many Arab American and Muslim American immigrant organizations are not explicitly political but are devoted to cultural awareness, community building, and solidarity. In Nagel and Staeheli's study of fifty-two websites of Arab American organizations, the researchers found that "only about one-third … have an overtly political message oriented towards civil rights advocacy, foreign policy issues or events in the Middle East" (2004:13).

14. In Los Angeles, for example, several different Japanese American groups, including Nikkei for Civil Rights and Redress, have participated with MPAC in Break the Fast celebrations for Ramadan in Little Tokyo. These began

in 2002 as a way of showing of solidarity with Muslims and are interfaith, multiracial, and multiethnic events. A Catholic priest, a Jewish rabbi, and Buddhist ministers also joined together with a Muslim imam in the Communities under Siege: Keeping the Faith celebrations, where an interfaith panel provided Jewish, Catholic, Buddhist, Muslim, and Native American views on civil rights. See www.ncrr-la.org/news/2–8–05/2html, accessed January 26, 2007.

15. For a contrasting view, see Okihiro 1984. Gary Okihiro's study of the Tule Lake camp suggests that religion fueled resistance by helping the Japanese Americans resist Americanization programs and uphold traditional values such as filial piety and family solidarity.

16. Historian David Yoo (2002:121) cites a 1930s Stanford University survey indicating that 78 percent of Issei, or Japanese immigrants, identified as Buddhist and 18 percent as Christian. A survey undertaken by the War Relocation Authority in 1942, believed to be more problematic because it was conducted under coercive conditions, suggests that 68 percent of all interned Japanese immigrants identified as Buddhist and 22 percent as Christian.

17. Yoo 2002:134.

18. Morris 1984:4.

19. The Southern Christian Leadership Conference (SCLC), according to Morris, served as the "decentralized arm of the black church," the organizational center for developing what would become the civil rights movement. The SCLC consisted of black ministers, many of them trained in theology in black colleges, and they maintained close, charismatic ties with their church followers. As Southern blacks moved from rural areas to big cities, churches became the primary community center and site of social recognition for black residents in the South, and the SCLC was able to capitalize on this and mobilize the masses of church congregational members into effective protesters.

20. Field notes from the Annenberg School workshop "Islam and Muslims in the Media," University of Southern California, November 9, 2005.

21. I attended the October 19, 2002, CAIR fundraiser banquet, held at the Hyatt Regency Hotel in Anaheim, California, just blocks away from Disneyland. After a banquet dinner, a series of speakers with very professional PowerPoint presentations reported on the annual activities of the local CAIR chapter. An esteemed imam from New York—one of the few African Americans in the crowd—took the floor and coaxed donations from the audience. Local businesses, he said, would be providing matching funds for donations raised at the banquet. "How many tonight will give $25,000 for this wonderful cause?" he asked the audience. "Who will raise their hand?" Slowly, and with hesitation, hands were raised and pledges of $10,000, $5,000, and $1,000 were made. Young women, many of them wearing headscarves, came by the tables to pick up the donations inserted in envelopes. Before the evening was over, the imam

announced that CAIR had exceeded its goal of raising a half a million dollars for the next year's operating costs.

22. Khan 2003:186.

23. www.mpac.org, accessed January 26, 2007.

24. The press release issued for this event by the Community Relations Service (which calls itself "a unique racial conflict resolution and prevention agency of the U.S. Department of Justice") stated, "The purpose of this town hall meeting is to reduce the level of anxiety in the Muslim American and Middle Eastern communities, as well as strengthening the direct access of the affected communities with key Department of Justice officials. Representatives from the U.S. Attorney's Office for the Central District of California, the FBI, and INS will attend the town hall meeting" (www.usdoj.gov/crs/pr01182002.htm, accessed June 10, 2007).

25. The forum where Randall Hamud reported this information, "Racial Profiling after 9/11," was held at a Jewish venue, the University Synagogue, in Brentwood, California, on March 12, 2002.

CHAPTER 3

1. There are, of course, competing Muslim American identity projects. For analyses of these, see Abdo 2006; Leonard 2003; Abdullah and Hathout 2003; Saeed 2002; and Haddad 2004. For an analysis of Arab American narratives of American assimilation, see Nagel and Staeheli 2005.

2. In Los Angeles, the prominent Masjid Omar ibn Al-Khattab Mosque, located across the street from my USC office, sponsors these types of community events. One such event included a public forum dedicated to a discussion of the possibility of forming an African American and Latino coalition of unity against the Minutemen (Gordon 2006:B4).

3. By October 2006 the Coalition to Preserve Human Dignity expected to serve over twenty thousand homeless people in twenty American cities. Islamic Relief, an international development organization, and the ILM Foundation (ILM signifies Intellect, Love, and Mercy), an L.A.-based nonprofit organization, are the primary coordinators of this effort. ("Southern California Muslims to Serve 3,000 Homeless and Hungry in Annual Ramadan Event," October 13, 2006, Listserv announcement sent by socal@cair.com.)

4. An organizational division of labor seems to prevail here. The Southern California Islamic Center, which I did not formally study because it provides social services (such as family counseling, educational programs, social and recreational events, etc.), not political advocacy, is involved in programs for second-generation youth and young adults.

5. John Esposito, cited in Hermansen 2004:77.

6. For an insightful discussion of the way the Israeli lobby and American political decisions after 9/11 have affected Muslim Americans, see Haddad 2004.

7. Associated Press 2006a: A29.

8. At the December 2005 MPAC convention, for example, a morning workshop entitled "U.S. Policy and Counter-extremism" featured Chuck Pena of the Cato Institute, a libertarian think tank, and Ron Nehring, chairman of the California Republican Party Committee in San Diego. Both speakers prefaced their remarks by stating that they were speaking on their own behalf, not their organizations', but they gave essentially Libertarian and Republican viewpoints, with Pena opining, "What should the government do about terrorism? The government should do nothing," and Nehring suggesting that private efforts against terrorism (such as the efforts of MPAC?) are more effective than government efforts. Salam Al-Marayati closed the session, and his initial remarks received spontaneous applause from the audience. "This discussion we're having here today couldn't happen at Capitol Hill. We need to have more dialogues like this there."

9. Abdullah and Hathout 2003:67.

10. Rudrappa 2004.

11. Kurien 2004.

12. The organizations that issued this statement included the following: the Islamic Society of North America, the Islamic Circle of North America, the American Muslim Political Coordination Council (which includes MPAC), and the Muslim American Society, among others (Elaasar 2004:97).

13. Kraul 2006.

14. "Interfaith-Update," Listserv message from Southern California CAIR, sca-interfaith-bounces@list.cair.com, accessed September 11, 2006.

15. *MPAC National Anti-terrorism Campaign Handbook*, 2004–2005, online at www.mpac.org/. See also "The National Grassroots Campaign to Fight Terrorism," www.mpac.org/ngcft/, accessed January 26, 2008.

16. Watanabe 2006:B2.

17. Quotes are taken from "American Muslim Community Announcements," email Listserv of sca-interfaith-admin@list.cair.com, accessed February 24, 2006.

18. Clark 2006:B4.

19. By contrast, the British government did form the Islamic Advisory Group to work together with British Muslims to deter terrorist violence.

20. Michel Shehadeh was one of the original LA 8, a group of seven Palestinians and one Kenyan (the wife of one of the group's Palestinians) who were arrested in 1987 for student activism. They were arrested at dawn, at gunpoint, and charged with supporting communism and the Palestinian cause. As Georgetown professor of law David Cole reports, "When the immigration judge

asked the government for evidence to support these allegations, the government responded that the evidence was classified and could be considered only in a closed-door hearing" (Cole 2003:162–63).

21. Basch, Schiller, and Blanc 1994; Levitt 2001.

22. Khan 2003:186.

CHAPTER 4

1. According to a CLUE fact sheet, in May 2000 thirty workers formed a union organizing committee at Loews. In response, the management hired labor consultants to discourage workers from supporting the union efforts. Six months later, HERE Local 11 filed charges with the National Labor Relations Board (NLRB), with testimonial evidence of violations of labor laws and protections. NLRB moved to prosecute, but Loews signed a settlement promising not to violate the labor laws—such as threatening employees with loss of benefits, wages, or jobs for their participation in union activities.

2. On the contemporary resurgence of labor and efforts to mobilize immigrant workers, see Brodkin 2007; Milkman 2000, 2006; Delgado 1995; Clawson 2003; Ness 2005.

3. In January 2004, CLUE organized the Grocery Workers Justice Pilgrimage to the exclusive Northern California suburban enclave of Alamo in an attempt to make its position known to the Safeway CEO, Steven Burd. The pilgrimage began with a rally and prayer session at a grocery store in Southern California, where clergy of various denominations offered blessings, prayers, and songs for the more than two hundred workers and the clergy who would be making the eight-hour bus ride pilgrimage. When they arrived in Alamo, they were met by security guards and police and prevented from meeting with Burd (White 2004). The labor dispute idled about seventy thousand grocery store workers in central and Southern California.

4. Wal-Mart Watch is a national campaign designed to expose the exploitation of Wal-Mart employees and the people who manufacture products sold by Wal-Mart. Wal-Mart Watch was formed in 2005, and CLUE is one of the many locally based supporters of it.

5. Sociologist Ruth Milkman's book *L.A. Story* (2006) adds to this list by noting important organizing efforts made by Los Angeles–based Latino immigrant workers employed as drywall hangers, port truckers, and garment workers. While the Justice for Janitors campaign and the drywall hangers' organizing efforts succeeded, organizing efforts among the Los Angeles–Long Beach port truckers and among garment workers proved to be less successful. Milkman argues that the more successful campaigns owe their success to, among other

factors, the ability to achieve broad community support (2006:186). Karen Brodkin's book *Making Democracy Matter* (2007) adds to this analysis by discussing organizing efforts outside of traditional unions and offers a finely nuanced analysis of a young generation of activists working for immigrant worker rights in Los Angeles during the 1990s. Curiously, however, neither Milkman nor Brodkin acknowledge the role of religion and religious people in these immigrant labor movements. In fact, "religion" does not appear in the index of either book, which is a bit reminiscent of how the immigration literature used to be.

6.   During the 2003 Immigrant Workers Freedom Ride, HERE began working with UNITE, which had formed in 1995 to organize garment workers. The union is today known as UNITE HERE and organizes workers in many service industries and also in garments and textiles.

7.   As historians Edwards and Gifford note, the "social gospelers perceived themselves to be acting on divine mandate as they marshaled public opinion, the tools of social science, and the power of the democratic political process in efforts to reconstruct society and its institutions, from the local to the global level, according to Christian ethical principles" (2003:3).

8.   Cornell 2006.

9.   Tranwick 2003.

10.   Today the Catholic Workers, among other things, shelter and feed unhoused immigrant workers in East L.A. On one of my visits to a meeting at the Los Angeles Diocese, I saw them with signs decrying the $2 billion allocated to build Los Angeles' new cathedral. They were protesting Cardinal Roger Mahoney's decision to allocate funds to this edifice at a time when millions in diocesan funds were paying for settlements in the pedophile priest scandals and cuts were being made to social, college, and ethnic ministries. The Catholic Worker placards read "Stop the Taj Mahoney."

11.   Catholic Workers took an broad view of who constituted a worker. As Day noted, "The Catholic Worker, as the name implies, *is* directed to the worker. But we use the word in its broadest sense, meaning those who work with hand or brain, those who do physical, mental, or spiritual work, and primarily the poor" (as quoted in Piehl 1982:126).

12.   On the importance of laity in the Catholic Workers, see Tranwick 2003:144.

13.   Piehl 1982:160.

14.   The historian Mel Piehl (1982:161) writes that in the midst of a 1940s strike against Barbara Hutton's Woolworth empire, the signs of Catholic picketers affiliated with the Association of Catholic Trade Unionists (ACTU) quoted the pope. One sign read "Babs gave $11,000,000 to charity, but 'the worker is not to receive as alms what is his due in justice'—Pius XI."

15.   Piehl reports that two radical priests affiliated with the Catholic Worker movement in Pittsburgh formed the Catholic Radical Alliance, which called for immediate realization of "the radical social program of the Labor Encyclicals" and criticized the CIO for being "content to sell labor for a wage" (1982:168). In Chicago, activists in the Catholic Worker movement formed the Catholic Labor Association (later called the Council on Working Life), which acted much like the ACTU during the 1940s and 1950s (Piehl 1982:167).

16.   César Chávez began incorporating popular religious elements into his organizing as far back as 1959, when, while at the Community Service Organization, a woman had asked if she could bring her banner of the Virgin of Guadalupe to a march. César not only said yes, but he sent her and the banner out marching in front (as reported to Jacques E. Levy, *Cesar Chavez: Autobiography of La Causa* [New York: Norton, 1975], and cited in Dalton 2003:35).

17.   As Luis Leon observes, "For the UFW, political revolt was a sacred action itself" (2005:61). And Frederick John Dalton declares that the UFW was not simply "'a political, economic, or social movement. . . . It was all of those and also a religious movement" (2003:86). Religion was central to the UFW. As Leon puts it, "Chávez preached a gospel of self-sacrifice, nonviolence, and social justice, and worked ecumenically with both Catholic and Protestant clerics, and deftly created and manipulated religious symbols to enlist the ultimate loyalties of the multitudes" (2005:54). Congregations declared their support of the grape boycott, many clergy came to work with the UFW, and a group of Catholic priests and bishops became intimately involved in the farm-labor negotiations after Chávez asked for their help (Dalton 2003; Bole 2001). By the time of his death, the Catholic Church claimed him as one of their own. Cardinal Mahoney eulogized him, as did an editorial in the *National Catholic Reporter*. When California honored Chávez by declaring March 31 as the official César Chávez holiday, the *National Catholic Weekly Newspaper* declared, "His Catholic faith led César Chávez to found the UFW" (Bole 2001). Many observers might disagree with this statement, but the Catholic Church's enthusiastic embrace of Chávez and the UFW struggle is notable.

18.   Leon 2005.

19.   Dalton (2003:86–87) reports that at this key juncture, some of the key UFW organizers did not embrace the idea of penance and atonement for past sins. He reports that Luis Valdez, then in charge of the UFW's theater, was a nonbeliever, and that Jewish organizers, such as Marshall Ganz, and some Anglo volunteers were ambivalent about incorporating traditions of penance, suffering, and La Virgen de Guadalupe. Moreover, the AFL-CIO leaders wanted to keep both religious and ethnic symbols out of the labor struggle.

20.   As quoted in Dalton 2003:44–45.

21.   Luis Leon reports that, in this paper, César Chávez stated that the Catholic Church "is a powerful moral and spiritual force which cannot be ignored by any movement" (2005:59).

22.   See Milkman 2006 and Brodkin 2007.

23.   Durazo 1999.

24.   When Mexican president Fox came to Los Angeles to discuss pending immigration legislation in the United States, he met with a triad of church, labor, and state representatives. As the *Los Angeles Times* reported, "Fox met first with [Cardinal] Mahoney, then with hotel workers and union leader in separate meetings" before meeting with Mayor Antonio Villaraigosa (Quinones and Gencer 2006:B1).

25.   Durazo served as president of UNITE HERE! Local 11 from 1989 to 2006, which represents nearly half a million hotel and restaurant workers. She was chief architect of the national AFL-CIO-sponsored Immigrant Workers Freedom Ride of 2003, discussed later in this chapter, and in 2006 she became the executive secretary-treasurer of the L.A. County Federation of Labor and the first woman to lead the nation's largest labor council. Durazo was by then the widow of Miguel Contreras, former executive secretary-treasurer of the council.

26.   At its inception, LAANE was called the Tourist Industry Development Council. With the success of LAANE, Local 11 then helped organized Santa Monicans Allied for Responsible Tourism, also dedicated to passing living-wage ordinances and reforming hotel practices.

27.   LAANE began with the victory of passing one of the nation's first citywide living-wage ordinances in 1997 but has since been involved in numerous projects designed to ameliorate employment-based poverty. Thereafter, together with the unions and CLUE, LAANE addressed the needs of low-wage LAX airport workers and initiated the Santa Monica living-wage movement, designed to raise the wages of workers in the tourism industry. In 2001 LAANE inaugurated the Community Benefits Program, a campaign designed to ensure that real estate developers who receive public benefits will offer quality jobs and community benefits in exchange for public subsidies. In 2004, together with CLUE support, LAANE launched a campaign against Wal-Mart's incursion in Inglewood and helped to pass the Los Angeles Superstore Ordinance.

28.   According to Nancy Cleeland (2002), writing in the *Los Angeles Times*, the waiters and waitresses were not allowed to speak to the press, who had gathered to cover the peaceful protest.

29.   These quotes come from fliers that CLUE distributed in 1998 and 1999. For a detailed analysis of this labor struggle at USC, see Wilton and Cranford 2002.

30.   The doctrine of Incarnation is the Christian idea that Jesus is the flesh of God. CLUE members extended this idea to advocate that all humans, regardless

of immigration status, are divine and deserving of justice on earth, and particularly at the workplace.

31.   I attended these meetings for slightly over a year, beginning in July 2000 until fall 2001, as did my research assistant, Kara Lemma, who even took a part-time job with CLUE during spring 2000.

CHAPTER 5

1.   An Interfaith Worker Justice (IWJ) letter of spring 2006 listed the following ways in which the group supported immigrant rights. Among these, the letter listed: "Participated in and supported immigrant rights rallies around the country; Recruited clergy to participate in actions aimed at influencing legislators for humane immigration reform; Distributed immigration reform action alerts to eight thousand people in the IWJ network; Created congregational resources for engaging people of faith in the immigration policy debates; Convened leading Hispanic theologians and scholars to discuss ways their important work could be more connected to on-the-ground justice struggles; Challenged the Department of Labor to more aggressively enforce labor laws in the Gulf Coast rebuilding work; Engaged seminary students in eight cities to support the struggles of immigrant workers." The letter also included the plea, "Pray for immigrants. Pray for employers. Pray for our nation's leaders to make just and responsible decisions."

2.   The observation that religious faith helps activists endure is echoed in the findings and analysis provided by Russell Jeung. He makes a similar argument in the case of a multiracial group of evangelical Christians organizing around housing issues for Laotian, Cambodian, and Mexican immigrants in Oakland (Jeung 2007).

3.   Jasper 1997:5.

4.   "An Invitation to Join the New Sanctuary Movement," in *Faith Works: Newsletter of Interfaith Worker Justice,* May 2007:5. In 2006 a new interfaith sanctuary movement arose, with CLUE and IWJ at the helm. The same newsletter article clarified that "secular immigrant and allied organizations will be invited to partner with the New Sanctuary Movement as needed, but the movement will be independent and faith-based" (2007:6). For more explanation on this new form of "prophetic hospitality" embraced by the new sanctuary movement and the direct legacy of it from the sanctuary movement of the 1980s, see p. 149 at the conclusion of chapter 6.

5.   The Labor in the Pulpit services of 2001 in Los Angeles also featured union leaders giving thanks to black congregations and clergy for the support they had offered during the previous year's thirty-two-day bus transit strike and

organizing campaigns at the airports. The *Los Angeles Times* reported that a small caravan of union leaders visited five predominantly African American churches to give thanks. "Whenever we need something, we come to the clergymen to get it done," said one transportation union leader. "The clergy brings the community together and strengthens the picket line" (Ornstein 2001:B3).

6. Daunt and Schoch 2001.

7. Daunt and Schoch 2001.

8. La Red de Lideres y Pastores del Sur de California, or the Network of Leaders and Pastors of Southern California, formed in 2006 and collaborated with other Latino evangelical and Pentecostal pastors seeking immigration justice around the nation. Their efforts were coordinated by Pastor Samuel Rodriguez, president of the National Hispanic Christian Leadership Conference.

9. The organization was called Los Angeles Committee against Plant Shut Downs.

CHAPTER 6

1. Posadas originated in colonial Mexico and incorporate both indigenous and Spanish-Catholic rituals. The posadas emerged as a conversion mechanism, a way for the Spaniards to evangelize and teach Christian biblical morals to Indians in the Aztec empire. These developed in the sixteenth century as rituals where the larger community, not only the clergy, could participate. Special prayers and a religious pageant were developed to commemorate Mary and Joseph's journey to Bethlehem. The posadas and *pastorelas*—miracle plays also introduced to the Indians by Spanish clergy—were initially very solemn, sacred affairs, but once they were removed from the church and came into the streets and people's homes, they gained a collective, joyous spirit (Elizondo 2000). The posadas vary across space and time, but they always include the reenactment of Mary and Joseph searching for shelter, their rejection at various homes, and the final extension of hospitality.

2. The annual Posada sin Fronteras in San Ysidro–Tijuana is a collective effort. On the program for the 2002 Posada sin Fronteras, entitled "Toward a World without Borders: Hacia un Mundo sin Fronteras," the cosponsors were listed on the back page. These include the American Friends Service Committee, Interfaith Coalition for Immigrant Rights, Catholic Diocese of San Diego, Ecumenical Council of San Diego, Southern California–Nevada Conference, United Church of Christ, Peace Resource Center, Immigration Ministry Team-Pacifica Lutheran Synod, Casa del Migrante, Casa YMCA de Menores Migrantes, El Centro Madre Assunta, Centro de Pastoral Migratoria, Frailes Franciscanos, and Procuraduria de los Derechos Humanos. Together with Genelle Gaudinez

and Hector Lara, I interviewed twenty of the initial and current organizers of the events, and they were drawn from eight of these organizations.

3. One Washington, D.C.–based interfaith group, the Border Working Group, has attempted to organize a national posadas campaign to draw attention to the rising number of human rights violations and deaths at the U.S.-Mexico border. Their website features a las posadas packet, with instructions on how to put a posada together and to issue press releases and write congressional representatives about border policies (www.rtfcam.org/resources/packets/posadas, accessed February 10, 2005).

4. Matovina and Riebe-Estrella 2002; Ramirez 2003.

5. See Ramirez 2003; Medina and Cadena 2002; Matovina 2002; Davalos 2002.

6. The University of Southern California students who joined me on these research visits to the Posada sin Fronteras include Kara Lemma, Genelle Gaudinez, Hector Lara, Billie Ortiz, and Maeve St. Leger.

7. Under the regime of President Bill Clinton and Attorney General Janet Reno, the INS budget tripled between 1993 and 1999, going from $1.5 billion to $4.2 billion. The Border Patrol—then under the jurisdiction of the INS—saw its budget increase rapidly, while the number of Border Patrol agents in the Southwest region more than doubled in a few years, reaching 8,200 in 1999 (Andreas 2000:89) and 11,000 by 2003 (Cornelius 2001).

8. See Massey, Durand, and Malone 2002:96. By 2006, several years after the 9/11 terrorist attacks prompted the United States to bolster national security and antiterrorism efforts, the FBI and the Border Patrol each numbered twelve thousand active agents. Politicians, however, continued to call for more Border Patrol agents. During the anti-immigrant backlash after the immigrant rights marches of spring 2006, President Bush visited the U.S.-Mexico border to brag that since taking office in 2001, the number of Border Patrol agents had risen from nine thousand to twelve thousand. That spring he also sought congressional support for an additional $1.9 billion to bolster militarization of the U.S.-Mexico border, which would include the deployment of six thousand National Guard agents to assist the Border Patrol agents.

9. The militarization of the border began with Operation Blockade (later renamed Operation Hold-the-Line) in El Paso, Texas, in 1993 and continued with Operation Gatekeeper in San Diego in 1994; Operation Safeguard in Nogales, Arizona, in 1995; Operation Hard Line in New Mexico in 1997; and Operation Rio Grande, complete with floodlights, twenty-foot watchtowers, and video cameras, in Texas in 1997. Most of these were expanded to nearby areas (Andreas 2000). During these years, the Border Patrol also adopted the navy's Deployable Mass Population Identification and Tracking System to keep records (Andreas 2000).

10.   See Huspeck, Martinez, and Jimenez 1998. Assaults have been committed by officers in the U.S. Border Patrol, the U.S. military, and sheriff's departments. The first and most notorious of the documented shootings by U.S. armed forces occurred on May 20, 1997, when Marine corporal Clemente Banuelos shot and killed eighteen-year-old Esequiel Hernandez, who was then tending his goats near Redford, Texas. According to Dunn (2001), the Marines failed to identify themselves or issue warning shots and then subsequently failed to administer aid to Hernandez. The U.S. federal government did not subpoena any of the Marines involved in the killing.

11.   See Eschbach, Hagan, and Rodriguez 2001; Cornelius 2001; Massey, Durand, and Malone 2002.

12.   A landmark study from the University of Houston estimates that there were more than sixteen hundred fatalities of would-be border crossers between 1993 and 1997 near Houston. See Eschbach et al. 2001; Eschbach, Hagan, and Rodriguez 2001.

13.   Marc Cooper, "The 15-Second Men," *Los Angeles Times,* May 1, 2005.

14.   Morosi 2006: B3; Associated Press 2006b: A16.

15.   Hondagneu-Sotelo et al. 2004; Hagan 2007; Menjivar 2007.

16.   Hagan 2007; Ruiz 2001.

17.   Personal communication with Scalabrinian brother Gioacchino Campese, March 6, 2006.

18.   U.S. Conference of Catholic Bishops and Conferencia del Episcopado Mexicano, "Strangers No Longer: Together on a Journey of Hope," section 3, January 22, 2003.

19.   "Humane Borders Water Stations," www.humaneborders.org/about/about_wstations.html, accessed March 1, 2006.

20.   In 2004 Morones told a reporter, "We do not answer to the Mexican government. We do not answer to the U.S. government. We respond to a Higher Authority." Cited in Perlita R. Dicochea, "Border Angels: A Politics of Humanitarianism," *La Prensa San Diego,* January 23, www.laprensa-sandiego.org/archieve/january04–23/angels.htm, accessed March 10, 2005.

21.   In July 2005, two Samaritans were arrested for assisting undocumented migrants, and felony smuggling charges were leveled against these border-ministry activists (Witherspoon website, www.witherspoonsociety.org/Global/borderlinks.htm, accessed March 10, 2005).

22.   www.witherspoonsociety.org/Global/borderlinks.htm.

23.   Cited in Menjivar 2007.

24.   Staudt and Coronado 2002:138.

25.   Golden and McConnell 1986.

26.   Golden and McConnell 1986:46.

27.   As quoted in Golden and McConnell 1986:48.

28. As quoted in Golden and McConnell 1986:48.

29. As quoted in Lorentzen 1991:39.

30. Lorentzen estimates that seventy thousand people in the United States helped about two to three thousand Central Americans, while Radar is more conservative, suggesting that by 1984, one hundred fifty sanctuary churches had been established with some thirty thousand church or synagogue members involved in supporting the effort (Lorentzen 1991:15; Radar 1999:331).

31. As quoted in Golden and McConnell 1986:47.

32. Napier 1985:36. Napier also cited biblical passages from Exodus, Leviticus, Joshua, Numbers, and Ezekiel to emphasize that under the law of God, unlike the laws of nation-states, there is no difference between the native and the alien or the refugee. "In Exodus 12:49," he writes, "'The same law shall apply both to the *ezrach* (the native) and to the *ger* (the alien).' In Leviticus 24:22, 'There shall be one law for both'" (1985:36–37).

33. Lorentzen 1991:16.

34. Blain 1994; Nepstad 2001.

35. Sociologist Sharon Nepstad (2001) argues that the narrative stories about Archbishop Romero, who was gunned down while saying Mass in El Salvador, facilitated the emergence of the transnational collective identity necessary for the mobilization of the Central American solidarity movement in the United States. She observes that stories couched in Christian faith and conveyed with melodramatic components, replete with innocent victims, vicious villains, and likeable heroes, were particularly effective in producing and sustaining mobilizations. Nepstad adds that personal stories are more effective than impersonal statistics in producing the proper emotional responses and that churches and other religiously affiliated settings are especially conducive to producing these responses.

36. Lorentzen 1991:42.

37. Coutin 1993:67.

38. Lorentzen 1991:42.

39. Eventually, U.S. Catholic bishops and mainstream Protestant denominations issued statements questioning U.S. policy in Central America. Other groups successfully challenged what they perceived as the unfair administration of asylum applications. In 1985 a group of churches filed a lawsuit against the U.S. federal government for the illegal application of asylum laws. The civil suit *American Baptist Churches et al. (ABC) v. Thornburgh* charged that the Reagan administration's policy of routinely denying Salvadoran and Guatemalan requests for asylum was in violation of the 1980 Refugee Act.

40. Sahagun 2007.

41. "An Invitation to Join the New Sanctuary Movement," in *Faith Works: Newsletter of Interfaith Worker Justice*, May 2007:5–8.

CHAPTER 7

1. Associated Press 2002.

2. Elizondo 1983:38.

3. The lyrics of the "Las Posadas del Barrio" song are reproduced here with permission from the songwriters, Rosa Martha Zarate and Francisco Javier Herrerra (phone communication, February 26, 2003).

4. Cornelius 2001; Massey, Durand, and Malone 2002.

5. Taylor 2002.

6. Jasper 1997:93.

7. Lowe 1996:167.

CHAPTER 8

1. In the United States and Europe, this has also prompted much hand wringing over presumed religiously based "clashes of civilizations" and, in particular, concern over the abilities of Western, Christian-established societies to mesh with Islamic-based immigrant groups and nations. The terrorist attacks of 9/11, the U.S. war effort and occupations in Afghanistan and Iraq, and the danger of Islamic terrorist cells forming in Western European cities have inflamed this discussion. In this era, Islam is associated less with the enrichment of pluralism and multiculturalism and more as a threat to national security.

2. In fact, a slate of books by conservative commentators has decried the embrace of Christian fundamentalism by conservatives. These include Andrew Sullivan's *The Conservative Soul* (HarperCollins 2006), Francis Fukyuama's *America at the Crossroads*, Kevin Philip's *American Theocracy*, and John W. Dean's *Conservatives without Conscience.*

3. Hondagneu-Sotelo 2007.

4. In October 2006, for example, members of CLUE joined with the hotel and restaurant workers' union to close the major avenues leading into Los Angeles international airport to draw attention to the low wages and hardships faced by airport hotel workers. Similarly, in 2000 they joined with union workers and leaders in an effort to shut down USC graduation to draw attention to the workers who were being denied a fair union contract. See Wilton and Cranford 2002.

5. For a discussion of the literature on new social movements, see Jasper 1997:70–74. For a discussion of the relationship between collective identities and social movements, see Polletta and Jasper 2001.

6. Simon 2006:A19.

7. Throughout my field work, I only saw three African Americans featured as prominent speakers at events. At the CAIR banquet in 2003, a well-known

African American iman from New York called the bids for donations. At a public forum at USC in 2002, an African American Muslim man spoke bitterly about
feeling invisible, as a black Muslim, because of the post-9/11 media focus on
foreign-born Muslim Americans. And at the MPAC 2006 convention, the
esteemed African American Muslim scholar Professor Sherman Jackson of the
University of Michigan opened his keynote speech in Arabic and gave a charismatic, well-received talk on Islamic reform to a predominantly immigrant
Muslim American audience.

8.   Karen Leonard (2007) argues that African American and immigrant
Muslim Americans were working toward convergence until 9/11 disrupted this
process. "African American Muslim efforts to seize the initiative and regroup
after 9/11 have widened the split between immigrant and indigenous Muslims,"
Leonard (2007:54) concludes. Moreover, she says that the African American leaders of the Muslim Alliance of North America, a group formed in 2001, have
"turned away from the national immigrant-led organizations because of their
failure to work for social justice for American Americans" (Leonard 2007:55).

9.   The CD *Posada sin Fronteras* features the eponymous composition that is
sung every year at the event. It was written by Rosa Martha Zarate and Francisco
Javier Herrera. This CD, as well as her others, *Yo Fuí Bracero* and *Señora del Canto*,
are available for purchase by telephone, (909) 875–1779.

10.   Gamson 2003:350.

11.   See Taylor and Rupp 1993.

12.   Jasper 1997:315.

13.   This includes CLUE as well as LAANE, which was discussed in chapter 4,
and Strategic Actions for a Just Economy (SAJE). For an analysis of how these
organizations work together and coordinate progressive economic action, see
Nicholls 2003.

14.   In fall 2006, Maher Hathout won the Human Relations Commission's
John Allen Buggs Award. The Zionist Organization of America and the American
Jewish Committee protested, and a new vote was taken. Hathout received the
award, but only after his reputation and legitimacy had been questioned.

15.   Khalil 2007:B9.

16.   Sahagun 2006:B3.

17.   See Hondagneu-Sotelo, Gaudinez, and Lara 2007.

APPENDIX

1.   My student and I were trying to do research and pioneer new service-
learning placement opportunities for USC students. We thought this would
broaden the perspective of what undergraduate students might be exposed to in

their community service-learning projects, and we thought that CLUE and various congregations could use student volunteers. Many of the clergy in CLUE were indeed interested, and some came to campus to meet with us and the director of the service-learning project but, ultimately, the limitations of hours of student volunteer availability precluded this plan from reaching fruition.

2.   I invested considerable time and effort in studying the Los Angeles section of a statewide organization called the Interfaith Coalition for Immigrant Rights (ICIR). Through this organization, I also spun off another satellite study of one of their projects, which advocated for affordable housing in Glendale through a Protestant church and in a neighborhood that included mostly Latino and Armenian immigrants. With ICIR, I also attended Immigrant Lobby Day in Sacramento, taking a bus with religious-based immigrant rights activists, many of them Latino immigrants, from Los Angeles for two days of interfaith lobbying efforts in the state's capital. I attended forums at a very activist Latino immigrant church in Boyle Heights, Mission Dolores, reputed to be the poorest parish in the archdiocese, and I attended immigrant social justice forums at a largely affluent, white Catholic parish in South Pasadena. During fall 2003, my graduate student and research assistant Genelle Gaudinez attended the AFL-sponsored Immigrant Workers Freedom Ride, which took her on a two-week-long bus trip from Los Angeles, throughout the Southwest and the South, to Washington, D.C., and New York City. When she returned, we designed and conducted phone interviews with clergy who had been active in the Immigrant Workers Freedom Ride. All of these research endeavors provided rich data and insights, but, in the end, the information proved too unwieldy to include in this manuscript, and including these other sources would have distracted from the book's narrative structure, which focuses on three separate cases.

References

Abdo, Geneive. 2006. *Mecca and Main Street: Muslim Life in America after 9/11.* New York: Oxford University Press.

Abdullah, Aslam, and Gasser Hathout. 2003. *The American Muslim Identity: Speaking for Ourselves.* Los Angeles: Multimedia Vera International.

"An Invitation to Join the New Sanctuary Movement." 2007. In *Faith Works: Newsletter of Interfaith Worker Justice.* May.

Andreas, Peter. 2000. *Border Games: Policing the U.S.-Mexico Divide.* Ithaca: Cornell University Press.

Associated Press. 2002. "Several Bodies Found in Rail Car in Rural Iowa." *Los Angeles Times.* October 15, A20.

———. 2006a. "Congressman Warns against 'Muslims Elected to Office.'" *Los Angeles Times.* December 21, A29.

———. 2006b. "Governors Stay Focused on the Border." *Los Angeles Times.* February 27, A16.

Balibar, Etienne. 1991. "Is There a 'Neo-racism?'" In *Race, Nation and Class: Ambiguous Identities*, edited by Etienne Balibar and Immanuel Wallerstein, 17–25. New York: Verso.

Basch, Linda, Nina Glick Schiller, and Cristina Szanton Blanc, eds. 1994. *Nations Unbound: Transnational Projects, Postcolonial Predicaments, and Deterritorialized Nation-States*. Amsterdam: Gordon and Breach Science Publishers.

Bellah, Robert N. 1970. "Civil Religion in America." In *Beyond Belief: Essays on Religion in a Post-traditional World*, 168–189. Berkeley: University of California Press.

Bender, Courtney. 2003. *Heaven's Kitchen: Living Religion as God's Love We Deliver*. Chicago: University of Chicago Press.

Bertbrier, Mitch. 2002. "Making Minorities: Cultural Space, Stigma, Transformational Frames and the Categorical Status Claims of Deaf, Gay and White Supremacist Activists in Late Twentieth Century America." *Sociological Forum* 17(4): 553–591.

Blain, M. 1994. "Power, War, and Melodrama in the Discourses of Political Movements." *Theory and Society* 23:805–837.

Bole, William 2001. "California Recalls Legacy of Farmworkers' Advocate." *National Catholic Weekly Newspaper*. March 18, 2001, www.osv.com, accessed May 4, 2006.

Brodkin, Karen. 2007. *Making Democracy Matter: Identity and Activism in Los Angeles*. New Brunswick, NJ: Rutgers University Press.

Burgat, Francois. 2003. "Veils and Obscuring Lenses." In *Modernizing Islam: Religion in the Public Sphere in Europe and the Middle East*, edited by John L. Esposito and Francois Burgat, 17–41. New Brunswick, NJ: Rutgers University Press.

"Bush Pushes Immigration Plan on Border Visit." 2006. www.cnn.com/2006/POLITICS/05/18/bush.border/index.html, accessed May 22, 2006.

Bustos, Rudiger V. 2005. "'In the Outer Boundaries': Pentecostalism, Politics, and Reies Lopez Tijerina's Civic Activism." In *Latino Religions and Civic Activism in the United States*, edited by Gaston Espinosa, Virgilio Espinoza, and Jesse Miranda, 65–76. New York: Oxford University Press.

Casanova, Jose. 1994. *Public Religions in the Modern World*. Chicago: University of Chicago Press.

Clark, Stephen. 2006. "Muslims Seek to Deflect Anger." *Los Angeles Times*. August 15, B4.

Clawson, Dan. 2003. *The Next Upsurge: Labor and the New Social Movements*. Ithaca: Cornell University Press.

Cleeland, Nancy. 2002. "Workers Have the Godly on Their Side." *Los Angeles Times.* February 11, www.cluela.org/old2/ClueNews/020211lat.html, accessed May 22, 2006.

Cole, David. 2003. *Enemy Aliens: Double Standards and Constitutional Freedoms in the War on Terrorism.* New York: New Press.

———. 2006. "Manzanar Redux?" *Los Angeles Times.* June 16, B11.

Cooper, Marc. 2005. "The 15-Second Men." *Los Angeles Times.* May 1, B7.

Cornelius, Wayne. 2001. "Deaths at the Border: Efficacy and Unintended Consequences of U.S. Immigration Control Policy." *Population and Development Review* 27(4): 661–689.

Cornelius, Wayne, James F. Hollifield, and Philip L. Martin, eds. 2003. *Controlling Immigration: A Global Perspective.* Stanford, CA: Stanford University Press.

Cornell, Tom. 2006. "A Brief Introduction to the Catholic Worker Movement." www.catholicworker.org, accessed April 24, 2006.

Coutin, Susan. 1993. *The Culture of Protest: Religious Activism and the U.S. Sanctuary Movement.* Boulder, CO: Westview Press.

———. 2000. *Legalizing Moves: Salvadoran Immigrants' Struggle for U.S. Residency.* Ann Arbor: University of Michigan Press.

Dalton, Frederick John. 2003. *The Moral Vision of Cesar Chavez.* Maryknoll, NY: Orbis Books.

Daunt, Tina, and Deborah Schoch. 2001. "Labor Unions March, Pray, Feel Stronger." *Los Angeles Times.* September 4, B3.

Davalos, Mary Kay. 2002. "'The Real Way of Praying': The Via Crucis, *Mexicano* Sacred Space, and the Architecture of Domination." In *Horizons of the Sacred: Mexican Traditions in U.S. Catholicism,* edited by Timothy Matovina and Gary Riebe-Estrella, 41–68. Ithaca: Cornell University Press.

Delgado, Hector L. 1995. *New Immigrants, Old Unions.* Philadelphia: Temple University Press.

Delson, Jennifer. 2006. "Church Abuse Screenings Easier on Undocumented." *Los Angeles Times.* June 22, B1–B3.

Demerath, N. Jay, III. 2003. *Crossing the Gods: World Religions and Worldly Politics.* New Brunswick, NJ: Rutgers University Press.

Dunn, Timothy J. 1996. *The Militarization of the U.S.-Mexico Border, 1978–1992.* Austin: Center for Mexican American Studies, University of Texas Press.

———. 2001. "Border Militarization via Drug and Immigration Enforcement: Human Rights Implications." *Social Justice* 28(24): 7–32.

Durazo, Maria Elena. 1999. Public Testimony. Subcommittee on Employer-Employee Relations Committee on Education and the Workforce, U.S. House of Representatives, July 21. www.house.gov/ed_workforce/hearings/106th/eer/ud72199/durazo.htm, accessed May 24, 2006.

Durkheim, Emile. 1995. *Elementary Forms of the Religious Life.* New translation by Karen E. Fieldo. New York: Free Press. (Orig. pub. 1912.)

Ebaugh, Helen Rose, and Janet Saltzman Chafetz, eds. 2000. *Religion and the New Immigrants: Continuities and Adaptations in Immigrant Congregations.* Walnut Creek, CA: AltaMira Press.

———. 2002. *Religion across Borders: Transnational Immigrant Networks.* Walnut Creek, CA: AltaMira Press.

Eck, Diana L. 2001. *A New Religious America: How a "Christian Country" Has Now Become the World's Most Religiously Diverse Nation.* San Francisco: Harper.

Edwards, Wendy J., and Carolyn De Swarte Gifford. 2003. "Introduction: Restoring Women and Reclaiming Gender in Social Gospel Studies." In *Gender and the Social Gospel,* edited by Wendy J. Edwards and Carolyn De Swarte Gifford, 1–17. Urbana: University of Illinois Press.

Elaasar, Aladdin. 2004. *Silent Victims: The Plight of Arab and Muslim Americans in Post 9/11 America.* Bloomington, IN: AuthorHouse.

Elizondo, Virgilio. 2000. *Galilean Journey: The Mexican-American Promise.* Maryknoll, NY: Orbis Books. (Orig. pub. 1983.)

Eschbach, Karl, Jacqueline Hagan, and Nestor Rodriguez. 2001. "Causes and Trends in Migrant Deaths along the U.S.-Mexico Border, 1985–1998." Working Paper Series 01–4. Houston: Center for Immigration Research, University of Houston.

Espinosa, Gaston, Virgilio Elizondo, and Jesse Miranda. 2005. *Latino Religions and Civic Activism in the United States.* New York: Oxford University Press.

Espiritu, Yen Le. 2003. *Homebound: Filipino American Lives across Cultures, Communities, and Countries.* Berkeley: University of California Press.

Freeman, Gary P. 1995. "Modes of Immigration Politics in Liberal Democratic States." *International Migration Review* 29(4): 881–902.

Fujiwara, Lynn H. 2005, "Immigrant Rights Are Human Rights: The Reframing of Immigrant Entitlement and Welfare." *Social Problems* 52(1): 79–101.

Gamson, Joshua. 1995. "Must Identity Movements Self-Destruct? A Queer Dilemma." *Social Problems* 42(2): 390–407.

Gamson, William A. 2003. "Defining Movement 'Success.'" In *The Social Movements Reader: Cases and Concepts,* edited by Jeff Goodwin and James M. Jasper, 350–352. New York: Blackwell Publishing.

Golden, Renny, and Michael McConnell. 1986. *Sanctuary: The New Underground Railroad.* Maryknoll, NY: Orbis Books.

Goldstein, Warren. 2004. *Warren Sloane Coffin Jr.: A Holy Impatience.* New Haven, CT: Yale University Press.

Gordon, Larry. 2006. "Meeting in L.A. to Discuss Views of Latinos and Blacks Draws Protestors." *Los Angeles Times.* June 6, B4.

Gutierrez, David G. 1998. "Ethnic Mexicans and the Transformation of 'American' Social Space: Reflections on Recent History." In *Crossings: Mexican Immigration in Interdisciplinary Perspectives*, edited by Marcelo M. Suarez-Orozco and Mariela M. Paez, 309–335. Cambridge, MA: Harvard University, David Rockefeller Center for Latin American Studies, and University of California Press.

———. 2004. "Demography and the Shifting Boundaries of 'Community': Reflections on 'U.S. Latinos' and the Evolution of Latino Studies." In *The Columbia History of Latinos in the United States since 1960*, edited by David G. Gutierrez, 1–42. New York: Columbia University Press.

Haddad, Yvonne. 2004. "The Shaping of a Moderate North American Islam: Between 'Mufti' Bush and 'Ayatollah' Ashcroft." In *Islam and the West Post 9/11*, edited by Ron Greaves et al., 97–114. Burlington, VT: Ashgate Publishing Company.

Haddad, Yvonne, and Jane I. Smith. 2002. Introduction to *Muslim Minorities in the West: Visible and Invisible*, edited by Yvonne Haddad and Jane I. Smith, v–xviii. Walnut Creek, CA: AltaMira Press.

Hafner-Burton, Emilie M. 2005. "Human Rights in a Globalizing World: The Paradox of Empty Promises." *American Journal of Sociology* 110(5): 1373–1411.

Hagan, Jacqueline Maria. 2007. "The Church vs. the State: Borders, Migrants, and Human Rights." In *Religion and Social Justice for Immigrants*, edited by Pierrette Hondagneu-Sotelo, 93–103. New Brunswick, NJ: Rutgers University Press.

Hagan, Jacqueline, and Nestor Rodriguez. 2002. "Resurrecting Exclusion: The Effects of 1996 U.S. Immigration Reform on Communities and Families in Texas, El Salvador, and Mexico." In *Latinos: Remaking America*, edited by Marcelo M. Suarez-Orozco and Mariela M. Paez, 190–201. Cambridge, MA: Harvard University, David Rockefeller Center for Latin American Studies, and University of California Press.

Hagopian, Elaine C., ed. 2004. *Civil Rights in Peril: The Targeting of Arabs and Muslims*. Chicago: Haymarket Books; Ann Arbor, MI: Pluto Press.

Herberg, Will. 1960. *Protestant, Catholic, Jew: An Essay in American Religious Sociology*. Chicago: University of Chicago Press.

Hermansen, Marcia. 2004. "The Evolution of American Muslim Responses to 9/11." In *Islam and the West Post 9/11*, edited by Ron Greaves et al., 77–96. Burlington, VT: Ashgate Publishing Company.

Heyman, Josiah. 2002. "U.S. Immigration Officers of Mexican Ancestry as Mexican Americans, Citizens, and Immigration Police." *Current Anthropology* 43(3): 479–508.

Hing, Bill Ong. 2006. *Deporting Our Souls: Values, Morality, and Immigration Policy*. Cambridge: Cambridge University Press.

Hitchens, Christopher. 2007. *God Is Not Great: How Religion Poisons Everything.* New York: Twelve Books, Hachette Book Group.

Hollifield, James F. 1992. "Migration and International Relations: Cooperation and Control in the European Community." *International Migration Review* 26(2): 569–95.

Holloway, Julian. 2006. "Enchanted Spaces: The Séance, Affect, and Geographies of Religion." *Annals of the Association of American Geographers* 96(1): 182–187.

Hondagneu-Sotelo, Pierrette. 1995. "Women and Children First: New Directions in Anti-immigrant Politics." *Socialist Review* 25:169–90.

———. 2007. "Religion and a Standpoint Theory of Immigrant Social Justice." In *Religion and Social Justice for Immigrants,* edited by Pierrette Hondagneu-Sotelo, 3–15. New Brunswick, NJ: Rutgers University Press.

Hondagneu-Sotelo, Pierrette, and Angelica Salas. 2008 (in press). "What Explains the Immigrant Rights Marches of 2006? Organizing, Xenophobia, and Democracy Technology." In *Immigrant Rights in the Shadows of United States Citizenship,* edited by Rachel Ida Buff. New York: New York University Press.

Hondagneu-Sotelo, Pierrette, Genelle Gaudinez, and Hector Lara. 2007. "Religious Reenactment on the Line: A Genealogy of Political Religious Hybridity." In *Religion and Social Justice for Immigrants,* edited by Pierrette Hondagneu-Sotelo, 122–140. New Brunswick, NJ: Rutgers University Press.

Hondagneu-Sotelo, Pierrette, et al. 2004. "'There's a Spirit That Transcends the Border': Faith, Ritual and Postnational Protest at the US-Mexico Border." *Sociological Perspectives* 47(2): 133–159.

Hoskins, Janet. 2007. "Caodai Exile and Redemption: A New Vietnamese Religion's Struggle for Identity." In *Religion and Social Justice for Immigrants,* edited by Pierrette Hondagneu-Sotelo, 191–209. New Brunswick, NJ: Rutgers University Press.

Huspeck, Michael, Roberto Martinez, and Leticia Jimenez. 1998. "Violations of Human and Civil Rights on the U.S.-Mexico Border, 1995–1997: A Report." *Social Justice* 25(2): 110–121.

Iwamura, Jane Naomi, and Paul Spickard, eds. 2003. *Revealing the Sacred in Asian and Pacific America.* New York: Routledge.

Jasper, James M. 1997. *The Art of Moral Protest: Culture, Biography and Creativity in Social Movements.* Chicago: University of Chicago Press.

Jeung, Russell. 2007. "Faith-Based, Multiethnic Tenant Organizing: The Oak Park Story." In *Religion and Social Justice for Immigrants,* edited by Pierrette Hondagneu-Sotelo, 59–73. New Brunswick, NJ: Rutgers University Press.

Joppke, Christian. 2005. *Selecting by Origin: Ethnic Migration and the Liberal State.* Cambridge: Harvard University Press.

Juergensmeyer, Mark. 2000. *Terror in the Mind of God: The Global Rise of Religious Violence*. Berkeley: University of California Press.

Khalil, Ashraf. 2007. "Boxer Rescinds Award to Islamic Activist." *Los Angeles Times*. January 6, B1–B9.

Khan, M. A. Muqtedar. 2003. "Constructing the American Muslim Community." In *Religion and Immigration: Christian, Jewish, and Muslim Experiences in the United States*, edited by Yvonne Haddad, Jane I. Smith, and John L. Esposito, 175–198. Walnut Creek, CA: AltaMira Press.

Kraul, Chris. 2006. "U.S. Muslims Rally for Hostage." *Los Angeles Times*. January 22, A10.

Kretsedemas, Philip. 2008. "What Does an Undocumented Immigrant Look Like? Local Enforcement and the New Immigrant Profiling." In *Keeping Out the Other: A Critical Introduction to Immigration Enforcement Today*, edited by David C. Brotherton and Philip Kretsedemas, 334–364. New York: Columbia University Press.

Kurien, Prema. 2004. "Multiculturalism, Immigrant Religion, and Diasporic Nationalism: The Development of an American Hinduism." *Social Problems* 51(3): 362–385.

Leon, Luis D. 2005. "Cesar Chavez and Mexican American Civil Religion." In *Latino Religion and Civic Activism in the United States*, edited by Gaston Espinoza, Virgilio Elizondo, and Jesse Miranda, 53–64. Oxford: Oxford University Press.

Leonard, Karen. 2003. *Muslims in the United States: The State of Research*. New York: Russell Sage Foundation.

———. 2007. "Finding Places in the Nation: Immigrant and Indigenous Muslims in America." In *Religion and Social Justice for Immigrants*, edited by Pierrette Hondagneu-Sotelo, 50–58. New Brunswick, NJ: Rutgers University Press.

Leonard, Karen, et al., eds. 2005. *Transforming Religious Life in America*. New York: AltaMira Press.

Levitt, Peggy. 2001. *The Transnational Villagers*. Berkeley: University of California Press.

———. 2007. *God Needs No Passport*. New York: Free Press.

Lloyd-Moffett, Stephen R. 2005. "The Mysticism and Social Action of Cesar Chavez." In *Latino Religions and Civic Activism in the United States*, edited by Gaston Espinosa, Virgilio Elizondo, and Jesse Miranda, 35–51. Oxford: Oxford University Press.

Lorentzen, Robin. 1991. *Women in the Sanctuary Movement*. Philadelphia: Temple University Press.

March, Charles. 2005. *The Beloved Community: How Faith Shapes Social Justice, from the Civil Rights Movement to Today*. New York: Basic Books.

Marchevsky, Alejandra, and Jeanne Theoharis. 2006. *Not Working: Latina Immigrants, Low-Wage Jobs, and the Future of Welfare Reform.* New York: New York University Press.

Marosi, Richard. 2006. "Feinstein Seeks to Criminalize Border Tunnels." *Los Angeles Times.* February 22, B3.

Massey, Douglas S., Jorge Durand, and Nolan J. Malone. 2002. *Beyond Smoke and Mirrors: Mexican Immigration in an Era of Economic Integration.* New York: Russell Sage Foundation.

Matovina, Timothy. 2002. "Companion in Exile: Guadalupan Devotion at San Fernando Cathedral, San Antonio, Texas, 1900–1940." In *Horizons of the Sacred: Mexican Traditions in U.S. Catholicism,* edited by Timothy Matovina and Gary Riebe-Estrella, 17–40. Ithaca: Cornell University Press.

Matovina, Timothy, and Gary Riebe-Estrella, eds. 2002. *Horizons of the Sacred: Mexican Traditions in U.S. Catholicism.* Ithaca: Cornell University Press.

McCarthy, John D., and Mayer Zald. 1977. "Resource Mobilization and Social Movements: A Partial Theory." *American Journal of Sociology* 82:1212–1241.

McRoberts, Omar M. 2003. *Streets of Glory: Church and Community in a Black Urban Neighborhood.* Chicago: University of Chicago Press.

Medina, Lara, and Gilbert R. Cadena. 2002. "Dias de los Muertos: Public Ritual, Community Renewal, and Popular Religion in Los Angeles." In *Horizons of the Sacred: Mexican Traditions in U.S. Catholicism,* edited by Timothy M. Matovina and Gary Riebe-Estrella, 69–94. Ithaca: Cornell University Press.

Menjivar, Cecilia. 2003. "Religion and Immigration in Comparative Perspective: Catholic and Evangelical Salvadorans in San Francisco, Washington, D.C., and Phoenix." *Sociology of Religion* 64:21–45.

———. 2006. "Liminal Legality: Salvadoran and Guatemalan Immigrants' Lives in the United States." *American Journal of Sociology* 111(4): 999–1037.

———. 2007. "Serving Christ in the Borderlands: Faith Workers Respond to Border Violence." In *Religion and Social Justice for Immigrants,* edited by Pierrette Hondagneu-Sotelo, 104–121. New Brunswick, NJ: Rutgers University Press.

Milkman, Ruth. 2006. *L.A. Story: Immigrant Workers and the Future of the U.S. Labor Movement.* New York: Russell Sage Foundation.

———, ed. 2000. *Organizing Immigrants: The Challenge for Unions in Contemporary California.* Ithaca: ILR / Cornell University Press.

Miller, Donald E., Jon Miller, and Grace R. Dyrness. 2001. *Immigrant Religion in the City of Angels.* Los Angeles: Center for Religion and Civic Culture, University of Southern California.

Mooney, Margarita. 2007. "The Catholic Church's Institutional Responses to Immigration: From Supranational to Local Engagement." In *Religion and*

Social Justice for Immigrants, edited by Pierrette Hondagneu-Sotelo, 157–171. New Brunswick, NJ: Rutgers University Press.

Morris, Aldon D. 1984. *The Origins of the Civil Rights Movement.* New York: Free Press.

Motomura, Hiroshi. 2006. "Immigration: How 'They' Become 'Us.'" *Chronicle of Higher Education.* September 8, B6–B9.

Murray, Nancy. 2004. "Profiled: Arabs, Muslims, and the Post-9/11 Hunt for the 'Enemy Within.'" In *Civil Rights in Peril: The Targeting of Arabs and Muslims,* edited by Elaine C. Hagopian, 27–68. Chicago: Haymarket Books; Ann Arbor, MI: Pluto Press.

Nagel, Caroline R., and Lynn A. Staeheli. 2004. "Citizenship, Identity and Transnational Migration: Arab Immigrants to the United States." *Space and Polity* 8(1): 3–23.

———. 2005. "'We're Just Like the Irish': Narratives of Assimilation, Belonging and Citizenship amongst Arab-American Activists." *Citizenship Studies* 9(5): 485–498.

Napier, Davie. 1985. "Hebraic Concepts of Sanctuary and Law." In *Sanctuary: A Resource Guide for Understanding and Participating in the Central American Refugee's Struggle,* edited by Gary MacEoin, 33–38. San Francisco: Harper and Row.

Nawyn, Stephanie. 2007. "Welcoming the Stranger: Constructing an Interfaith Ethic of Refuge." In *Religion and Social Justice for Immigrants,* edited by Pierrette Hondagneu-Sotelo, 141–156. New Brunswick, NJ: Rutgers University Press.

Nepstad, Sharon Erickson. 2004. *Convictions of the Soul: Religion, Culture, and Agency in the Central American Solidarity Movement.* New York: Oxford University Press.

Ness, Immanuel. 2005. *Immigrants, Unions, and the New U.S. Labor Market.* Philadelphia: Temple University Press.

Ngai, Mae M. 2004. *Impossible Subjects: Illegal Aliens and the Making of Modern America.* Princeton, NJ: Princeton University Press.

Nicholls, Walter Julio. 2003. "Forging a 'New' Organizational Infrastructure for Los Angeles' Progressive Community." *International Journal of Urban and Regional Research* 27(4): 881–896.

Nussbaum, Martha C. 2007. *The Clash Within: Democracy, Religious Violence, and India's Future.* Cambridge, MA: Belknap Press / Harvard University Press.

Okihiro, Gary Y. 1984. "Religion and Resistance in America's Concentration Camps." *Phylon: Review of Race and Culture* 45(3): 220–233.

Ornstein, Charles. 2001. "Labor Says Thank You to Black Churches." *Los Angeles Times.* September 3, B3.

Palacios, Joseph M. 2007. "Bringing Mexican Immigrants into American Faith-Based Social Justice and Civic Cultures." In *Religion and Social Justice for Immigrants*, edited by Pierrette Hondagneu-Sotelo, 74–90. New Brunswick, NJ: Rutgers University Press.

Passel, Jeffrey S. 2005. *Unauthorized Migrants: Numbers and Characteristics*. PEW Hispanic report, June 14, http:pewhispanic.org/files/reports/46pdf.

Peterson, Anna, Manuel Vasquez, and Philip Williams. 2001. "The Global and the Local." In *Christianity, Social Change, and Globalization in the Americas*, edited by Anna L. Peterson, Manuel A. Vasquez, and Philip J. Williams, 210–228. New Brunswick, NJ: Rutgers University Press.

Pickus, Noah. 2005. *True Faith and Allegiance: Immigration and American Civic Nationalism*. Princeton, NJ: Princeton University Press.

Piehl, Mel. 1982. *Breaking Bread: The Catholic Worker and the Origin of Catholic Radicalism in America*. Philadelphia: Temple University Press.

Polletta, Francesca, and James M. Jasper. 2001. "Collective Identity and Social Movements." *Annual Review of Sociology* 27:283–305.

Pulido, Laura. 2006. *Black, Brown, Yellow and Left: Radical Activism in Los Angeles*. Berkeley: University of California Press.

Quinones, Sam, and Arin Gencer. 2006. "Fox Makes the Rounds for Immigration." *Los Angeles Times*. March 3, B1–B10.

Ramirez, Josephine. 2003. "A Tale of Los Angeles: Posadas, Nourishing Community." *ReVista: Harvard Review of Latin America* 2(2): 73–75.

Rudrappa, Sharmila. 2004. *Ethnic Routes to Becoming American: Indian Immigrants and the Cultures of Citizenship*. New Brunswick, NJ: Rutgers University Press.

Ruiz, Olivia Marrujo. 2001. "Los riesgos de cruzar: La migracion centroamericana en la fronteras Mexico-Guatemala." *Frontera Norte* 13(25): 7–33.

Saeed, Agha. 2002. "The American Muslim Paradox." In *Muslim Minorities in the West: Visible and Invisible*, edited by Yvonne Haddad and Jane I. Smith, 39–58. Walnut Creek, CA: AltaMira Press.

Sahagun, Louis. 2006. "Muslim Leaders Demand Inclusion." *Los Angeles Times*. August 5, B3.

———. 2007. "A Mother's Plight Revives the Sanctuary Movement." *Los Angeles Times*. June 2, B2.

Shupe, Anson, and Bronislaw Misztal, eds. 1998. *Religion, Mobilization and Social Action*. Westport, CT: Praeger.

Simon, Stephanie. 2006. "A New Face for Islam in North America." *Los Angeles Times*. September 21, A19.

Smith, Christian. 1996a. *Disruptive Religion: The Force of Faith in Social Movement Activism*. New York: Routledge.

———. 1996b. *Resisting Reagan: The U.S.–Central America Peace Movement.* Chicago: University of Chicago Press.

Staudt, Kathleen, and Irasema Coronado. 2002. *Fronteras No Mas: Toward Social Justice at the U.S.-Mexico Border.* New York: Palgrave Macmillan.

Stohlman, Sarah. 2007. "At Yesenia's House . . . Central American Immigrant Pentecostalism, Congregational Homophily, and Religious Innovation in Los Angeles." *Qualitative Sociology* 30(1): 61–80.

Taylor, Charles. 2002. *Varieties of Religion Today: William James Revisited.* Cambridge, MA: Harvard University Press.

Taylor, Verta, and Leila Rupp. 1993. "Women's Culture and Lesbian Feminist Activism: A Reconsideration of Cultural Feminism." *SIGNS* 19(1): 32–61.

Thomas, William Isaac, with Dorothy Swaine Thomas. 1928. *The Child in America: Behavior Problems and Programs.* New York: Knopf.

Tranwick, Robert. 2003. "Dorothy Day and the Social Gospel Movement: Different Theologies, Common Concerns." In *Gender and the Social Gospel,* edited by Wendy J. Edwards and Carolyn De Swarte Gifford, 139–149. Urbana: University of Illinois Press.

U.S. Conference of Catholic Bishops. 2000. "Welcoming the Stranger among Us: Unity in Diversity." Washington, DC: U.S. Conference of Catholic Bishops.

U.S. Conference of Catholic Bishops and Conferencia del Episcopado Mexicano. 2003. "Strangers No Longer: Together on the Journey of Hope." Washington, DC: U.S. Conference of Catholic Bishops.

Vasquez, Manuel A., and Marie Friedmann Marquardt. 2003. *Globalizing the Sacred: Religion across the Americas.* New Brunswick, NJ: Rutgers University Press.

Warner, Stephen R., and Judith Wittner. 1998. *Gatherings in Diaspora: Religious Communities and the New Immigration.* Philadelphia: Temple University Press.

Watanabe, Teresa. 2006. "Muslims Take Bigger Role in Terror Fight." *Los Angeles Times.* February 22, A1.

White, Ronald D. 2004. "Workers Are Stopped Far from Safeway CEO's Home." *Los Angeles Times.* January 29, www.cluela.org/old2/ClueNews/040129lat.html, accessed May 24, 2006.

Williams, Rhys H. 2002. "From the 'Beloved Community' to 'Family Values': Religious Language, Symbolic Repertoires, and Democratic Culture." In *Social Movements: Identity, Culture, and the State,* edited by David S. Meyer, Nancy Whitier, and Belinda Robnett, 247–265. New York: Oxford University Press.

———. 2003. "Religious Social Movements in the Public Sphere: Organization, Ideology and Activism." In *Handbook of the Sociology of Religion,* edited by Michelle Dillon, 315–330. Cambridge: Cambridge University Press.

Wilton, Robert D., and Cynthia Cranford. 2002. "Toward an Understanding of the Spatiality of Social Movements: Labor Organizing at a Private University in Los Angeles." *Social Problems* 49(3): 374–394.

Wood, Richard L. 2002. *Faith in Action: Religion, Race, and Democratic Organizing in America.* Chicago: University of Chicago Press.

Wuthnow, Robert, and John H. Evans, eds. 2002. *The Quiet Hand of God: Faith-Based Activism and the Public Role of Mainline Protestantism.* Berkeley: University of California Press.

Yoo, David. 2002. "A Religious History of Japanese Americans in California." In *Religions in Asian America: Building Faith Communities,* edited by Pyong Gap Min and Jung Ha Kim, 121–142. Walnut Creek, CA: AltaMira Press.

List of Interviews

Richards, Rev. Sandie. November 10, 2000.
Salvatierra, Rev. Alexia. March 30, 2001.
Smith, Rev. Don. August 10, 2000.
Villacorta, Borris. November 11, 2002.
Walsh, Father Mike. November 11, 2000.

IWJ ORGANIZERS

Bobo, Kim. May 25, 2004.
Heine, Joy. May 25, 2004.
Mohammed, Richard. May 25, 2004.
Olivas, Jose. May 25, 2004.

MUSLIM AMERICAN AND CIVIL RIGHTS ORGANIZERS

Abuljebain, Nader. March 3, 2002.
Al-Marayati, Salam. February 25, 2002.
Anonymous. July 20, 2002.
Ayloush, Hussan. February 26, 2002.
Eltantawi, Sarah. February 25, 2002.
Faraj, Ra'id. March 19, 2002.
Frenzen, Niels. March 5, 2002.
Hathout, Samer. April 1, 2002.
Kennedy, Rusty. September 6, 2002.
Khan, Hamid. June 3, 2002.
Lafferty, James. March 29, 2002.
Muro, Irene. April 28, 2002.
Narro, Victor. July 29, 2002.
Nashashibi, Tareef. July 17, 2002.
Shehadeh, Michel. February 27, 2002.
Sood, Samera. May 20, 2002.
Toma, Robin. April 22, 2002.
Upadhyay, Pradeepta. June 3, 2002.

POSADA SIN FRONTERAS ORGANIZERS

Arreola, Linda. December 7, 2004.
Campese, Bro. Gioacchino. May 22–23, 2004.
Canton-Self, Betty. December 10, 2004.

Cribbs, Pastor Art. May 18, 2004.

Dunn, Bro. Ed. July 26, 2004.

Gates, Rev. Jamie. December 15, 2004.

Herrera, Francisco. December 23, 2004.

Johnson, Rosemary. November 10, 2004.

Kendzierski, Padre Luis. May 18, 2004.

Lisot, Madre Gema. May 18, 2004.

Martinez, Roberto. November 10, 2004.

Myers, Ched. June 30, 2004.

Raditz, Rev. Bill. December 7, 2004.

Schroeder, Bro. Mark. May 24, 2004.

Sullivan, Noreen. December 12, 2004.

Thing, Bro. Tom. May 24, 2004.

Trujillo, Maria Lourdes Arias. May 23, 2004.

Zarate, Rosa Martha. October 10, 2004.

Forty-seven short interviews with participants at Posada sin Fronteras, December 14, 2002.

ADDITIONAL INTERVIEWS

Moreno, Rev. Ricardo. April 7, 2004.

Zavala, Bishop Gabino. March 26, 2007.

Index

Text: 10/14 Palatino
Display: Palatino
Compositor: International Typesetting & Composition
Indexer: Ruth Elwell
Printer and binder: Maple-Vail Manufacturing Group